HOW TO HEAL YOUR WEIGHT

A 16-Step Mind, Body, Spirit
Approach to Fat Freedom

TAMARA PITELEN

Blue Dea Books

Blue Dea Books
35 Morgan Way, Peasedown St John
Bath BA2 8TT, United Kingdom

The information in this book is not intended to treat, diagnose, cure or prevent any disease. This information is not intended as a replacement or substitute for medical advice nor does it prescribe the use of any technique as a form of treatment for physical, emotional, or medical problems without the advice of a physician, either directly or indirectly. The material in this book is for educational and entertainment purposes only. The intent is to offer general information with regards to emotional well-being. In the event you use any of the information in this book for yourself, the author and the publisher assume no responsibility for your actions.

For information contact:
hello@howtohealyourweight.com
www.howtohealyourweight.com

ISBN13: 978-1-9160116-0-1 (print)
ISBN13: 978-1-9160116-2-5 (eBook)

10 9 8 7 6 5 4 3 2 1

Patrons and Supporters
I would like to thank and acknowledge the following people for putting their faith in me by pre-ordering a copy of the book while it was still being written. It was this act of kindness and support that got me to the finishing line. Much love and gratitude to each of you. Tamara

Patrons
The Union Health Project
www.theunionhealthproject.org

Supporters
Adrian Maul
Annette Davison
Anne Toth
Debbie Hucker
Gabriela Awad
Georgia Briata
Jacquie Valentine
Jaspal Sira
Katja Gloeckler
Kristian Reiss
Lisa Pascoe
Lisa Thomas
Marianci Baba
Nicolas Descharnes
Oona O'Shea
Polly Shelton-Lowe
Rachel Smith
Raymond Ware
Sue Deere
Vanya Silverten

For Adrian

You are my one and only. Thank you for your rock-solid support and love, and for your unwavering belief in me.

I bloody love you.

CONTENTS

INTRODUCTION

WOULD YOU LIKE to finally get to the bottom of your struggle with your weight?

Are you open to the possibility that the 'advice' you got to 'just eat less and exercise more' is horribly missing the point?

Are you ready to escape from diet prison and break the dieting cycle of self-blame, self-shame, self-punishment, deprivation and general misery that comes with it? Not to mention failure.

I was on that miserable hamster wheel for decades, I'll tell you my story in the next chapter but the gist of it is that you have been sold a lie, my beautiful friend. Diets not only don't work—they are a sure-fire way to get fatter, sicker and crazy obsessive! (Oh yeah, I got that tee-shirt, binged on those cookies...)

So if you're ready to explore the idea that calorie-counting for weight-loss is woefully flawed and if you're ready to go on a journey to uncover the spiritual, emotional, and mental solution to your physical issue of excess weight, let's do it.

There might be a few tears along the way but I'll hold your hand and I promise that we'll have some laughs as well. Ultimately though, I'm here to tell you that you've done your time in what I like to call the Guantanamo Bay of Calorie Counting. If you want to ride off into the sunset of weight liberation, let's saddle up.

The boiled down gist of this book is that if you're carrying excess body fat, it's because a subconscious part of you wants it there. Badly wants it there. And it will fight hard and fight clever to keep it there because it is doing this to protect or serve you in some way. This subconscious part of you has very good reasons for keeping this extra fat padding on your body. In fact, this deep down, well-hidden part of you believes it's doing this for your own good. Your subconscious either believes that losing the weight carries risk, or that keeping it on offers a benefit, or pay-off. So you can count your calories and tot up your carb grams till the cows come home but you're not going to permanently shift this fat unless your subconscious mind decides the weight is surplus to requirements. What do you do? To change your body, you must first change your mind.

Healing your weight, and healing your obsession with your weight, is about taking on a radically new way of looking at health and wellness. It's the idea that everything—absolutely everything—is profoundly connected.

The body is a whole dynamic integrated living organism where every part affects every other part. Where everything is irrevocably intertwined in a sophisticated symphony. All the pieces of your biology and your unique genetic code interact with your environment to determine how sick or well, fat or thin, you are in this moment.

Your weight 'problem' does not exist in isolation to the rest of your body, brain, life, environment, and ancestral lineage. So it cannot be successfully tackled by only focusing on the physical aspect, namely food consumption and exercise.

Your body and mind are profoundly connected. They have a bi-directional relationship. What you do to one, has enormous impact on the other. What you do to your body, you do to your brain, and what happens in the brain impacts the body.

We know that our thoughts, beliefs, attitudes, traumas, life experiences directly impact our biology. We know that stress and other psychological factors have a major impact on our health. We now know that most illness is either caused, or worsened, by stress. What you think can influence how sick or well you are—the mind influences the body. This is known as mind-body medicine.

Successfully and permanently shedding this excess body fat is about uncovering and transforming all your various and valid subconscious reasons for holding onto it. Those subconscious reasons are rooted in your mental, emotional, physical and spiritual bodies. As well it's about healing your body so it's able to release excess weight. It's only by accessing the different layers of your subconscious self that true transformation and weight liberation can occur. I'll go into specific detail about how you can do that but this conundrum is actually just the beginning.

What you and I will also explore, as you gently peel back the layers of your weight, is the link between the rise of global obesity and our disconnection from both the natural world and ourselves as spiritual beings.

For about 200,000 years or so, our ancestors managed to maintain a normal weight without diet shakes, low fat muesli, calorie counting phone apps, Fitbits, and Zumba classes.

Our ancestors knew how to live in harmony with the natural world but we've messed it up. We're the only species on the planet that has lost the ability to automatically regulate our body weight. For every other species, automatic weight adjustment is effortless and as natural as breathing—with the exception of the unfortunate creatures who are unlucky enough to be fed by humans. We've even managed to give diabetes to elephants in captivity, a condition that's unheard of in the wild.

What's happened? We've profoundly lost our way.

We've forgotten that we are an intrinsic part of the natural world and pretended that we're somehow 'better' than Mother Earth. We've allowed the toxic values of 'dominate or destroy, compete and conquer' be applied to the way we treat our planetary home.

As a result, we're out of harmony and disconnected from each other, from nature, from the land, the seas, the animals, the air, planet Earth, the sun and moon, God... and ultimately from ourselves.

This disconnection has left us believing we are alone and separate. So we behave as though our actions have no impact on the circle of life. We fill the soil with poisons and dump plastic and chemicals into the oceans. Just like the boomerang though, we're now getting whacked in the head by the consequences of our actions. Unfortunately, other species that we share this planet with are also suffering immensely from the consequences of our actions.

The micro is the macro. Everything is connected and our global challenges with the explosion in rates of obesity, and other 'lifestyle' diseases like diabetes and cancer, reflect just how disconnected we've become from our natural selves.

Our ancestors did not need someone to tell them how many grams of protein they should eat at each meal nor how often they should eat. We've now got more information about dieting, food, nutrition, and biology than ever before in history and yet we're collectively fatter than at any time in human history.

This is because addressing obesity with all the focus on food and exercise is akin to manually pulling a dog's tail from side to side to make the dog happy. It works the other way around. Make the dog happy and the tail will wag. The epidemic of obesity and lifestyle diseases is a red herring because the real epidemic is disconnection and separation, isolation, despair, emptiness, and loneliness. We've created a world where we prioritise business profits from cheap, processed fast foods over public and planetary health. When we get connected back to who we really are and to the rhythms of the Earth; when we find a sense of meaning and purpose; when we get happy and release the emotional baggage... then the extra physical weight will resolve itself. Based on my own years of research and life-long experimentation on myself, here is what I believe in a nutshell:

If you're carrying excess weight, your subconscious mind wants it there, perhaps as part of its survival safety net or perhaps as some kind of defense against emotional or mental stress, pain or trauma. Your subconscious mind does not view the excess weight as a problem—it views the weight as the solution to a problem. So when your body stores excess fat and refuses to let go of what it's got, it's just following orders from your subconscious mind and doing its utmost to keep you safe.

Calorie-focused dieting does not work for permanent, sustainable fat loss. In fact, on-going calorie reduction triggers the body's fat storage systems. This is now scientific fact. Your subconscious mind and body are far too intelligent and resourceful to be manipulated by your efforts to regulate calories. As soon as you reduce your calorie intake, your body-brain reduces its energy expenditure. It's your body-brain's way of budgeting. Its version of 'switching off the lights' to save money on electricity. And the more often it has done that, the more efficient a budgeter it has become. So all that low calorie dieting you've been doing has just trained your body into being a powerful fat storage machine.

If you have been on and off the diet treadmill for years, you've re-set your body's chemistry, so that your internal weight set-point is now higher. As well, you've triggered a number of real physical issues that will need to be healed before weight-loss is even possible. This includes conditions like low stomach acid, gut dysbiosis (microbiome imbalance), food intolerances and allergies, thyroid dysfunction, sluggish metabolism, chronic inflammation, leptin and insulin resistance, leaky gut, constipation and digestive issues, and more.

Self-blame, shame, guilt, self-punishment and critical negative self-talk all make you fatter. Mentally whipping yourself for not getting to the gym or feeling guilty about eating that chocolate bar makes you fatter in the long run. Why? Because this type of behaviour perpetuates your 'I'm useless' programmes, which triggers the hormonal stress response that turns you into a fat-storing machine. It also feels punitive so at some point you'll revert to childhood and rebel against this 'punishment' by eating that slab of lemon meringue tart with ice-cream. This is part of a battle with your parents or authority that you internalised as a child and continue to subconsciously play out. I like to call it the 'submission rebellion see-saw'.

Your subconscious mind always wins. If your subconscious wants that extra padding to stay on your frame then it will battle your conscious mind tooth and nail to keep it there. And it will win because the subconscious accounts for 90 to 95 per cent of all your actions, decisions, behaviours and patterns. So if your subconscious has good reasons for keeping the extra padding, you'll ultimately keep the extra padding no matter what your conscious mind decides needs to happen in time for that wedding, beach holiday or milestone birthday. If your body-brain does allow you to lose weight for the special occasion, it will then rapidly recreate the weight in the weeks or months after the event.

Willpower doesn't work. Trying to change your behaviours with grim, white-knuckled willpower is a waste of time. Again, this is because when willpower is involved, the conscious mind is fighting the subconscious mind and the subconscious mind has an armoury of top-class weapons at its disposal. For example, the subconscious can set off a storm of hormonal havoc to turn you into a fat-storing machine. It can lower your metabolism, induce lethargy, and burn muscle tissue for energy instead of fat. It can silence signals to the brain such as the hormone leptin so the brain doesn't register satiety nor 'see' that the body is already carrying plenty of excess fat. It'll also flick the cravings switch, which explains why you suddenly find yourself jumping into the car at 11pm in your slippers (just me?), trawling the fast food joints and 24-hour convenience stores at midnight then inhaling French fries and sundaes in the car park despite vowing a few hours earlier that this was going to be the day when you'd stick to that (depressing and pointless) diet. Cue more self-hate and the cycle continues.

The very good reasons that your subconscious mind has for holding onto the excess weight come down to a mix of physical, mental and emotional stresses from your childhood and current life experiences, as well as from the subconscious beliefs and programming you've formed as a result of these experiences. In addition, you may also have the beliefs and programmes of your ancestors playing a role. We inherit so much more than we realise through the coding of our DNA. Somewhere along the way, usually childhood, we've formed subconscious beliefs like, '*I need this fat to avoid inappropriate sexual attention*', '*If I'm too attractive, I'll cheat on my husband*', '*food is love so this excess fat is love*', '*I nurture and reward myself with food*', '*I'm scared there might be a famine so I need to keep fat reserves to survive*', '*the body is shameful and dirty*', '*being emotional is a weakness*'... and many, many more. If you really want to initiate permanent changes you need to install and run new programmes on your 'brain computer'.

HMS FATTY U-TURN

How do you start turning the good ship HMS Fatty around?

For a start you slowly back the truck up from dead-end diet street and quit with all the beating yourself up that you've been doing for so long. Instead of criticising and finding fault with your body, it's time to change the filters through which you view yourself and start appreciating your incredible body and listening to it in a new way. It's time to begin a new and kinder dialogue with your body because it's been trying to get your attention for ages. It's got so much to tell you.

When you start really seeing this sophisticated suit of flesh and bone that you inhabit as the miracle it really is, you'll start to support and heal your body so that it is well enough to automatically regulate your weight and you won't have to even think about it.

So dump the diet, change the self-hate record, snap that 'must try harder' whip over your knee and throw it away.

Happiness, health and weight-loss does not come via whipping or criticising yourself, nor from punishing yourself with deprivation.

Ultimately, it's about giving up your addiction to constantly scanning yourself for flaws, constantly searching yourself over for things that are wrong with you, constantly finding fault with yourself. When you can stop all that, you can start to find wonder, beauty and delight in your body and yourself.

Does that sound easy? All you have to do is give yourself a break, cut yourself some slack and like yourself as you are. You just have to stop punishing yourself. Surely that would be easy, wouldn't it?

Lordy no! You're a woman[1] brought up in the modern world—self-criticism has been tattooed onto your psyche. The irony is, my beautiful friend, that while you continue to loathe, criticise, and resist the way your body looks now, the more you ensure that the parts you have decided are unacceptable and must change—will not change.

So, are you ready to turn your back on the miserable merry-go-round of self-blame, deprivation, punishing exercise regimes, obsession with counting calories, points, grams, yada yada? Are you ready to hear that 'calories in and calories out' is the 20th Century's Flat Earth theory of weight-loss? Are you ready to nourish your body in a way that will undo and heal the damage done by your past dieting efforts?

Are you open to the idea that grimly sticking to a traditional calorie-controlled, low-fat diet is actually a sure-fire, can't-fail way to get you fatter in the long run?

Are you ready to take your first steps on a journey of self-love, self-acceptance, and self-exploration so that you can give your incredible body the opportunity to truly heal from a cellular level?

Most importantly, are you ready to do the work to find and release the real, subconscious reasons for your weight issue?

Even if you're not feeling ready yet, that's okay, hear me out and then just mull it over for a while. The diet industry isn't going anywhere. They'll happily welcome you back with open arms if you still think that's the answer for you and if it is I wish you well, I really do. Or maybe you like some of the ideas in this book but others seem like a load of woo woo talking-to-angels nonsense*. No problem. Take the bits you find helpful and leave the rest.

Before we continue though, I do want to make one thing crystal clear. Right now, exactly as you are in this moment, you are brilliant, courageous, beautiful and inspiring. I see your pain and I see your shame and I see your despair and I see your fear of even daring to hope that this might be a way out of the prison. I see all that because I lived it too. For decades. Let's do this, you beautiful soul...

Full disclosure: I do talk to angels, spirit guides, dead grannies, and other non-corporeal or discarnate entities who exist in alternative

---

[1] *You're probably a woman but maybe not. Maybe you're a man. Maybe you're a non-binary who doesn't identify as a specific gender. Maybe you're gender fluid... whatevs, I'm not bothered. Please assume 'she' etc. includes every human being.*

dimensions. For this book, I channelled information from Spirit, which you will see at the start of some of the Steps in part two.

Or I'm just a hippie with an over-active imagination. You pick whichever you want to believe.

CHAPTER 1
A FAT GIRL'S TALE

"Weight that disappears from your body but not from your soul is simply recycling outward for a while but is almost certain to return."— Marianne Williamson, author, spiritual teacher, lecturer and activist. @marwilliamson

I WAS AGED NINE when a doctor put me on my first diet.

"You're too heavy for your age," said the doctor. *"Let's try putting you on a calorie-controlled diet..."* and so it began.

It was the late 1970s and the billion-dollar dieting industry was just starting to get into full swing. We were all buying into the theories about how low-calorie diets and low fat Frankenfoods were the answer to weight loss. 'Fat-free', 'low fat' and 'lite' were stamped on everything from sausages to crisps, cake and cola.

On the surface, it seemed to make all the sense in the world—just stop eating fat and you'll stop having fat on your body, we were told. *'Easy peasy!'* we thought.

We were all happily chowing down on fat-free cookies, fat-free cereals, fat-free muffins, skimmed milk, zero per cent fat yogurt, and so on. The fat had been removed from these foods and replaced with sugars and starchy fillers but we thought that was okay back then.

How wrong we were.

If the past 50 or so hysterical, fat-phobic years have taught us anything it's that such a simplistic view of the human body and metabolism is just wrong.

Fast forward from the 1970s to today and where has all that calorie counting and zero per cent fat yogurt got us? It's drop-kicked us straight into a global obesity crisis that's unprecedented in human history. Despite about 200,000 years of managing our weight without aspartame-sweetened fizzy drinks, it's taken us just 50 or so years to monumentally screw it all up.

Let's go back for a moment, though. to that fateful day when the nine-year-old me was walking home with my mum from that doctor's surgery.

My mum had taken me to the doctor because she was worried about my supposedly inexplicable weight gain over the previous few months.

Being fairly obsessed with her own weight, having a fat daughter was simply not acceptable to my mother. I don't mean that she was ashamed of my size (she probably was a little but she'll go to her deathbed denying that, bless her), what I mean is that my mum's main motivation for me losing weight was so that I wouldn't go through the wretched misery that she'd gone through as a young woman who got teased about her weight.

Anyway, as we walked home from the doctor's that day, I remember feeling chastened and a little ashamed. But sitting alongside the shame in my little breast was also a newly formed flicker of hope that this might be the answer to getting thin.

In my hand I clutched a joyless bit of paper that ordered me to eat half a grapefruit for breakfast, or one thin slice of toast with a scraping of butter, and a cup of tea, ideally black but a small dash of milk would be permitted if absolutely necessary for the weak-willed, fatty guzzlers who couldn't manage without it.

This diet allowed me about 1000 calories a day—which was the accepted wisdom in the 1970s. Never mind that I was rapidly growing into a young woman with all sorts of nutritional needs for the development of my brain, my bones, my organs, reproductive system, nervous system and more. Nutrition? Pah! No, that didn't matter in comparison with the holy grail of thinness.

'Just consume 1000 calories a day,' the experts told us, 'and you will lose weight. We guarantee it,' they said.

'It's that easy, no arguments, it doesn't matter if you're nine years old or 79.'

The subtext of this message was that, if you can't do it, there's something wrong with you – you're lazy/ not trying hard enough / lying about it / in denial / kidding yourself / have no willpower. It was the lie we all bought. Today's massively profitable diet industry was built on that premise.

What was the result of that low calorie, low fat dieting?

At 19 years old, after 10 years of dieting, I peaked at my heaviest weight, which was about 20kgs (45lbs) more than I weigh today. And I picked up a host of eating disorders and neuroses along the way.

Instead of helping me shift that little bit of excess fat off my nine-year-old body, all that angst and dieting triggered real problems—physical, mental and emotional. Plus, it ignored the real reasons for the extra weight that had so quickly manifested. Reasons that had nothing to do with food and everything to do with love and security. I actually dieted myself fatter, sicker and obsessive.

The nine-year-old me could never have foreseen that those first tentative steps into the world of dieting started a journey that was to unfold into decades of deprivation, calorie counting, punishing exercise regimes, and weight-gain. This journey would make me a compulsive eater. It would make me obsessive and miserable, and make me feel like a failure. It would screw up my microbiome (gut flora bacteria balance) and trigger a storm of eating disorders, cravings, and binges that led to metabolic syndrome, insulin resistance, leptin resistance, famine response, thyroid and hormonal disorders, sluggish metabolism, digestive disorders, lethargy... it was a cascade of knock-on issues that led to more weight gain as well as a load of other conditions that came with the territory such as an under-functioning thyroid, brittle nails, dry skin, acid reflux, digestive issues, and memory loss.

I didn't know all that back then though. Back then, I put my faith and trust into the medical establishment and the health experts. So I stubbornly and blindly persevered with the low-calorie-low-fat dieting advice because that was the accepted wisdom of the time—and still is in many quarters.

'Eat less and exercise more' was the mantra. *'It can't fail,'* we were promised. *'It's all about calories in and calories out, simple maths...'* they said. But it's not and it did fail.

Over and over and over again this approach failed to get me the results I wanted. However, instead of blaming the advice, I, like millions of others, blamed myself. Every expert and authority and media platform told us that more dieting and more exercise was the only solution to excess weight so I spent about 35 years following that 'advice'. The promised results obstinately failed to transpire permanently and I kept blaming myself for the failure. Albert Einstein said that the definition of insanity is doing the same thing over and over again and expecting a different result. By this definition, I was insane.

On top of the low calorie and low-fat dieting, I also engaged in excessive and rigorous exercise for years and years. I ran marathons, completed triathlons and clocked up thousands of kilometres in my running shoes. I dragged myself out of the door in all weathers to pound the pavements almost every day in the name of elusive thinness. I also certified as an aerobics teacher and taught classes at a local gym a few evenings a week on top of my marathon training and my full-time day job—a day job to which I cycled usually via a 7am stop at the gym for 30 to 45 minutes of treadmill running.

Along the way, I also did long distance cycling and once spent three months cycling around a whole country (albeit a smallish one – Ireland). Did I lose weight? That would be a big, fat, freaking NO. I just couldn't understand why the excess weight wouldn't budge. I racked my brain trying to figure it out.

'What am I doing wrong? What part of the puzzle is missing?' I asked myself for the millionth time. 'How on earth could I even fit more exercise into my life without giving up my job?' And I came back with the usual answer, 'I'm obviously not trying hard enough or I'm doing something wrong...' which is something I hear today from the people that come to me for help with their own weight issues.

In their first session with me, I can just about guarantee that a new client will blame their extra weight on 'needing to try harder' or 'not having enough willpower'. These are all intelligent, hard-working, resourceful and motivated people. These are people who get up at 6am to do a gym class before taking the kids to school and then going to their own workplace. They raise families and hold down demanding jobs. These people are amazing. They just don't see it.

Like them, I was trapped in a vicious cycle of self-blame, self-punishment and self-criticism. I put parts of my life on hold until that glorious day when I would be thin (cue angelic choir singing 'Hallelujah') and I was darned if I was going to let myself relax and enjoy life until I was. I was obsessed with my weight, with calories, with what I ate. Ironically, this was why I could never enjoy cooking, or appreciate good food, because I was always thinking of food and eating in terms of guilt and calories.

Every single morning from the age of nine to 19, I'd tentatively step on the bathroom scales, praying for the needle to shift downwards. Yet, no matter how 'good' I'd been the day before, it wouldn't move or it would even show a gain. On the rare occasion when the needle did move downwards, I was rapturous with joy but as sure as the sun sets in the west, it would have pinged back up again in a week or so. If I ever did just let go and indulge for a celebration such as Christmas Day, I could gain two kilograms (4.5lbs) in a single day.

'It's not fair!' I would cry, wiping away hot tears of despair and frustration and anger because it felt like my body was battling with me every step of the way... and therein lay the clue. My body *was* battling me every step of the way. Or, more precisely, my subconscious mind was battling with my conscious mind and my body was simply following orders from the vastly more powerful of the two. This is at the heart of what needs to be addressed.

Before we get into that though, let's just return again to that doctor's appointment I had at age nine. I was at the doctor's because my mother couldn't figure out why I'd suddenly gained a noticeable amount of weight. It was a mystery!

Then again, maybe it wasn't really such a mystery when you looked at what was going on in my life at the time—trauma, divorce, abandonment, bullying and intimidation.

This was back in the 1970s though. A time when mainstream western wisdom did not generally make any connection between emotions and the physical body.

Conventional wisdom of the day was that you had emotions on one side and the physical body on the other and never the twain shall meet. In fact, there was still the suggestion that there was something 'wrong' with showing or having emotions. Women had emotions; men did not. And as we all knew in the 1960s and 1970s, men were far superior to women so what they did must be better. Having emotions must be wrong and weak. God must have made some sort of mistake when He gave them to us and we all needed to deny and suppress our emotions as much as possible. The good old British stiff upper lip.

At any rate, no one thought to wonder if the traumatic events and huge upheaval in my young life may have played a part in my rapid weight gain. No, I was simply a greedy little girl, said my doctor. At least that's the impression I got. In fairness to him, he perhaps wasn't so unenlightened and may not have used the word 'greedy'. I just remember feeling humiliated and chastised. Even if the word 'greedy' wasn't actually uttered, it was hovering heavily in the air. The message I heard was that my weight was 'wrong' and it was my own fault. I was doing something wrong, I was lazy and I ate too much. I was unacceptable as I was. I needed to change and I needed more self-control and discipline. That was what little nine-year-old Tammy heard. This made me sad and anxious and ashamed. It also forged a steel-like determination to follow the rules set out to me in the hope of achieving what was required of me in order to be accepted (and loved) again. I was nothing if not a 'good girl' who craved approval.

But what was really going on? About 18 months before that fateful doctor's appointment to discuss my 'weight problem', my parents' marriage had broken up. My father had been unfaithful to my mother.

The divorce was messy and vicious and raw. It splintered the hearts and cracked the souls of all concerned. I would hear my mother sobbing alone in her bedroom after Dad had left us. By then, we were living in a small two-bedroom flat down in the city. The large family home with the amazing views at the top of the hill had been sold and the profits divided between my mum and dad so they could start new lives apart. This new residence was like a geographic symbol of my mother's 'fall' in society.

From being the respectable wife in a loving nuclear family living in a large, new house right at the top of the hill overlooking the city, she'd become a struggling, single mother living in a little flat down amongst the folk she had viewed from above. It was a rapid and painful tumble. My mother crumbled and for a while her women friends would need to come over in the middle of the night to look after her.

Aged just seven, I didn't have the mental or emotional tools to process that kind of searing pain and anxiety. Emotions that were so palpable, I felt them like a physical ache in my gut.

This is why, flying in the face of logic and reason, children find a way to blame themselves for things like divorce and abuse—it's the only reference they have for making sense of it: *'Bad things happen when I'm bad and good things happen when I'm good so this must be my fault. Daddy isn't here because I was a bad girl and he doesn't love me enough. I'm not enough...'*

When they grow up, these girls may wander down the promiscuity road and make themselves sexually available to any male who'd have them. They're motivated by a jumble of needs including the need to feel desirable, the yearning for something similar to the intimacy of love-making and the belief that jumping quickly to the sex act will somehow fast-track an emotional relationship—when in fact it usually does exactly the opposite.

(Obviously I'm speaking hypothetically here. I have no personal knowledge of such desperate, tragic behaviour. Honest. No, really... this wasn't me at all, heaven forbid! Promiscuous? [cough] How very dare anyone suggest such a thing... ooh, look over there!)

Ironically, these beautiful little girls often end up staying single for decades or they have a string of unsuccessful pseudo-relationships or a bizarre knack for always attracting damaged and emotionally unavailable men. Some of these little girls then spend the rest of their lives subconsciously seeking Daddy's love and approval, often from emotionally unavailable or abusive men. They don't realise that it's because they've been programmed with corrupted beliefs about love and men such as *'men who love me, leave me, so I'd rather stay alone to avoid the hurt...'* or *'men can't be trusted'* or *'relationships are painful'* or *'love is abusive'*, *'I'm unlovable'* or *'I must be submissive to get love'* and so on. These types of subconscious beliefs can be the drivers for why we hold onto extra weight.

My mother's marital split, her bitterness over the profound betrayal and the enormous panic about how she would raise two small children on her own caused my mum to have a nervous breakdown – this was on the back of suffering post-natal depression after giving birth to my younger brother, who was age two. My mum felt desperate, vulnerable, alone and scared. She didn't know how she'd manage financially or emotionally to raise my brother and me by herself. So it wasn't a huge surprise when she quickly rebounded into a new relationship.

Unfortunately, this new man had his own baggage and it manifested as a tendency towards controlling and domineering behaviour.

Now aged in her 70s, my mother tells me that back then, at the age of 32, she'd felt old and past it, as though no one else would have her. She thought this man was her last chance. Which is so tragically sad because my mother was—and is—beautiful, kind and fiercely intelligent. She would have had her pick of men but her confidence was so crushed, she couldn't see it at the time.

In that two years, my family crumbled around me, my beloved dad abandoned me (it seemed to me), we moved house three times, I changed schools and found myself living with an intimidating man as well as his 13-year-old son. A boy who never passed up an opportunity to call me a fat, ugly or stupid pig. Usually all three. This boy was going through his own turmoil of course. Like me, his life had also been wrenched apart by his parents' divorce but that doesn't occur to you when you're a child whose world has crumbled.

Is there any wonder my emotional pain showed up in my body as excess weight?

At nine years old, you don't have substances like vodka, cigarettes and cocaine to turn to. All you have is cocoa pops, cookies and ice cream. Food became my drug of choice. Over the next few years, I used it to stuff down my misery, I used it to feel loved and I used it to rebel. That's the thing about issues with food misuse and abuse, they're not rational and they're often conflicting. I would eat to feel better but I would also eat as a form of self-harm. I would starve myself to feel better and starve myself to self-harm. I would eat as an act of defiance and rebellion against the adults telling me I mustn't because I wasn't good enough as I was and I would diet as an attempt to adhere to social mores and expectations. I would mindlessly binge-eat because my body-brain thought I was starving to death after days of surviving on apples and crispbreads.

Yes, it's complicated. It was complicated even further because all this stress and trauma, plus the sudden increase in the amount of sugar I was consuming, triggered adrenal fatigue and an under active thyroid. So before you could say 'low-fat freaking nightmare', I had a slow motion metabolism thrown into the mix.

Back then, the first thing I did every morning was hold my breath and tentatively weigh myself on the bathroom scales. My mum wanted to know that the needle was moving in the right direction. More mornings than not, however, this did not bring happy news and I would start the day gripped by feelings of despair, failure and shame as well as by a determination to make today different because I did not want to be a disappointment to my mum.

'Today I will stick to the diet!' I vowed yet again to myself, to God, our cat... before slinking in to the kitchen to break the bad news to Mum and assure her it would be different today. Then I'd work out the lowest calorie breakfast possible—this was often five dry crispbreads or rice crackers, coming in at 30 calories each with another 30 calories spent on milk in my cup of tea. This breakfast feast totaled 180 calories, which left me 820 calories for the rest of the day. I'd dip the crackers in my cup of tea to make them edible. Then the aim would be to eat nothing till I got home from school at 4pm, which is when I could have a 'sensible snack' worth 140 calories of a boiled egg and a medium-sized apple. (*'Don't go crazy and have a large apple!'* Says the diet industry. Small aside: I remember being at a Weight Watchers meeting in my teens and hearing the leader telling a frustrated woman, who couldn't understand why she wasn't losing weight because she was following the plan to the letter, that her failed weight-loss was likely due to her eating a large banana every day instead of a regular one. *"That can add an extra 100 calories every day!"* the leader said. Ridiculous.)

So maybe for a few days, through grim determination, I'd survive on 1000 calories a day. Every mouthful would be written down and calculated in a notebook. Maybe after the first or second day of a renewed effort, the scales would show a drop of half a kilo or a kilo but then the needle would stay stubbornly still for days. On the fourth or fifth day of semi-starvation, my sensible afternoon snack would blow out into a mini binge. This regime was the dieting equivalent of hanging by your fingertips on a mountain's ledge. You're hanging on for dear life but you can't keep hold forever. Eventually your fingers slip and you fall like a rock into the canyon below. A binge session takes hold and you find yourself shovelling food into your mouth like an eating robot on auto-pilot. The numbers on the scale fly up. Cue more self-loathing and self-flagellation. You pick yourself up from the canyon floor and climb back up the mountain to hang off the ledge again, promising yourself that this time your fingers won't slip...

Back then I'd never heard of the famine response. I didn't understand that my body-brain had noticed the reduced amounts of fuel and assumed there was a famine situation to get through. So, to protect me from perceived starvation, it had triggered cravings and was holding onto every ounce of body fat for dear life, as well as choosing to burn muscle tissue for energy instead of stored fat as I persevered with the self-starvation strategy called a 'diet'.

THE BEAST OF BINGEING

Over time the bingeing escalated. I fell into a pendulum swing pattern of starve and binge. The bingeing got crazy as well. It started out with extra pieces of toast and jam or raiding the biscuit tin but at the worst of my bingeing I would shovel tablespoons of butter heaped with sugar into my mouth. First, I would scrape the spoon through the block of butter then use it to scoop a heaped spoon of white sugar from the big bag of sugar Mum kept for baking. Other times I'd spoon the butter into my mouth along with a mound of breakfast cereal.

This was not about enjoying food. This was a type of mental illness and I was self-medicating with food. You don't hack slices of frozen bread from a stale loaf in an ice-covered plastic bag in the freezer and chew on the corners out of a love and appreciation for food.

Nor do you stand inside the open fridge door with your head back and mouth open to squirt whipped cream from a can directly into the back of your throat.

Other times I'd just pile a load of different foods together like it was some strange eating game. I might cover a slice of cheese with whipped cream then top it with strawberry jam and chocolate sprinkles. Or I would fill a bowl with cottage cheese and then cover it in white sugar. I was using food as a reality escape drug in the same way that a junkie uses heroin.

When a binge kicked in, I became a mindless automaton just pushing food in as fast as possible. The next mouthful was ready to go in before

I'd finished chewing the one I had. Although I didn't chew much either. I would swallow as quickly as possible. It was like there were two versions of me and the one that wanted the food was stronger than the me who was already hating herself for having it.

In a way, there *were* two versions of me. Probably more than two. Subconsciously, I was using food to numb all the emotions I couldn't process. I was also using extra weight to hide behind. I was using it to put a buffer between myself and the hostile strangers with whom I suddenly found myself living. Men who left piles of pornographic magazines sitting on the coffee table. [How reading *Penthouse* and *Playboy* magazines from cover to cover as an eight-year-old girl screwed up my understanding of female sexuality is a whole other book.]

I was also mirroring behaviours and attitudes I'd learned from my mother and her friends. My mum had always been weight conscious— thanks to her own childhood issues and the cultural messages of the day (Twiggy, Audrey Hepburn, Jean Shrimpton et al)—but in the wake of the divorce this became a much bigger monster. During her nervous breakdown, mum survived on coffee and toast, possibly thinking at some level that if only she'd been thinner, my father wouldn't have cheated on her.

I didn't realise all that at the time, though. I was an impressionable child of the 1970s and 80s. A time when the diet industry was just shifting into top gear, salivating with excitement as the realisation started to sink in about the vast and deep oceans of money that were there for the taking from armies of women who thought there was something wrong with their amazing, incredible bodies because that was the message from the dominant mainstream culture.

I wasted decades of my life on the flawed information put out by the billion-dollar dieting industry. I wasted a lifetime on the dieting and self-blame game. Don't do that, it really sucks.

Those 20kgs (45lbs) of excess body fat cast a long and dark shadow over my whole life and they consumed my every waking moment. I know that there are many people who are battling with much larger amounts of excess weight whilst for others it's a much smaller amount, perhaps that last 10lbs, or 5kgs, that has refused to budge for the last 20 years. However, the amount of excess fat you're dealing with is not the main concern. What's more of a concern is how this extra weight is impacting your mental health and life quality. Someone with 'just' 10lb (4.5kg) to release can be more mentally and emotionally impacted by it than someone who is carrying four times as much excess fat.

I was obsessed with my weight and with food. While I was growing up, it was all I could think about all of the time. Even when on the surface I was talking about something else, it was always there, this critical self-hate-speak chattering in my head like a sinister soundtrack to my life.

This obsession ruined countless special times in my life from celebrations to milestone moments to holidays and travel, it clouded every moment of my life until I worked out how to extricate myself from the tangled emotional and physical mess that is obesity and eating disorders.

What was the turning point? Everything started to slowly shift when I realised my body and mind wanted this extra weight. No, I didn't believe it at first either. Could it really be true that some part of me wanted to keep this extra weight?

Yes.

Because if some part of me didn't want the excess weight, it wouldn't be there. And until I got in touch with that part of me, and got it on board with what I consciously wanted, I was never going to win this fight. I wasn't even in the boxing ring. I was shadow boxing up dead-end diet alley.

For me, getting to a place of peace with my weight took many years spent on a healing journey that meandered through a variety of healing modalities including kinesiology, ThetaHealing, EFT Tapping, hypnotherapy, life coaching, Spiritual Response Therapy, yoga... and more.

It's been a journey that has expanded my mind and enriched my life in ways I could never have imagined. So my invitation to you is to see this as a beautiful healing journey and an exploration of yourself. Open your mind, be curious and find what works for you. Most of all though, take off your 'it's all about diet and exercise' blinkers. Because it's effing not.

CHAPTER 2
THE DIET INDUSTRY'S
EPIC FAIL

"We don't know shit. Correction. We know lots and lots about why people are getting fat. We can tell them all about their night eating and their insulin levels and the horrible impact of the obesogenic food environment. But we don't know the first thing about what to do about it. There isn't a single intervention that has been shown to work long-term. We have absolutely nothing of substance to offer people who are overweight or obese and trying to lose weight."

—Dr. David Levitsky, Professor of Nutrition and Psychology at Cornell University speaking at the Psychology of Eating Conference, Manhattan, 2013

WE SPEND BILLIONS each year on books, diet magazines, gadgets for weight-loss and fitness, gym memberships, lite foods, gluten-free foods... yet two thirds of us are overweight or obese and this figure is going up year on year. We are drowning in information about how to lose weight and yet the percentage of overweight and obese people in the world is rising.

Through the 1970s, 80s and 90s, the 'eat less exercise more' message was hurled at us from every angle. It was shouted at us from the covers of glossy magazines and explained to us on the basis of flawed science in the pages of newspapers and bestselling books.

We were force fed this advice in the TV and radio commercials paid for by organisations like Weight Watchers Ltd, Jenny Craig, and Thompson Medical Company, which was the then-owner of SlimFast diet drinks (the same company that sold the controversial Dexatrim supplements, which are basically caffeine pills).

In various boardroom meetings, eyes began to gleam as the realisation sunk in that there was an inordinately huge and exciting amount of money to be made from making women believe there was something wrong with them and then selling them the 'solution'. It is the default position of the advertising industry generally.

All the diet industry had to do was convince us we needed to be ashamed of our bodies and that it had all the answers to 'curing' these shameful things about our bodies.

Essentially, we've been brainwashed on mass into believing there is something wrong with a perfectly normal and natural female body. You've been steeped in this diet mentality and blasted with its message, both subliminally and overtly, for your entire life.

BRAINWASHING THE MASSES

So, while I'm not at all denying that obesity levels have skyrocketed, I do question whether women have been sold an unrealistic idea of what they 'should' look like. If you're a woman aged in her fifties or sixties, is it really so awful to have a soft belly? Do you really need to get into that pair of jeans you had when you were 25? Is that what it's going to take to feel validated as a woman? Or could we get to a place where it's okay for our bodies to soften a little with age and for our hair to turn silver? Could we embrace and value each phase of a woman's life as she unfolds into a deeper wisdom and different type of beauty? From girl to maiden, to mother, to wise woman, to goddess.

Yes, we could but we have a way to go because when women don't buy into the notion that there is something wrong with them, they cannot be controlled and they cannot be sold a 'solution' to their 'problem'.

What better way to ensure women stay subservient and oppressed than by convincing them they're intrinsically flawed? Ensure that they spend every waking moment thinking they're not good enough, not pretty enough, not thin enough, etc. Hungry women don't think straight. And all that endless pedalling around the dieting hamster wheel ensures we're too distracted, exhausted, and lacking in self-confidence to claim our rightful role in shaping the world. When Susie Orbach wrote her groundbreaking book, *Fat is a Feminist Issue,* in 1978 she was on the money.

The diet industry grew rapidly as more women began entering the workforce and earning our own money. The strangling patriarchal choke hold began to loosen some of its grip. So methods of controlling women had to evolve and shift into new areas if we were still to be manipulated in ways that suited the capitalist patriarchal system. Is it coincidence that the rise of the diet cult came hot on the heels of the women's liberation movement of the 1960s and 70s?

As women's lib gained momentum, women began vociferously rejecting the centuries-old 'Madonna or whore' stereotypes as well as the notion that a woman's value was based on her virginity; that women didn't have the same sexual appetites as men; that a woman who enjoyed sex was a slut; that women should not have numerous sexual partners, and the idea that sex outside of marriage was sinful, even criminal.

[Fun fact: At time of writing, adultery is still illegal in 21 states of America, including New York, the home of current President Donald Trump.]

Anyway, not long after women began more actively throwing off the shackles of suppression, mainstream culture of the day began offering up flat-chested, thin and asexual, androgynous-looking women like Twiggy and Jean Shrimpton as female role models. It was a dramatic swing away from the voluptuous and smouldering stars of the 1950s and 60s like Marilyn Monroe, Sophia Loren, Brigitte Bardot and Elizabeth Taylor. Just as women began stepping into their sacred feminine and sexual power, the message they got back was *'no, you must shrink, starve, go back to being pre-pubescent skinny girls with no sexual appetite'.*

Suddenly everybody was desperate to be rail-thin. Boobs and big bums were out of fashion and for about 30 years having a small, flat bum was the ideal. How were we all going to get so emaciated? By starving our arses off!

An early wave of diet books got pumped out. I owned most of them. There was the grapefruit diet, the VLCD diet (Very Low Calorie Diet), and the frankly soul-crushing Scarsdale Medical Diet, which was a two-week regime allowing just 700 calories a day that became a bestselling book in 1978. I tried that diet countless times. It is a recipe for misery.

About the same time, in 1977, the meal replacement shake SlimFast hit the shelves as the calorie obsession got into full swing. The belief was that it didn't matter what you ate as long as you controlled the calories. So, if you ate three chocolate bars of 300 calories each and nothing else all day, you should be congratulated.

At this time, the importance of calorie counting was the king of the diet theories. I remember reading a magazine article about the chocolate cake diet. The writer of this article claimed you could lose weight by eating a big piece of chocolate cake for breakfast, lunch and dinner. The theory being that this would equate to about 1200 calories so would result in quick and easy weight-loss! This was based on the notion that all calories are created equal. Guess what, they're not and the chocolate cake diet didn't work but I think you knew that.

It was the start of a global mania and insanity that's helped lead the world into the grip of a global obesity epidemic. The western world became fanatically committed to calorie counting and a hysterical rejection of dietary fat in foods. The experts told us that if we could get every drop of fat out of the foods we were eating, we would be thin. *'Definitely,'* they said. *'This will work!'* Mysteriously though, we all kept getting fatter.

In 1978, Weight Watchers International was sold to the H.J. Heinz Company and specially prepared diet foods and ready-meals hit the market. The fat taken out was replaced with sugars but no one was worried about that then.

Then in 1980, the Cabbage Soup Diet came along and was hailed the 'can't fail' method. Essentially, it's elective starvation.

In the 1980s, the F-plan diet swept the globe and had its 15 minutes of diet fame. The F stands for fibre and the premise was that eating an excess of dietary fibre keeps us feeling full and therefore less likely to overeat. You also had to restrict calories to 1500 per day. For a while we all shovelled down All Bran cereal and baked beans by the bucket-load thanks to its creator Audrey Eyton, founder of UK's *Slimming Magazine*. Heinz had never had it so good.

In 1982, Coca-Cola Company launched Diet Coke (aka Coca-Cola Light) and I remember thinking *'Hallelujah! This is the answer! This is the breakthrough I've been waiting for!'*

It seemed like a miracle, I could drink an entire 1.5 litre bottle of the artificially-sweetened, brown liquid and it amounted to no calories! NO calories! OMG praise the Lord!

'This cannot fail,' I thought to myself.

'I'll just live on this stuff, I'll be thin in no time...'

And I did live on it. I drank gallons of Diet Coke as a kind of meal replacement. But no. It didn't turn out to work that way and again I just couldn't figure out why it wasn't working. Some days the only substance that passed my lips was Diet Coke. I'd buy two to three 1.5 litre bottles and drink them throughout the day. How could I not lose weight from living on Diet Coke? But I didn't. Again, I told myself that it must be my fault and that I just needed to try harder. [Sigh.]

The 1970s and 80s were the start of us being sold the message that if low-fat and low calorie wasn't working, you were doing it wrong, and the answer was more self-flagellation, deprivation, self-punishment and more calorie counting and exercise until you do get it right.

'If it's not working, it's your fault, you don't have enough willpower...' was the bullying and erroneous message. I can't tell you how many times I paid for the services of a dietician or nutritionist for whom I would faithfully fill out food diary sheets. On a follow up appointment, when the diaries revealed that my average daily calorie intake was between 1000 and 1500 calories but I still wasn't losing weight, I would inevitably hear something like, *'Okay, now, are you sure you've really remembered to write down everything? You're only cheating yourself if you're not being honest...'*

Coincidentally (or not), the 1980s was also the decade when we saw the rise of the 'dieting disease' called anorexia nervosa. It was firmly stamped on our cultural map with the death in 1983 of Karen Carpenter—one half of successful brother and sister musical duo The Carpenters. Karen was the first famous person to 'diet herself to death'. I remember the shock and confusion rippling around the world. *'How can you die from dieting?'* We asked each other. It was bewildering.

The condition was tragically misunderstood. I remember many women I knew having conversations that would invariably involve a theatrical sigh followed by saying something along the lines of wishing they could catch this anorexia disease for a few weeks.

Like many other desperate dieters, I tried fasting as well. On one occasion I ate nothing but apples for three long days. Yes, I was lighter on the scales at the end of the three days but a few days after that and, surprise, surprise, the weight was back. This gave me another reason to blame myself for being weak and gluttonous and 'letting all that good work go to waste'.

On another occasion, I remember buying some kind of diet shake powder from an overweight woman in a shopping mall who wore a big badge on her ample chest that read 'Lose Weight Now, Ask Me How'. So I did ask her and the 'how' was the aforementioned meal replacement shakes for a rather hefty price. I remember her telling me all about how wonderful these products were and how they were a sure-fire way to finally get to my goal weight. Then she averted her eyes and quickly said, "although it doesn't work for me but that's my fault, it'll definitely work for you..." that should have been a loud, clanging, warning bell. But I was so desperate for a solution, I stuck my fingers in my ears against the screeching siren of the bullshit alarm and paid her the money, happily going home with a couple of boxes of processed, chemical-laden powders in three 'flavours' – chocolate, strawberry and vanilla.

I don't think I need to tell you that the promised results eluded me yet again.

The diet industry is a killer of joy. The diet industry is happiest when you believe there is something wrong with you and when you believe that they have the answer to your pain. But they don't. And they don't want you to find a real and lasting solution because then you'll stop buying their useless products and services.

That's my view when I'm feeling cynical and bitter.

In my more reasonable moments, I realise that there are many, many people who work in the various sectors of the diet and weight-loss industry who really do have the best intentions and do want to help you get thinner and happier. The trouble is that many of them have been taught the 'calories in calories out' and 'just try harder' myth as well.

NATIONAL OBSESSION

However it wasn't just the profit-making diet industry that fuelled our low calorie and low-fat diet frenzy. Even governments and insurance companies got on board, wagging their fingers at us and ordering us to cut our fat intake, reduce calories, and take up activities like Jazzercise in order to lose weight. (Remember Jazzercise? Amongst the first wave of group classes of exercise to dance music, also called Step Aerobics. Must admit though, I loved Jazzercise. I had a Jazzercise record—that's right, a vinyl Jazzercise album—that I would play over and over again while doing all the moves as shown in an illustrated booklet that came with the album. To this day, if I hear the opening bars to 'Another One Bites the Dust' by Queen, I start doing squat lunge pulses in time with the beat (*sing it with me now: 'boom boom boom—another one bites the dust...'*).

And, of course, losing weight was talked about ad-freaking-nauseum amongst the general public, particularly amongst groups of women who seemed to bond over this shared 'problem'.

Women friends would gather in groups in cafes, at work, the hairdressers, kids' playground, at dinner parties and barbeques, or wherever, and invariably the conversation would turn to the latest efforts at weight-loss as well as what the cousin of a friend's neighbour's dogsitter who had lost weight was doing. Details would be shared, new hope sparked, and another diet plan started. It was the pass-it-on evil chain letter of dieting.

Baby girls of the time grew up listening to their mothers talk about diets before they could even speak. Those babies grew into little girls who had been programmed to think it normal for women to be concerned to the point of obsession with dieting and striving to be thin—all wrapped up with a big ribbon of self-criticism and self-judgment. This self-judgment invariably leaks out into judgment of others as well. What we internalise, we externalise, or project. So when a woman has a brain loop running on repeat about how her thighs are too fat, she'll be judging other women's thighs as well.

Men, of course, face their own pressures that lead to feelings of inadequacy and inferiority that can be the road to excess weight. They judge themselves as failing to meet the unrealistic pressures on men to be staunch and emotionless at all times. Those ridiculous, so-called 'movies 4 men' spawned by Hollywood perpetuate the inane and narrow stereotype of a one-dimensional 'real man'. These fake 'real men' grunt, kill, avenge, blow things up, shoot guns, and drive recklessly. They never eat, cry or go to the toilet. I would argue that they are not real men. They are dull impersonators and poor substitutes. I wish our amazing boys and men would not measure themselves against these grunting, emotionally stunted Barbie dolls for boys. I wish they felt free to feel and express the full complement of human emotions as opposed to being limited to varying degrees of one emotion, namely anger.

If we, as a species, gave our children the safe space to express their feelings and have those feelings validated, as opposed to silenced or dismissed or ridiculed, maybe we wouldn't end up wearing our emotions, pain, trauma and defences as body fat later in life.

DIETING AS A MENTAL ILLNESS

This desperation and misery about my weight coloured every moment of my life and impacted everything I did and said, as well as what I didn't do and didn't say.

It was an acceptable mental disorder.

No one ever thought there was a problem with me endlessly agonising about my weight because, apparently, this is an appropriate thing for a woman to do—whether she's 13 or 63, a woman should hate her body for something. It's like an unwritten rule.

Admittedly, I don't think anyone understood the full extent of just how obsessed I was with my weight, unless they'd read the pages and pages of angst and self-loathing scribbled in my private diaries.

However, instead of anyone questioning the sanity or happiness of a young woman being so focused on weight and dieting, it was the opposite. I received approval and encouragement when I agonised about my weight. It was even a way of bonding with other women and engendered a sense of belonging.

Men have sport and cars; women have body hate and diets. Because of course I should be worried about my weight! That's what women do! It would be a problem if I WASN'T constantly criticising my hips, thighs, waist... then people would be like, 'who does she think she is? Going around thinking there's nothing wrong with the size of her belly, she should be ashamed of herself! Why isn't she ashamed of herself? She has no thigh gap and her upper arms wobble. It's mortifying. No, I'm sorry, but she really does need to start hating herself more...'

So with all this self-criticism, endless calorie counting and obsessive exercise, did the weight come off? No, of course not. Quite the opposite. It felt like I spent my life in constant battle with a body that wanted to be fat and I was terrified that if I stopped all my efforts, I would end up enormous. I believed that the dieting and exercise may not have gotten me thin *(Yet! Keep trying Fatty Pants!)* but if I stopped, I would be engulfed by a tsunami of body fat. I felt like I was just barely holding back the floodgates of blubber with this regime of self-loathing and calorie counting. My body seemed to be fighting me every step of the way. It was like my body wanted to be fat. And if I ever dropped my guard for a day or two, I would gain two to four kilograms virtually overnight—thus confirming my worst fears about being consumed by a tidal wave of fat if I took my foot off the self-hate and diet-obsession brake. I was trapped in a miserable cycle and I didn't know how to break it.

So what was the issue? My body DID want to be fat. Well, more precisely, my subconscious mind wanted to hold onto a certain amount of adipose tissue, which is the proper name for the intelligent and essential substance we call body fat. My subconscious perceived that this amount of adipose tissue was necessary for my optimal wellbeing. My body was just following instructions.

While the conscious thinking part of me wanted the weight off, so I could finally have the life and love of my dreams, my subconscious mind didn't see it that way. My subconscious had a whole range of very good reasons for keeping on that extra padding. It was trying to keep me alive and safe. So, no matter what I did with regards to reducing calories and increasing exercise, my subconscious had weapons to combat my efforts. From lowering my metabolism and increasing my appetite, to silencing the hormonal signals to the brain that control fat storage and satiety, my efforts with the latest diet plan never stood a chance. So, here's the crux: If you're holding onto excess body fat, your body and brain have good reasons for doing so. Good subconscious reasons. And the subconscious always wins.

It doesn't matter what you consciously want and yearn for. Cognitive neuro-scientists conclude that the conscious mind contributes only about 10 per cent of our cognitive activity. That means that 90 per cent of our decisions, actions, emotions, and behaviours are derived from the processing of the subconscious mind. This is why relying on white-knuckled willpower is useless and counter-productive.

FOUR-SIDED SOLUTION

What, then, needs to happen for you to release your excess body fat? The solution lies in a mental, physical, emotional and spiritual response.

Mentally, the key is in figuring out how the weight is serving you and uprooting the old core beliefs attached to this so that your subconscious mind no longer perceives a benefit in holding onto the excess weight.

Physically, the key is in undoing the diet damage and nourishing yourself properly with real foods so that your body-brain can finally turn off its famine response and regain the ability to burn fat. Like the combat troop that's been fighting in the trenches, your body-brain can at last stand at ease because the enemy has receded. With this battle finished, the troops can now get on with other work, like repairing, maintenance, rebuilding and strengthening.

Emotionally, the key is in processing any feelings, pain and trauma that send you running into the comforting arms of warm scones slathered in jam and cream, or toasted crumpets dripping with butter. Over-eating can cause you to gain weight, we all know that, but we're not asking the most obvious question of all... *why are you over-eating in the first place?*

Over-eating and lethargy are symptoms of the problem, not the causes.

The number one issue? Stress—in its many guises. Mental and emotional stresses cause a chain reaction that create hormonal imbalances that literally force your body to gain and hold onto weight.

Spiritually, it's about remembering who you really are; reconnecting with the Source Consciousness (aka God, Creator, the Universe, Great Spirit, Allah, Great Mother, Him Upstairs, Source Consciousness, All That Is, Buddha, Yahweh... whatever you wish to name the intelligent

31

consciousness that is everything) within you and comprehending your own awesome powers of co-creation. It's about feeling safe to step into your full power.

Once your subconscious mind no longer wants the weight for, say, your physical survival or emotional safety, it will change all the settings in your body to begin releasing the excess fat. It will raise your metabolism, decrease your appetite and turn off your cravings. It'll start burning fat for fuel instead of muscle, it will start laying down more muscle, and it will activate your satiety messages and trigger your desire to move your body. And more. Your subconscious mind has all sorts of powerful tools up its sleeve for changing your physicality.

What kind of beliefs might be hidden in your subconscious mind that are sabotaging your weight-loss efforts? In truth, the possibilities are endless because every one of us is different with a unique set of circumstances and life experiences.

My reasons for holding onto body fat are unique to me and to my life experiences and my inherited genetic coding, as your reasons are to you. The best person to find all the reasons buried in your subconscious that perceive excess body fat as a benefit is you. The purpose of this book is to help with that.

Shall we get on with it then? Yes, let's...

CHAPTER 3
HOW DIETING MAKES YOU FATTER

"This idea that you can just put less [calories] in and the body will just give up fat like some kind of cash machine for fat is quite possibly the most naive assumption we've made in the world of dieting." — Dr Zoe Harcombe, obesity researcher and author of The Obesity Epidemic and The Diet Fix. @zoeharcombe

Dear Diet,
It's over between us. It's not me; it's you. I tried, God knows I tried! I've wasted years on you. But you're boring and you're useless. You promise the world but you deliver nothing but abuse and unhappiness. You don't work, you never do what you say you will and you tell me everything is always my fault. You make me miserable. I've changed the locks and I never want to see you again. Goodbye.

Yours sincerely,
Me.

THE REASONS FOR why we weigh what we weigh are complicated and multi-layered. So many factors come into play that contribute to excess weight, including hormones, inflammation, gut microbiome, medication, unexpressed emotions and unprocessed trauma, sleep, and genes. All these factors and more influence your ability to lose weight and keep it off.

But before we really start exploring what will work for transforming your physical body, let's just knock the final nails into the coffin of the calories-in-calories-out theory.

This belief that reducing calories is the key to weight-loss needs completely dismantling, unpacking, deprogramming, and uprooting as the first step to weight-freedom. And I know that part of you doesn't believe this. Yet.

The 'calories-in-calories-out' thing has been hammered into you too deeply for too long. Don't worry, that's okay. You're welcome to hold on to this for as long as you need it. Like me, you've been so completely indoctrinated with this message that it's going to take some shifting.

Thankfully, the dogma of dieting is starting to be seen as flawed but like the snowball that triggered an avalanche, it will take some effort to redress the damage of the diet snow job.

First though, let's recap the spiel that you now have engraved in your subconscious mind due to decades of incessant mainstream culture brainwashing. It goes like this: *'To lose weight you must eat less and exercise more. To lose one pound of fat, you must create a deficit of 3,500 calories...'* blah blah.

It might sound plausible at first glance but here's the big fat truth—it does not work and it's not true. It is improperly applied science because the human body cannot be compared to the coal-fuelled engine of a steam train.

We were also told that all calories were created equal—so it didn't matter whether you got 500 calories from broccoli or from a family-size box of chocolates.

'A calorie is a calorie,' we were told. Happily, this piece of nonsense is now widely recognised as such but if you're too young to remember that being accepted wisdom, I promise you that this 'all calories are equal' theory was put about like an absolute truth.

Anyway, I'm thinking that chances are you've already let that piece of misinformation go because it really just doesn't make any sense, does it? So maybe if that was nonsense, then the 'eat less do more' theory could be flawed too? Or overly simplistic? Or misleading?

THE CALORIE FALLACY

According to Dr Zoe Harcombe, author of *The Obesity Epidemic*, the calorie deficit formula that's been spouted by government agencies and weight loss authorities for decades is based on a flawed understanding of our bodily processes and it fails to correctly apply the laws of thermodynamics.

Interestingly, no one in a position of authority seems sure about exactly where the calorie formula originated.

Dr Harcombe approached the leading seven UK health organisations that espoused this '3500 calories equals a pound of fat' theory and asked, first, if they could explain it and, second, if they knew where the formula originated. Bodies she approached included the Department of Health and The National Institute for Health and Care Excellence.

None of them could tell her.

"The calorie formula is our conversion between weight and energy," explains Harcombe in a public lecture you can see online[2] that she gave at Cardiff Metropolitan University.

"The British Dietetic Association definition is that a pound of fat contains 3,500 calories. So, to lose a pound a week, you need a deficit of 500 calories a day. Five hundred x seven equals 3,500 calories," Harcombe says.

"There are three problems with this. The first is that one pound of fat does not equal 3,500 calories, not even close. A deficit of 3,500 calories will not lead to a weight-loss of one pound. Never has and never will. The body can and does adjust."

"This idea that you can just put less [calories] in and the body will just give up fat like some kind of cash machine for fat is quite possibly the most naive assumption we've made in the world of dieting," Harcombe says.

"When we tell people to eat less and do more, we think that the body is just going to give up fat. But the body can and does adjust. When you put less in, the body says, 'You know what, I was going to be busy today building bone density, fighting infection, cell repair, but I'm not going to do that now because you haven't put enough energy in. I was also going to walk the dog and maybe do some ironing but I'm not going to do that either,'" Harcombe says.

Starving the body of the energy and nutrients it needs to keep you thriving is basically the most efficient way to get fat, quick. The body-brain views adipose tissue as a precious commodity for survival in times of food scarcity so when it feels its fat stores are under threat, it will bring everything to the table to protect and grow those stores. The body-brain reacts to your efforts to remove your body fat stores in the same way that you would react to someone trying to steal money from your purse. It protests loudly, fights back, and clings to the weight with all its might.

When does the body-brain assume we're in a famine period? When it senses a prolonged, reduced calorie intake. So our dieting efforts are

---

[2] https://www.youtube.com/watch?v=ysoScJ2Q5RQ

triggering our body-brain to implement measures that fight to protect our fat at all cost. Isn't that ironic! It's almost hilarious.

And, boy, the body-brain has some awesomely powerful weapons, cleverly evolved over thousands of years, to keep us safe. For the body-brain, being 'safe' equates to having plenty of precious adipose tissue stockpiled to survive periods of famine. The more often it perceives 'famine' (i.e. dieting), the more fat it wants in storage. Prolonged caloric restriction, which is defined as more than 21 days, puts extra strain on your body, causes metabolic damage, increases cortisol[3] and causes changes to thyroid function (further reducing your metabolism).

When treating adrenal and cortisol-related problems it's important to consume enough calories and nutrients to provide your body with the building blocks for energy production. Dieting is the last thing you should be doing. Ironically, your years of dieting have methodically trained up and strengthened your famine response. You now have an Olympic performing famine response. In tennis terms, your famine response is a powerful and determined Serena Williams.

So, while your body is stubbornly holding onto body fat, it gets the fuel it needs from breaking down your muscle tissue. Your metabolism will be dialled down so you'll feel lethargic, which is why getting to the gym is such a struggle. Your cravings switch will be flicked on, which is why you are preoccupied with food and why, when you do give in and allow yourself *'just one slice of pizza because I've been so good'* you end up inhaling the whole thing and then ordering garlic bread and fries. You hoover this up like you're in a trance-like eating frenzy (because you are) then as you finish the last bite and sit back, you look at the dieting crime scene in front of you and think, 'oh God, why did I do that...' and the self-shame cycle begins.

But here's the thing, you did that because your body-brain made it nigh on impossible not to do it. Your brain had pressed the red panic button and everything within you was set to *'Eat! Eat Now! Eat the most sugary foods you can find! Quick get a donut! Get pizza! Make toast...'* Your body-brain pressed the red button because it had sensed famine through your attempts to reduce your calorie intake.

FLAT EARTH THEORY OF WEIGHT-LOSS
Another voice speaking up against the calorie formula is Jonathan

---

[3] https://www.ncbi.nlm.nih.gov/pubmed/20368473

Bailor, author of New York Times bestseller *The Calorie Myth*. Bailor says that counting calories is the 'flat earth theory of weight-loss'.

"The assumption that your body works like an equation, and that just dropping 500 calories out of your diet creates a 500-calorie deficit, is 100 per cent, unequivocally, not-disputed-by-anyone-who-knows-anything-about-human-biology, false," Bailor said during an online interview.

"Telling someone they just need to 'eat less and exercise more'— think about using that logic in any other area of our lives. Let's say you're trying to start a business and your mentor's advice was 'make more money than you spend'. Or perhaps you're coaching your child's soccer team and you lose and you're asked why and you say, 'we didn't score enough goals and the other team scored too many goals'. Yes, that's true but it's not explaining the issue and it's not particularly helpful," Bailor says.

"Obesity is a disease caused by eating too much of the wrong quality of foods. You cannot become chronically obese by eating too much of the right kinds of foods because your stomach would explode before you over consumed them," says Bailor.

"If you eat 500 fewer calories, you will burn fewer calories. Bottom line, you will be cold, you will be tired, you will be hungry, your brain will be foggy. Your base metabolic rate will drop. If your body is in a caloric shortage state—what does it want? More calories. What burns a lot of calories? Muscle tissue. So, what is it going to burn off first? Muscle tissue.

"So, maybe after you've slowed your body down radically and burnt off a load of muscle tissue, then maybe, your body might burn some fat. But, now, if you ever stop starving yourself, you have a body and brain that is slower, and that has less calorie-hungry muscle tissue on it, so guess what happens? You gain it all back, and then more," Bailor says.

THE HIGH CALORIE CHALLENGE

One man who really wanted to put the calorie deficit formula to the test is UK-based health activist Sam Feltham. In 2013, he set out to test the calorie formula for himself and went on a 21-day, high calorie challenge that he posted on YouTube[4].

For three weeks, Feltham followed a real foods, low carb, high fat

---

4   http://live.smashthefat.com/why-i-didnt-get-fat/

diet, consisting of eggs, nuts, fatty fish, steak and green vegetables equalling 5,794 calories a day.

Based on his daily energy needs of about 3,500 calories and using the conventional theory of 'calories in calories out', he should have gained 7.3kg as the result of a surplus 56,654 calories. However, after those 21 days, he had gained 1.3kg but lost three centimetres from his waist. A 6kg discrepancy.

Why didn't Feltham gain the weight that he should have, according to the calorie formula? The very low carbohydrate intake meant there was little to no insulin being triggered and without insulin there's no fat storage. Also, Feltham's body-brain didn't want any extra adipose tissue because no famine was sensed so it increased his metabolic rate to burn up the excess because adjusting like this is what it does so brilliantly.

This, my beautiful friend, is why you can cut your calorie intake to 1000 calories a day and not shed fat—your body-brain makes the necessary adjustments.

Interestingly, Feltham went on to do a similar 21-day experiment where he ate exactly the same number of calories as the first experiment— about 5,794—but this time the foods were all low fat, high carb and highly processed foods like bread, cereal, low fat yogurt, crumpets, skim milk, etc. The result? This lean, muscular, young man-machine chubbed up like a fatty pants.

Over just 21 days, Feltham gained a massive seven kilograms (15.5lbs) while eating a diet high in processed carbohydrates. The typical western diet, in other words. He gained weight because it is not the calories in food that count, it is the nutrients and quality of the food that counts. Although I would like to add in a caveat here. Feltham was a fit, lean, 20-something male, which is, hormonally speaking, a planet away from a 50-something menopausal female.

LARDY LABOURERS

As well as the calorie myth, it's time to examine more closely the oft-repeated assumption that we're all so much fatter because we're eating more and exercising less than we did 50 years ago. This is a fallacy, wrote journalist George Monbiot in an article called Obesophobia[5] for The Guardian newspaper in August 2018. Monbiot found that 1976 was the year that we all started getting fatter but

---

[5] https://www.monbiot.com/2018/08/17/obesophobia/

incredibly, we're actually eating fewer calories than we did back then and we are just as physically active.

"According to government[6] figures," wrote Monbiot, "we currently consume an average of 2131 kcals per day, a figure that appears to include sweets and alcohol. But in 1976, we consumed 2280 kcal,[7] excluding alcohol and sweets, or 2590 when they're included."

Monbiot also looked at the assumption that we're exercising and moving less than we used to in the past. The general perception being that the decline in manual labour and voluntary exercise is a contributor to our weight woes.

Again, this seems to make sense, writes Monbiot but the data doesn't support it.

"A paper in the International Journal of Surgery[8] states that 'adults working in unskilled manual professions are over 4 times more likely to be classified as morbidly obese compared with those in professional employment'."

In other words, our labourers are lardier than our lawyers. Go figure. But if we can't blame calories and cardio, where then lies the root of our problem?

Just follow the money into the pockets of the corporate food giants, writes Monbiot.

"We have been deliberately and systematically outgunned. Food companies have invested heavily in designing products that use sugar to bypass our appetite control mechanisms, and packaging and promoting them to break down what remains of our defences, including through the use of subliminal scents. They employ an army of food scientists and psychologists to trick us into eating more junk (and therefore less wholesome food) than we need, while their advertisers use the latest findings in neuroscience to overcome our resistance.

"They hire biddale scientists and thinktanks to confuse us about the causes of obesity. Above all, just as the tobacco companies did with smoking, they promote the idea that weight is a question of 'personal

---

[6] https://www.gov.uk/government/statistical-data-sets/family-food-datasets

[7]

https://assets.publishing.service.gov.uk/government/uploads/system/uploads/attachment_data/file/549223/ Domestic_Food_Consumption_and_Expenditure_1976.pdf

[8] https://www.ncbi.nlm.nih.gov/pmc/articles/PMC5673154/

responsibility'. After spending billions on overriding our willpower, they blame us for failing to exercise it," writes Monbiot.

THE CALORIE CONUNDRUM

So yes, the calorie counting approach had us all fooled for a while, and yes, we all went along with it but that theory has now proven to be obsolete. Instead of getting back on that old broken bike and insisting it's 'absolutely fine' even when the wheels are falling off, we all just need to draw a line under that whole sorry mess, pick ourselves up and move on. We got it wrong. Badly, horrifically, wrong and millions of people all over the world are now suffering the consequences of that mistake through chronic illness and obesity.

When you think about it, the idea that we can manipulate our body-brains by regulating our calorie intake is insulting to the intelligence, design and brilliance of our body-brains. This is an ignorant model that treats the body-brain as stupid, passive and easily manipulated.

The truth is that the body-brain is powerful and resourceful beyond our realisation. It can, and does, adjust its calorific requirements based on what it receives.

To give you an example, 70 to 80 per cent of the calories you burn have nothing to do with how much you exercise. It's your organs—your liver, heart, kidneys and brain—that soak up a massive amount of energy every day to keep you alive and functioning. Your liver alone burns between 400 to 700 calories a day. This is why you can never completely control 'calories out'. Your body will auto adjust how it burns calories based on how you fuel it. If you eat less, it is a fact that your body will burn fewer calories. Everything you do to your 'calories in' impacts how your body handles 'calories out'. Then, when you manipulate calories out by exercising more, what happens? It makes you hungrier. So by burning more, it drives you to want to eat more.

Does that mean exercise is pointless? No, definitely not, our bodies were designed to move and they thrive on it. However, the most important reasons to exercise and move your body have nothing to do with burning calories. The importance of moving is because it dramatically and quickly shifts the hormonal dance constantly going on in your body.

That is what brings about physical transformation—not to mention mental and emotional transformation. This all-important hormonal dance decides whether you're a fat storer or a fat burner.

Moving your body and weight-resistance activity is important because it builds muscle tissue and causes our body-brains to squirt

40

out a completely different cocktail of hormones. This is why you can lose weight from a meditation practice. That's right, just sitting around meditating can make you thinner. Again, it's not about calories, it's about the effects of the meditation, which is to remove fat-storing, stress hormones like cortisol from your system.

Unless you're being chased by a tiger, cortisol is basically a 'store fat' switch. If you are being chased by a tiger, all that screaming and running for your life will burn up all the glucose being pumped into your system by cortisol and no fat will be stored. However, if you're in an ongoing state of low grade or chronic stress (like about 98 per cent of us) from financial worries, marital stress, sleep deprivation and so on, then that glucose isn't getting burned up and so your blood sugar levels remain high because the available energy is not being used for vigorous physical exertion.

Your pancreas senses the high levels of glucose in the blood stream and releases the insulin hounds to get rid of it. Pancreas doesn't care what insulin does with the glucose, as long as it's removed from the blood stream. So insulin pushes as much as it can into your liver and muscles then all the rest is packed up into the fat cells for storage where it can do the least harm, which is generally around your belly.

Here's the sciencey bit to remember: Insulin makes you fat and insulin is triggered by the presence of sugars (aka glucose) in the bloodstream.

How do sugars sneak their way into your blood stream? Cake, pasta, bread and biscuits are one sure-fire route but there's another major culprit as well, stress. When you're stressed, your body pumps out cortisol, which triggers the breaking down of muscle tissue into sugars to be burnt for energy in running away from that tiger. Again, when there's no tiger and the sugars don't get burnt up in a life-dependent sprint, pancreas steps up to tell insulin to push those sugars into fat cells. So cortisol makes you gain weight too.

Let's really boil that down to the bones. Sugars and stress make you fat because of the hormonal shifts they trigger, mainly the release of insulin. If there's insulin around, your body is storing fat. When is insulin around? It comes hand in hand with stress and sugars.

LEPTIN RESISTANCE

The traditional view of body fat, or adipose tissue, is that it's just some blubbery, butter-like, unsightly storage bin for excess energy that is packed onto our frame under our skin and on top of our muscles like a type of insulation cladding or the padding that's used in protective sportswear. We haven't given our fat stores much credit for having any intelligence or any real use. However, we now know that body fat stores are in fact an active endocrine gland, which means they make stuff like hormones and inflammatory chemicals. Our fat isn't just sitting there going 'duh,' it's busy with all sorts of important work.

One of the hormones made by our fat cells is leptin. This hormone is part of our hard-wired starvation defence system, in other words our famine response system, aka our 'diet resistance system'. Why? Because our ancestors lived in a world of feast or famine. For thousands of years, the human body had to adapt to regular periods of famine and to survive these times, body fat was a very precious commodity that could literally mean the difference to you between surviving the winter or not. For our ancestors, it was more relevant in a way to talk about survival of the fattest than it was to talk about survival of the fittest. Our 21st Century bodies and brains are still operating under this famine response system.

How does the body-brain know that it needs to baton down the hatches and prepare for a tough period of famine? One of the signals it reads is a lower intake of calories over extended periods of time—in other words, when the human goes on a reduced calorie diet.

The body-brain notices the reduced calorie intake, senses the threat of starvation and goes all out to preserve the precious fat stores. As well, it ensures the human becomes hyper aware of food opportunities and, should they come up, the human is hard-wired to make the most of them. In other words, binge eating and cravings.

When your average dieter gets locked into this cycle of 'starvation' and binge-eating, the body-brain takes this as validation that it has correctly assessed the famine-feast situation and proudly notes how well it did in keeping as much fat stores in place as well as making as much more fat as possible from the feasting opportunity.

'Gold star for me!' Thinks body-brain.

'We got our human through this famine and she's even fatter than when we started! Damn, I'm so good at this survival stuff...'

The human stays alive to face another famine and the body-brain gives itself a high-five, completely unaware that their female human was enduring the whole low calorie torture in the hope of getting into a smaller dress for an upcoming birthday party of an old school friend. A number of ex-boyfriends would also be attending this party, not to mention that naturally skinny old frenemy, Michelle, who used to say things to this human like, *'oh, I wish I could gain weight on my belly and hips like you, it's so very womanly to be pear-shaped, isn't it?'*

Nope, body-brain is blissfully unaware of party dresses and back-handed bitchiness. Body-brain is still running on operating software developed in the time of Neanderthal woman and it has not yet been updated to the 21st Century version of 24/7 supermarkets, food delivery phone apps, and drive-thru diners.

So, our body-brains are all about survival and this is where the leptin comes in. Your fat stores are in constant communication with your brain. They are constantly sending messages to the hypothalamus in the brain and leptin is the crucial messenger.

If you haven't heard much about leptin, it could be because as far as hormones go, this is the new kid on the block. The science bods didn't even discover it until 1994 but even with this late start, this is the hormone that's now considered to be the master hormone when it comes to your body weight. This one hormone can control your hunger and satiety, your cravings, your metabolism and how much weight you carry on your body. So you can imagine how excited everyone was when they realised they'd at last found this amazing hormone that is really in the driving seat when it comes to how fat or thin we are, as well as our energy levels.

Like with insulin, we ideally want to be extremely sensitive to leptin. When this hormone messenger reports to the the brain that there is too much fat being stored on the body, we want the brain to sit up and take notice.

Because have you ever wondered how the brain knows that the body is, or isn't, carrying too much fat? The brain can't 'see' the fat, it relies on all its various hormonal messengers to report back on what's going on in the different parts of the body then, like a central HQ, the brain or, more specifically, the hypothalamus, will send out whatever resources are needed to address the situation at hand.

All your organs and glands produce hormones that communicate with all the other cells, that's how everyone knows what's going on in the body.

In the case of fat cells, the more fat you have, the more leptin is produced. This leptin travels via the bloodstream to the brain and basically says, 'hey Brain, look, sorry to bother you, I know you're busy but just to let you know, there's a whole heap of extra fat being stored around the belly of our human today because it's their birthday and you know the deal with all the chocolate and cake... we have way too much fat on our body, you need to do that stuff you do to burn it.'

And the brain replies, 'OMG there's so much of you Leptin! That means our body is too fat. Damn that cookie dough ice-cream cake.

How ironic, this human tradition of celebrating life with the over-consumption of this processed white sugar toxin that actually kills life... [Brain can be very cynical].

'Ok, we have to get this fat off our body asap, thanks for the heads-up Leptin, I'll tell the whole team to get on to it... Thyroid, please speed up the metabolism. Liver, please burn more fat. Stomach, please reduce your capacity and I want satiety signals ramped up to maximum. Attention everyone, all desire for carbohydrates and sugars is to be turned off effective immediately...'

When your brain and body is working together in this way to release excess fat, it's easy to maintain your ideal weight. So why doesn't this process kick in to keep all of us thin all of the time? Because just like with insulin resistance, our brains can become resistant to leptin. The brain just doesn't hear leptin knocking at the door anymore. This is why it doesn't work to simply take leptin injections to lose weight. Severely overweight people already have plenty of leptin in their bloodstream; the problem is that the brain has gone 'leptin deaf'.

Just like with Goldilocks and the three bears, there is an optimal 'just right' level of leptin—not too much and not too little—that facilitates weight-loss. Too much leptin means the brain goes 'leptin deaf'. It thinks the human is starving so flicks all the switches for storing fat.

Too little leptin and, again, the brain thinks the human is starving so turns on fat-making and fat-preserving mode. Leptin levels need to be somewhere in the middle for the brain to be able to hear what leptin has to say and to regulate body weight as appropriate.

So obviously if you've become leptin resistant, reversing that condition is a number one priority for losing weight. What causes leptin resistance? A number of factors. One of which is, as I've already said, calorie restriction or dieting, which the brain views as a famine situation and takes immediate steps to redress. Other factors that cause, or contribute to, leptin resistance include chronic stress and inflammation, toxicity, triglycerides, polyunsaturated fats, over-eating, sleep deprivation, food intolerances, refined carbs and sugars, and also insulin resistance.

That's right, being insulin resistant can make you leptin resistant as well. If you've got both of these bad boys playing at your fat party, it's impossible to lose weight permanently until you get rid of them.

So again, our not-so-good friend sugar is lurking in the background of the whole sorry mess.

Other causes are chronic stress and chronic inflammation because the hormones involved in stress and inflammation can prevent the brain from sending the commands that it would normally send in its response to leptin.

Chronically elevated triglycerides will also cause leptin resistance, which can arise from stress and processed foods. The triglycerides ambush leptin and stop it from getting to the brain to deliver its message.

So, a whole host of paths lead us to leptin resistance and many of us are walking more than one of these paths.

CHAPTER 4
BITTERSWEET HORMONAL SYMPHONY

"Fat is a social disease and fat is a feminist issue. Fat is not about lack of self-control or lack of willpower. Fat is about protection, sex, nurturance, strength, boundaries, mothering, substance, assertion and rage. It's a response to inequality of the sexes. Fat expresses experiences of women today in ways that are seldom examined and even more seldom treated." —Susie Orbach, author, Fat is a Feminist Issue. @psychoanalysis

I'VE TOUCHED ON IT already but let's really go deep into hormones now because it is a KEY issue. That's right, this point is so vital to the weight-loss conundrum that I spelt 'KEY' in capitals. That's how serious I am about this piece of information. In fact, this issue could easily be a book on its own. So, are you ready? More capital letters are coming. I'm basically yelling this at you. Here it is:

YOUR HORMONES ARE KEEPING YOU FAT!

That is so important that I'm going to say it again.

SUCCESSFUL WEIGHT-LOSS IS ABOUT HORMONAL BALANCE!

Calories schmalories. One of the biggest secret keys in unlocking the door to your fat trap is getting to grips with your personal hormonal dance. When it comes to releasing and regulating the amount of body fat you're carrying on your frame, hormones are a major brick in the obesity wall.

A hormone is a chemical messenger. It's the job of your hormones to communicate messages around your body. These hormones are how different parts of the body 'talk' to each other.

A hormone is a messenger that travels through the blood while neurotransmitters are messengers that travel through the nervous system. So cortisol, leptin, ghrelin and insulin are hormones, while dopamine, serotonin and endorphin are neurotransmitters.

Our hormonal balance decides whether we're horny, hungry, sleepy or moody, and so on. Hormones, or chemical messengers, are produced in the glands and organs of the endocrine system, which includes the thyroid, pancreas, pineal, pituitary, and ovaries and testes. They then hitch a ride through the bloodstream to deliver messages to tissues and organs throughout the body, including the brain.

So far, scientists have identified about 50 different hormones in the body and you've probably heard of some of them, there's estrogen, progesterone, testosterone, thyroid, cortisol, insulin, leptin, ghrelin, and more.

Hormones control most of our body's major systems including heart rate, metabolism, appetite, mood, sexual function, reproduction, growth and development, sleep cycles, and more. So our bodies are a 24/7 hormone producing factory. Every second of every minute, a thousand times a second, your body-brain is pumping out the hormones and chemicals that it needs to function properly.

With just a thought, your body can respond by squirting out a particular hormone or neurotransmitter. If it's a stressful thought like *'Oh my god I'll never meet this deadline...'* or *'how will I pay for new school uniforms?'* then that hormone may be cortisol, which as you know is the Big Daddy of the 'fight or flight' survival response.

If it's a loving thought then that response may be a squirt of dopamine, which is one of the 'feel good' neurotransmitters, along with serotonin and oxytocin.

The science bods call this 'hormonal dynamics', a phrase that refers to the changes in our hormonal state in response to factors such as what we consume, our thoughts and emotions, our stress levels, toxin exposure, our environment, and more. What's particularly pertinent though is that it's our thoughts—both conscious and unconscious—that profoundly alter our hormonal dynamics.

So we are no longer looking at food in terms of calories. We are now looking at food in terms of what information that food is communicating to our body.

The crucial question, therefore, is not: 'How many calories does this thing I'm about to eat have?' The crucial question is: 'What kind of hormonal changes will take place in my body in response to this thing I'm about to eat? And to how I feel about eating it?'

Interestingly, different people can respond differently on a hormonal level to the same foods, which is why one way of eating works for someone while it doesn't work for another. In the same way, one person can happily eat peanuts while someone with an allergy can die from inhaling peanut dust.

When you dig down, most people are overweight because they have one or more ongoing hormonal imbalances in their body.

A number of hormonal-related conditions cause weight-gain. These include Hashimoto's thyroiditis and hypothyroidism, estrogen dominance, and adrenal fatigue.

Hormonal imbalances can be triggered by a variety of factors—stress, sugar, thyroid function, dieting, environmental toxins, etc. Once a hormonal condition develops, it must be healed before weight-loss can happen.

This is where us chronic dieters make our cataclysmic mistake. We continue to be obsessed with weight-loss above all else and do not realise that we need to heal our systems before the body is even capable of burning up fat stores. And the more we attempt to diet, which is read by the body-brain as starvation, the more out-of-whack our hormonal dynamics becomes as the body-brain goes into battle to save us from this 'starvation'.

INSULIN RESISTANCE

You've probably heard of insulin. Most of us associate insulin with diabetes since that is what diabetics inject themselves with to manage their condition. All of us, though, have insulin naturally produced by our bodies and this hormone plays a vital role in controlling our blood sugar levels.

Insulin is the big hitter of the fat-making hormones. The big chief of the fatty tribe. When this guy is around all the time, there's almost nothing you can do to release excess weight because insulin is all about creating fat.

Insulin gets released by the pancreas when it senses sugars in your bloodstream. The pancreas is kind of like a farmer who sees rabbits (sugars) in his fields and releases the dogs (insulin) on them.

That's not all though. There's another side to the fat-making insulin coin. When your body is in fat-making mode, thanks to the work of insulin, it is not possible for your body to burn fat. Why? Because insulin instructs glucagon to pull back and let him get on with what he's doing.

Glucagon is the fat-burning hormone but when insulin is around, glucagon takes a break from fat-burning until insulin buggers off. It's a double whammy, slap in the face, then, for anyone hoping to shed body fat.

While insulin is on a fat-making rampage, fat-burning glucagon takes a holiday.

Things get really bad for the hopeful weight-loser though when insulin just doesn't ever go away. That's a condition known as insulin resistance, it means our insulin levels are perpetually raised and your body is locked in a fat-making state—you've basically lost the ability to burn fat. If you're someone who regularly consumes more sugars than the body can easily process and, as a result, has developed insulin resistance from exhausting the pancreas, the next stop is type 2 diabetes. How much sugar does it take to trigger the release of insulin? A teaspoon. That's right, just one little teaspoon, or 4gm, of sugar kicks off the fat-storage process.

We develop insulin resistance when there is simply too much sugar for too much of the time, especially if it's quickly absorbed or 'fast' sugars like high fructose corn syrup. Insulin resistance is basically when the insulin comes along to push sugar into the cells of the muscles and liver but his key no longer unlocks the cells' door. 'Oh no!' thinks insulin. 'Where can I put all this toxic sugar to get it out of the bloodstream? I know! I'll dump it all in the fat cells around the belly. Phew! Disaster averted.'

Of course your waistline gets a bit bigger each time insulin has to leave extra sugar with the fat cells (well, hello there Pot belly and Muffin top).

Along with the ongoing presence of sugars, the other factors that contribute to insulin resistance are chronic stress and chronic inflammation. The stress hormones, such as cortisol, basically drown out the insulin messages. The stress hormones are yelling 'don't listen to insulin, listen to us, it's urgent that you listen to us!' and so the cells do.

REVERSING INSULIN RESISTANCE

One of the keys in reversing this is making our bodies sensitive to insulin again. Obviously one of the main factors in doing this is, like, duh, drastically cutting your consumption of 'fast' carbohydrates and processed sugars. As well, it's important to deal with the reasons that your brain is flicking on the 'fight or flight' switch, aka your stress response. This includes the stress of reduced calories on an ongoing basis but it also means looking at lifestyle stresses like financial and relationship worries, and unresolved trauma from your past.

In addition, you can consume more foods that make your cells sensitive to insulin again and that improve the body's ability to store the carbs you eat as muscle glycogen instead of fat. Here are some tips:

1. Massively, enormously, increase your vegetable intake, especially green vegetables.

2. Eat healthy fats full of omega 3 such as coconut oil, avocado, nuts, oily fish.

3. Drink a cup of green tea before every meal.

4. Start the day with the juice of a lemon in hot water.

5. Use spices such as cinnamon, turmeric and fenugreek, in cooking or as herbal tea

6. Eat a handful of almonds and walnuts every day or so.

7. Eat high magnesium foods like leafy greens, pumpkin seeds, almonds, cashews, and broccoli. Magnesium is a natural insulin sensitiser.

I guess that maybe you're now thinking *'oh wow, great, all I need to do is cut out sugar and drink some green tea and I'll be thin'*. Because that's what I thought when I first learned about insulin sensitivity. Here's the reality check though. If you're not dealing with your stress, beliefs, and emotional health, you won't do that because the human relationship with sugar is much more complex than just our insulin response.

If you're an emotional eater who uses sugars and fast carbs as self-medication to numb painful feelings such as worthlessness, anxiety, grief, regret, or resentment... you can try drinking all the green tea you want but when that emotional tsunami hits, or those subconscious switches are flicked, all the scientific data on insulin sensitivity and hormonal dynamics is out the window and you're driving to the 24-hour convenience store for a loaf of white bread, peanut butter, chocolate spread and ice-cream.

Yes, there is absolutely no doubt that we should all be aware that the amount of sugar the world is consuming now is a staggering 230 times the amount our ancestors were consuming 200 years ago.

And, yes, if you haven't already I would suggest you make changes now to reduce the amount of processed sugars you're consuming but also know that this is not the whole story. So if you've been trying to do that and still you haven't succeeded, don't fall back into that self-blame guilt cycle. It's a waste of time and doesn't get to the root of the issues.

If all it took was being aware of the damage that the various substances were doing to our bodies to make us change our ways then no one would smoke cigarettes, no one would take heroin or cocaine, no one would drink alcohol. But we do. Why? There are many reasons but one of them is because it feels good. Another is because it numbs our pain and makes us forget. Sugar dulls our pain, that's why we take it.

Let me illustrate this point with an anecdote about one of my clients, a man named Matt, who lives in the UK.

Matt is a very clever, fifty-something, high achiever with an important job who had given up smoking some years earlier. He felt great about having given up smoking and hadn't been a smoker for about five years when he started coming to me for sessions for a different issue. As far as he was concerned, smoking was conquered and no longer any kind of issue.

Yes, he'd had the odd puff of a single cigarette at parties but he could count those occasions on one hand in five years and even that he hadn't done for a good 18 months so he was baffled when, on a two-week work trip to Munich in Germany, he had sudden and intense cravings for cigarettes.

By this time, there was definitely no physiological addiction because all the substances like nicotine had long since left his system and he'd also shifted his psychological triggers because he'd had absolutely no desire to smoke for 18 months even when he was with friends in bars and pubs. Yet suddenly, when he was in Munich for work, it was all Matt could do not to buy a packet of cigarettes and smoke the lot. In fact, this craving was so strong he did give in to it, he bought a pack of cigarettes, sat in a bar by himself and smoked half the packet in one sitting. After which, he was engulfed with feelings of shame, regret and disappointment in himself.

What was going on? During an energy healing session, we uncovered some old beliefs and insecurities that had triggered Matt's desire to smoke cigarettes. Specifically, this concerned some old, deeply buried subconscious beliefs that Matt had about not fitting in, not belonging, being isolated and feeling lonely.

The reason these old limiting beliefs had surfaced on his work trip was because he was living in a hotel by himself for those two weeks. He would spend his days at a workplace where he knew no one and was the only native English speaker. He felt ignored and left out when everyone around him carried on conversations in German. Then he'd go back to the hotel and either stay in his room by himself or eat alone in the hotel restaurant. He missed his wife back in the UK, he felt lonely and isolated and as though he didn't belong.

These kinds of feelings and beliefs were exactly the same motivating factors for why Matt had first started smoking at the age of 11 when his family had moved to another country and he found himself the new boy and a foreigner in a challenging school environment. How did he find a way to fit in with the other boys at school? By smoking with them behind the bike sheds in school breaks and after school.

So, using healing techniques such as EFT Tapping and ThetaHealing, I worked with Matt on clearing his limiting beliefs and the attached emotions from that time in childhood when he had felt like an outcast and cigarettes had come to his rescue. We replaced them with positive beliefs and feelings of being accepted, and of belonging, in order to dissolve the triggers that caused the urge for cigarettes.

My point being that we reach for substances and distractions like tobacco, food, alcohol, porn, television, social media, and so on, for reasons that are beyond our conscious mind. So yes, by all means slash all processed sugars and refined foods from your life, drink your green smoothies with spirulina, eat your chia seed and flaxseed porridge with organic unsweetened almond milk, cover your steamed vegetables with kale pesto, and get to your yoga class three times a week. All that stuff is wonderful and will have your amazing body looking and feeling healthier but if you're supplementing your kale breakfast smoothie with a mid-morning bar of chocolate and a croissant then don't beat yourself up. There is something going on in your system that is triggering that craving and your body has a good reason for it. Just like Matt with his cigarettes, you are not weak and lazy and hopeless, it's just that the human relationship to food—and your relationship to food—is a great deal more complex than it's given credit for by a straight nutrition-only-focused approach.

Are you a little closer to deleting the *'eat less do more'* file that's playing on endless repeat in your subconscious mind? If you're not convinced yet, don't worry, we'll come back to this later but in the meantime let's push on and go on a journey into your head because that's where all the fun's happening.

CHAPTER 5
YOUR SUBCONSCIOUS WANTS THE WEIGHT

"You will find a lot of naturally thin people saying 'just don't eat'. This is like telling an insomniac to 'just get into bed and you'll fall asleep'."— Marisa Peer, behavioural psychologist and therapist @MarisaPeer

TARA TAYLOR WEIGHED 606lbs when she first appeared on the reality tv show My 600lb Life, a programme that follows super morbidly obese people through the process of having bypass surgery for weight loss. This kind of surgery has about a five per cent chance of long-term success and it's often fatal. People still have this kind of procedure because they simply don't know what else to do.

When Tara was 15, her father died suddenly. Then at age 26, she was raped and as a result fell pregnant and then had a miscarriage. From that point on, Tara's weight kept rising.

"Food doesn't judge me," Tara said.

"Whether I'm happy or sad, I'll always have food. Food has always been my safe haven.

"I got a lot bigger after [the miscarriage]. I thought if I gained a lot of weight, no man would want to touch me and I would be safe."

So Tara had some really good subconscious reasons for masking her sexuality beneath a suit of body fat armour but still she loathed herself for her 'weakness' around food and over-eating.

"After I eat, I feel angry with myself and I beat myself up for it," Tara says to the camera.

Of course she does because, as a society, we have failed Tara.

Instead of having systems in place that offer her love, support and healing in the wake of personal trauma or tragedy, we give her judgment. Oh and we offer her low calorie dieting—a sure-fire way to gain more weight and loathe yourself.

When a person is morbidly or significantly obese, they're beaten up, ground down, and constantly punishing themselves.

Living life in a morbidly obese body is incredibly difficult. It creates all sorts of other problems, from the ever-present pain of the weight wearing down the cartilage in the knee joints to the constant exhaustion from never sleeping properly due to sleep apnea, the open skin sores that develop from over hanging 'apron' skin or from 'chub rub' when the thighs chafe, to the oedema, or swelling, in the feet and legs. The icing on the cake of course is the public humiliation and criticism.

We look at the super morbidly obese people on our screens and shake our heads in bewilderment of how that person, who is clearly desperate to have their mobility and life choices back, is still pushing buckets of chicken nuggets and boxes of donuts into their mouths.

'How can they do that to themselves? What's wrong with them?' We ask in disgust, disbelief and pity.

It is the same reason why the man who has gambled away his family's life savings and destroyed his marriage as a result is still driven to place another bet. The same reason why the alcoholic with chronic liver disease cannot resist another drink despite it having cost their job, their relationships, and their health. It is the same reason why the woman with emphysema eating away at her lungs still can't resist lighting up another cigarette.

Does it really sound like the best advice here is 'just stop it!'?

The subconscious drivers involved in this kind of behaviour are powerful and complex and we all have some version of them to a greater or lesser extent.

Which brings me to the main point of this section. I will put it as simply and bluntly as possible: If you're carrying excess body fat that just won't budge, or might go away but always comes back, it's because some part of you, your subconscious mind, has reasons for this extra weight.

These reasons could include saving you from famine or from financial hardship, or by offering emotional support or physical protection, or by playing out some inherited ancestral coding or past life vow, commitment, trauma, obligation, or similar.

I know. It's hard to swallow, isn't it (unlike that tub of delicious cookie dough ice-cream with hot chocolate sauce...).

Consciously, up here on the surface at the tip of the iceberg where logic and reason reign, it is clear that the extra weight is unwanted and it must go. So you go to all sorts of ridiculous and expensive lengths to get rid of this excess body fat—from starving yourself on cabbage juice for a week to buying some abdominal-crunching machine and diet snack bars 'in three exciting flavours!' off the shopping channel at 2am.

It doesn't matter what physical actions you take, though, because if your subconscious wants the excess adipose tissue to stay where it is on your hips or belly then, ultimately, that's what's going to happen. Even if you have all the fat sucked out by surgeons with expensive machines. If your body-brain sees a benefit in having it, it will replace it over time.

When your subconscious drivers shift and the weight is perceived by your brain as more of a detriment than as a benefit, then it will be released from your frame.

PRIMAL URGES

Have you ever noticed how people who've broken up from their partner often lose a lot of weight and get a new hair cut? After the obligatory week of sobbing in bed with a tub of ice-cream and an Adele album on repeat, that is. That's their subconscious survival drivers kicking in.

If you're a heterosexual woman aged somewhere from 20 to 40, your lizard brain survival programmes might be saying something like *'oh no, I must find a new mate who will protect and provide for me and our children. I must be as appealing as I can in order to attract the strongest, most virile male...'*

If you're a heterosexual man, your genetic survival drivers may be saying, *'I must spread my seed to continue my lineage! I must be attractive to the opposite sex to beat out the competition and secure a faithful mate who will nurture my offspring...'*

It's not just about going forth to multiply though.

People from the LGBT+ community also have strong drivers to partner up and create their own family unit, as do heterosexuals who are beyond the breeding age. As humans, we're hard-wired to crave companionship, connection, and intimacy.

So, suddenly, recently-singled 21st Century man and woman find they look forward to getting to the gym every day and, strangely, their efforts at last seem to be reaping results.

They might think to themselves, 'Wow, I'm finally getting the hang of this fitness and weight-loss thing, I feel unstoppable! Is it the daily tablespoon of apple cider vinegar that's making the difference? Or that new maca powder in my breakfast green smoothie...'

Perhaps they strut around the gym feeling smug about this surge of granite-like determination while looking down on all the other poor fatties who just don't have their super-sized willpower.

What's really happened though is that something in the singleton's subconscious has shifted. Priorities have changed so the brain has reset the body's chemistry to shed excess weight and generally appear younger. It's also brewed up a heady cocktail of pheromones that's now coming off the looking-for-a-mate gym-goer in waves. They are on the human version of heat and it's probably just a matter of time before they'll once again be comfortably coupled up. That's when the gym membership will lapse and, mysteriously, they'll not have the same drive to do those Body Pump double classes three times a week. Instead, they'll spend their evenings snuggling on the sofa with their new partner and a DVD box set of *Peaky Blinders.*

My husband, Adrian, says this was his experience. He says that, when his first marriage of 25 years came to an end, he became a man possessed with getting back into shape. Things got a bit extreme. He started living on not much more than bananas and went to the gym for an hour to two hours every single day for months. He said this level of commitment took no willpower on his part, he was driven by a primal determination and a need to get 'back in the game'. If he hadn't had to go to work, he says, he would have spent all day in the gym.

In just three months, Adrian had shed the 20kg (45lb) that had been seemingly impossible to budge for the previous decade. Sporting his newly trimmed waistline, he then began online dating. The rest is our happy history. [In case you're wondering, Adrian has gained about 10kgs of it back and stabilised at this new weight.]

The weight rollercoaster is not just about finding a mate though. I've had several male and female clients come to me with mysterious weight gain that, on digging, we realised coincided with them losing their jobs or feeling that their job was not secure.

All of them found that the weight melted away again once they got a new job, or felt secure in their role again. Why? Again it's our inbuilt primitive survival response. Our Neanderthal lizard brains are programmed to store excess body fat so that we have enough energy in reserve to survive through times of famine. So far so clear but here's where it gets more complex because, as far as our subconscious is concerned, a threat to the salary we get from our 21st Century office job is perceived in the same way as a brutal winter in 40,000BC. They're both about survival and having enough food to eat. A job threat or financial worries can trigger the famine response of 'Stockpile fat now! We might need it!'

These inbuilt subconscious drivers have done us proud as a species. They are the reason that humans can thrive and survive in just about every corner of the planet no matter what the climate or the environmental challenges.

THE SUBCONSCIOUS ALWAYS WINS

In a battle between the two minds, the subconscious always wins. It doesn't matter what you consciously want. Your conscious mind has the firepower of a cigarette lighter in comparison to your subconscious mind's fleet of nuclear warships. This is why putting your faith in willpower is setting yourself up for failure. Needing to apply willpower to achieve something is a sure sign it's not fully in alignment with your subconscious belief system in some way. This is a signal to you that there is an issue that needs exploring.

Every single behaviour that you demonstrate, whether it be good, bad, frightening, or ridiculous, is run by your subconscious mind. So if you want to change a behaviour, you cannot do it by willpower alone, you have to get into the subconscious mind and change it there. That's when transformation takes place.

If you're one of the people who've been battling the bulge for decades, and would literally sacrifice a limb to be thin if offered the chance, it can be hard to digest the idea that you're fat because something in your subconscious perceives a benefit in keeping the fat.

And I'm not exaggerating when I say 'sacrifice a limb'. Studies have shown that formerly morbidly obese people who lost weight would actually prefer to have a limb amputated or their vision or hearing sacrificed, rather than be fat again.

One such study[9], carried out by researchers at the University of Florida led by Dr. Colleen Rand, was done on a group of people who had lost an average of 100 pounds (45kg) each through intestinal bypass surgery. The majority of these people said they would rather have a leg amputated or be blind than have the weight back. The precise numbers were that 100 per cent of those researched would rather be deaf, 89 per cent would rather be blind and 91 per cent

---

[9] www.researchgate.net/publication/21319699

would rather have a leg amputated—than be obese. Interestingly, all the patients also said they would rather be normal weight than be a morbidly obese multi-millionaire. This offers some small inkling of how profoundly traumatic it is to feel helplessly trapped in a morbidly obese body.

The imaginative and desperate lengths that humans resort to in search of the magical secret to weight-loss is extraordinary. This is how we ended up with jaw wiring and liposuction. Sometimes these lengths are even fatal, such is the desperation to be thinner. Many of us are so determined to be rid of this excess body fat that we go under the knife to have expensive and dangerous surgery.

We pay to have our fat sucked out, or sliced off, as well as to have parts of our stomach cut out. We'll even take out crippling bank loans or re-mortgage our houses to pay for this kind of treatment even though the long-term success rates are depressingly low.

Other people swallow handfuls of pharmaceutical drugs that come with all sorts of nasty and dangerous side effects. *'Who cares if my bones crumble, my hips seize up, or my liver fails in a few years*,' they cry, *'at least I'll be thin!'*

Others of us spend an eye-watering fortune on weight-loss programmes that basically involve being starved in exotic locations whilst getting wrapped in clingfilm and covered in seaweed. And yet, globally, we are fatter than ever.

Desperate, morbidly obese and overweight people are having their bodies carved up in the vain hope it'll leave them thinner. They would literally try anything to reduce weight because life as an obese person is incredibly tough. Every second of living life in a super morbidly obese body is difficult. It is physically painful and emotionally harrowing. Being so large robs a person of their life, their joy, their relationships, their health. It creates all manner of problems from not being able to play with their children to not fitting in public seating, to not being able to dress or bathe themselves. To the humiliation of not being able to wipe themselves after going to the toilet. These people are beaten up, ground down, and all the time punishing themselves. It's no wonder they resort to expensive and risky surgery.

Remember this the next time someone trots out that old line about how overweight people just *'aren't trying hard enough'* or someone smugly sneers about dropping a so-called 'truth bomb' like *'just stop eating so much'*. Or when some troll spits out something vitriolic and moronic like *'step away from the donuts ya big fat pig'*. These offerings are about as insightful and compassionate as telling an addict to 'just say no' to heroin or alcohol. They ignore the breadth, depth and complexity of an issue that is now seeing children as young as five struggling with obesity and diabetes.

Yet, despite all this cost and pain and shame, still the fat stays. Or it leaves temporarily (usually taking a load of muscle with it) before reappearing with a gang of fat friends. The end result is the same because the weight-loss information of the last 50 or so years has not addressed the real causes of excess body fat—quite the opposite, it's added to the problem with all the low calorie nonsense.

Our attitudes to obesity must change because too many children and adults are truly and profoundly suffering. Too many people feel hopeless, desperate, depressed and sad. Offering them *just try harder'* and *'eat less, do more'* is brutally stupid and unhelpful.

BIG FAT WITCH HUNT

Society is extremely unkind to severely overweight people. I remember going away for a long weekend break at a holiday camp with some friends from Australia. My husband and I went with this married couple, both of whom work in the healthcare industry. This couple are very close friends, we've known them for decades. We love them dearly, they are kind and decent people. The wife, Cath, is a surgical nurse who does a great deal of work with people who need joint surgery such as hip and knee replacements.

The husband, Trevor, is a porter. Part of his job is to transport people in wheelchairs, or on stretchers, to and from the various departments in the hospital for treatment or bed rest. Although both Cath and Trevor are intelligent and compassionate people, they have both developed some harsh views about morbidly obese patients.

During a conversation we were having one afternoon, Cath called the obese people she has to work with "these wretched creatures". Why? Because she's strained and injured her own body as a result of having to manually handle the weight of others.

For example, in the operating theatre during a typical surgical procedure, it will be Cath's job to hold the overweight patient's leg up while the surgeon works. She says that, after a few minutes of holding the dead weight of the leg up high enough, and still enough, for the surgeon to do their precise work, the muscles in her arms and back are screaming. She blames injuries she's incurred on her own back down to the moving and lifting of the bodies of severely overweight patients.

Cath says the surgeons are similarly exasperated with the obese patients. She was in one surgery when the irritated surgeon ordered her to "get me a ruler!" He then measured the depth of the stomach fat he'd had to cut through on the patient in front of him before he could even start work.

"Ten centimetres!" he cried in exasperation to everyone in the operating theatre. "I've had to cut through 10 centimetres of fat before we can even start..."

Trevor is even more condemning of fat people. A fit and trim man himself with a passion for long distance running, he doesn't understand how people "let themselves get like that" and puts it down to "just being lazy". Even more telling, he describes how he and the other hospital porters have discussed how to deal with the national obesity epidemic. They 'joke' that they would cover the beaches with donuts as bait for "all the fatties" then club them to death like seal hunters.

I would argue that this is not the most helpful or compassionate response to the obesity crisis.

Trevor says he's "just joking obviously" but the sentiment is real and it reflects a wide and pervading attitude in the community—even amongst the people tasked with caring for obese people.

Just as with drug and alcohol addiction, the mainstream view of obesity is that it's simply a sign of weakness, laziness and generally inferior, stupid people who could sort themselves out if they really tried and they should be shamed into trying.

I don't believe in the concept of laziness. I don't believe anyone is lazy but I do believe people are demotivated, despairing, traumatised and numb. I believe people feel hopeless, broken and overwhelmed.

I believe people get depressed. And I believe they turn to substances and habits to numb their emotional pain or relieve the soul crushing tedium of a dehumanising job. These substances, or 'drugs', can be food, alcohol, sex, illegal drugs, medication, television, computer games, shopping, gambling, pornography, social media, DVD box sets, adrenalin sports... anything that takes us out of our present reality and alters our brain chemistry even just temporarily. We are essentially self-medicating, which is why focusing on the 'drug' or the addiction is missing the point. The 'drug' is serving a purpose. Focus instead on the emotional conditions that are fuelling the addiction. When they have gone, the addictive substance has no more attraction.

What kind of emotional conditions underpin eating disorders like compulsive eating, bulimia, anorexia, orthorexia (obsession with healthy eating), binge eating, and so on? According to spiritual teacher Teal Swan, eating disorders root back to boundary violation, which is the result of relentless intrusion experienced as a child.

"Someone relentlessly doing something to you and you cannot say *'stop, enough is enough!'*

This is a boundary violation," Swan says. This could be someone who grew up in an environment where they had no say over what happened with or to them. This can be overt disempowerment as a result of, say, physical or sexual abuse but it can also be the result of a rigid upbringing where the child's decisions and feelings were regularly invalidated.

For example, 'I don't care if you're not hungry, you will sit at the table until you've finished your dinner...' or 'what do you mean you're sad? No, you're not, you've got nothing to be sad about!'

The child learns that she cannot trust her own feelings, that her feelings are of secondary importance and that she should feel what others tell her to feel. Hello eating disorders!

FABULOUS FAT

Let me hammer this point home one more time: All the fat that is on your body is there because there's a part of you that believes this fat is of benefit to you. And this part of you is much stronger than the part that doesn't want the weight, which is your conscious mind. This is why we conscientiously count calories, tot up points and calculate grams of carb or fat or protein, and we say things like, *'oh no, not for me, I'm trying to be good'* when someone offers us a chocolate but then, later that night, when everyone's gone to bed, we stand inside the pantry door pushing handfuls of sugary cereal into our mouths, straight from the box, faster than we can taste it. That's what I used to do. You may have a different food-drug of choice.

Then we hate ourselves for being weak-willed and so we punish ourselves with threats of deprivation and the withholding of love. We talk to ourselves like we are a disobedient child with proclamations like, *'Right Fatso! Nothing for you tomorrow but green juice! You're on a juice fast...'*

The situation you have is that, as far as your subconscious mind is concerned, your extra weight is not the problem; it is the solution to a perceived problem.

If a three-year-old child picks up a pair of shiny, sharp scissors and starts running about the house waving them wildly, the child's mother will do whatever it takes to get those scissors off the child to keep them safe. No matter how much the child cries and screams.

Your subconscious mind is like that mother and you're that child running with scissors when you attempt to shift body fat. Your subconscious mind/mother senses a threat to you and will do everything it/she can to make sure that extra weight stays exactly where it is for your own good, for the sake of your very survival.

You, however, the three-year-old, are kicking and screaming to keep hold of the scissors, and you are red-faced with fury that you're not getting your way. You may even shout, *'I hate you!'* at your mother and hit at her with your angry little fists. But it won't work. She still won't let you have those scissors because she loves you completely and believes she knows what is best for your safety.

It's not the best analogy in the world but I hope you get the point. So, yes, your body-brain is fighting back against all your efforts to release your excess body fat. It's not doing so because your body hates you and wants you to be miserable. Quite the opposite. It loves you and wants to keep you alive.

Shaming and punishing yourself will never lead to positive, sustainable change. You cannot guilt yourself thin. You cannot hate yourself happy. You can't think, *'if I just punish and berate myself long enough I'll get to the place where I can love myself'.*

Obesity is not cured by shame. We cannot bully ourselves to a place of self-love and self-acceptance. It works the other way around. Turns out that The Beatles were right, Love IS all you need and love is always the answer.

Let's continue, then, our journey around the various long and winding roads of weight loss.

CHAPTER 6
FAT BEEBS—BELIEFS, EVENTS, EMOTIONS, BENEFITS

"Weight is only the outer effect of a fear that is inside you. When you look in the mirror and see the fat person staring back, remember that you are looking at the result of your old thinking. When you start to change your thinking, you are planting a seed for what will become true for you."— Louise L. Hay (1926-2017), author of The Power Is Within You and founder of Hay House Inc.

IN ORDER TO HEAL your weight and your anxiety around your weight, the four main avenues to explore are beliefs, events, emotions, and benefits. In other words, the BEEBs.

Now, for the sake of bringing the highly complex workings of your body-brain, as well as the whole universe and the meaning of life itself, into something that we can understand for the purposes of our weight-love plan, I'll take each of the four aspects of the human experience in turn and seeing how they fit together but just bear in mind that, in practise, it's not so simple.

As far as the mysterious depths of your subconscious mind, the specific beliefs, events, emotions, and benefits, that are relevant to why you're struggling with excess weight (or perceived excess weight) don't usually come in a nice, structured, linear way. They're jumbled together and they're overlapping, as well as self-perpetuating. The human experience is not so easily shoved neatly into these four boxes but for the sake of comprehension, we will do what we can.

To put it another way, we form limiting or negative beliefs as the result of experiences or events in our life. But wait, there's more. We also inherit beliefs and programmes from our ancestors via the coding in our genetic material. So yes, believe it or not, your great grandmother's experiences and beliefs can be influencing your body's fat stores. For now, though, let's just deal with the experiences in your own present life that have resulted in beliefs and programming that are underpinning your weight struggle.

In addition, these subconscious beliefs and programming that we have running in the background have emotions attached to them. As well, there is always a pay-off, or benefit, in holding onto this belief.

It may be a dysfunctional benefit such as *'people are kinder to me when I am ill'* or *'my mum only looks after me when I'm sick so I have to create sickness to feel loved'* but there is still a subconscious benefit. Over time, we become our beliefs. The more we repeat a thought, the denser the neural pathway becomes. First, we form our beliefs, then our beliefs form us.

Your mind doesn't judge whether what you believe is 'good' or 'bad' it simply follows your orders about what you expect to have in your life—most of these orders are subconscious. How do you know what they are? You start by looking at what keeps showing up in your life. This could be illness, money worries, relationship failures, conflicts, accidents, and so on.

To give you an example of how we form beliefs, let's say you were three years old when you were in the car with your mother. While you and your mother were waiting at an intersection for the lights to change, another car struck yours from behind. Your car jolted forward, your mother screamed, her body jolting forward and slamming on the car horn. You were very afraid for your life and extremely distressed. Maybe you and your mother were both badly injured and in hospital for weeks.

This event encoded a number of beliefs into your brain computer. Such beliefs could include, *'the world is not safe'*, *'cars are not safe'*, *'driving is scary'*, *'I am vulnerable'*, *'I'm not in control'*, and so on. The benefits of holding onto these beliefs could include being an alert and defensive driver as an adult, to even forming your whole approach to life if, say, you're someone who makes the most of every minute because you never know when disaster will strike.

Let's take this a step further. Let's say the car that crashed into yours was a red one and, at the moment of the collision, the song playing on the radio was 'Like a Virgin' by Madonna. As an adult, you have no memory of this accident but if you did remember, it might explain why you've always disliked red cars and why hearing that song by Madonna always has you feeling uneasy.

Let's add in some more detail. Maybe you and your mum had been doing something really fun together and, just before the accident, you were feeling happy and carefree and secure in your mother's love. In an instant you went from feeling happy and loved to terrified for your life. As a result, you may have laid down beliefs in that instant along the lines of, *'it's dangerous to be happy'* or *'something terrible happens when I feel loved'*.

Let's say that you take on the belief deep in your subconscious that *'disaster strikes when I'm having fun with someone I love'* so you grow up and you meet a wonderful person. You begin to fall in love but at some deep, subconscious level, this terrifies you because of that belief brick laid in the foundations of your psychology, which asserts that something terrible happens when you feel loved. So you do something to sabotage that relationship.

Alternatively, you may ensure you side-step this disaster by ensuring you're never happy and in love. You always attract emotionally distant people who don't fully love you and, although on the surface, this leaves you feeling unfulfilled and unhappy, that subconscious belief is working on the premise that it's better for you to be safe and alive—albeit romantically unfulfilled—than in love but in danger of your life.

Are we really such complex creatures? Oh yes, we are. We are all, women and men, walking this world and living our day to day lives being aware of just 10 per cent of the thoughts, beliefs and cultural imprints running behind the scenes in our bodies and unconscious minds. This is our 'operating software', the algorithms driving our decisions, behaviours, habits, feelings, and actions. These, in, turn shape the unfolding of our experience in this 3D physical reality.

BOILING DOWN THE BEEBS
Let's take a closer look at each of these four factors as they can relate to food and weight:

Beliefs:
There are hundreds of thousands of subconscious beliefs that can result in excess body fat. These root beliefs operating in your subconscious can be anything from: *'Being fat protects me from sexual abuse...'* to *'I'll never be happy until I lose weight so I will never lose weight because it's not safe to be happy'* or *'I need to punish myself'*... and the list goes on.

The crucial, life-transforming key is finding the bottom beliefs, also called core or root beliefs, and replacing them with beliefs that do support what you want in life. The challenge in finding the root belief, or beliefs, is that they are generally buried under a pile of other beliefs that have sprung out of that bottom belief, kind of like the branches of a tree. We may need to follow the trail backwards. For example, maybe you start with a very top level surface belief such as *'I need to lose weight'*. Just below this you find beliefs like *'weight-loss is a struggle'* and *'I never win in life's battles'*.

Beneath this you could find the belief that *'life is a constant struggle'* which leads you to *'nothing ever happens easily for me', 'I must struggle to get anywhere'*... and so on.

When you dig further into these beliefs, you might find the belief that *'I have to struggle to prove myself worthy'*. This is linked to the belief that *'without the need to struggle I wouldn't achieve anything'* and *'people approve of me when they see me struggle'* along with *'people only help me when they see me struggle', 'the need to struggle in life shows how resourceful and capable I am', 'I need struggle to prove I'm not a quitter', 'I need struggle to motivate myself to achieve'*.

On digging a bit deeper, maybe you find a deeply subconscious belief like, *'people only love me when I struggle'*. This is the kind of bottom belief that may be holding someone's weight in place – the 'benefit', or perceived pay-off, of the weight is that it keeps you locked in a struggle. This is a benefit because, as far as your subconscious mind is concerned, as long as you're locked in a struggle, you feel loved, or you feel useful, or you have a purpose.

This belief may have been formed when, as a small child, you were struggling with something and a parent, who was usually distant or aloof, took the time to help you with whatever it was and in the process perhaps they hugged you and told you that they loved you. Maybe they praised you for not giving up.

Because here's the red herring, healing excess weight is never achieved by putting all your focus on the weight. The weight is a symptom. Thinking that you'll heal the weight by focusing on the weight is like thinking you can change your reflection by wiping at the mirror. Your physical body is a reflection of your emotional body.

Events:
This aspect is about what has happened in your life so far. For example, it could be with regard to situations that left you feeling violated or unsafe. Maybe you had a traumatic childhood experience such as sexual, emotional and mental abuse, or the divorce of your parents, or living with an alcoholic parent or guardian. Or it could be 'smaller' events like the way a family friend looked at your breasts

when you hit puberty or a comment someone made in the school playground. If we do not heal our wounds and scars from childhood, part of us stays emotionally stuck at the age of these earliest wounds, living inside us as an inner child. This causes us to repeat the cycle of suffering by attracting adult versions of these childhood wounds into our lives (*'Why do I keep attracting men who reject me...?'*). They're showing up so they can be healed and reintegrated. The way out is via forgiveness but we'll get to that later.

By the way, don't fall into the trap of rating your trauma and deciding whether or not you're allowed to be affected by something. This is a common trap. It's where we say things to ourselves like, *'but it wasn't that bad, other people have worse experiences, I need to get over it...'*

This kind of thought process is just more self-abuse and denial of our right to feel the way we feel. As babies and children, there is no telling what experience will leave us feeling vulnerable and alone. Some babies experience a trauma when their mother takes away the breast, or bottle teat, before they were finished drinking. There is no blame to apportion when we go back to examine our lives for the experiences that form who we are today. When we are weeding our gardens, do we stop to apportion blame about how each weed was seeded? No, we just pull it out at the root and plant something beautiful in its place.

Emotions

There are different aspects to the emotional component of weight. One of these involves how some of us use food to numb negative feelings. Another is the effects of stress on the body and how it triggers a strong desire for food. In these situations, we use sugary, starchy foods in a similar way to how junkies use heroin and alcoholics use alcohol—these substances all stimulate the brain's pleasure zone; temporarily silencing feelings of anxiety, worry, boredom, self-doubt, depression, and so on. Some of us literally become addicted to food— we are fooddicts. So we reach for foods that alter our brain chemistry in a way that makes us feel calmer and happier.

Cravings are another branch of the emotional eating tree. This is when our feelings get stuck in a particular food, or foods, that remind us of being loved, or of good times, like Grandma's shortbread biscuits.

Benefits:

This is where we'll look at how we are benefiting from the extra weight; how it serves us, what's the perceived pay-off?

Your first thought is probably *it doesn't bloody well benefit me!* but if the weight is on your body, then your subconscious believes there is a benefit to having it there. For example, our subconscious may be literally putting distance between you and someone who bullies you. Of course, this 'benefit' is often dysfunctional. The key lies in convincing the subconscious mind that the so-called benefits are no longer required, or can be achieved without excess weight.

ROLLING BACK THE BEEBS

All of the BEEBs interlink and overlap with each other. For example, if you experienced sexual abuse as a child (an Event), the Emotions that may have been triggered could include confusion, terror, violation, betrayal, guilt, shame, resentment, vulnerability and insecurity, etc.

In that moment, your brain lays down trillions of new neural pathways that we can also call learnings, or conclusions, or beliefs. One of these beliefs may be *I am not safe*.

To your body-brain, the feeling of *I am not safe* is viewed as a threat to your survival in the same way as a famine is a threat to your survival. For the body-brain, thousands of years of evolution have resulted in an efficient and swift response to a survival threat. Registering this kind of danger is like breaking the glass on the fire alarm and flicking the switch.

Your body-brain perceives a threat and triggers the preservation mode. It launches the fight or flight response. Your blood stream is flooded with cortisol and adrenalin while non-essential systems like digestion, repair and immunity are dialled down to low, or even off, so that all resources can be funnelled into the systems necessary for survival as the result of abuse.

Among the many responses your body-brain has to feeling unsafe, packing on extra body fat is a primary and primal response. Your body's boundaries have been violated and, because your body is a physical representation of your emotional, mental and spiritual boundaries, a response to this violation is accumulating extra body fat to both strengthen your boundaries and put distance between yourself and the abuser.

Other potential reactions to some kind of abuse in childhood can include reverting to childhood comforts such as thumb-sucking, or using food to numb your feelings.

If this trauma is unprocessed, the beliefs formed as a result usually become even more deeply embedded and branch off into other areas.

For example, the subconscious Belief that being fat keeps you safe from unwanted sexual attention. A benefit of the extra weight then, or the pay-off, is avoiding unwanted sexual attention.

Here's another hypothetical example. Say that when you were aged two years old, your parents had a huge, blazing row in front of you about money. Perhaps it started while you were all sitting at the dinner table with you sat in a special child's high chair. Suddenly, they were yelling and screaming at each other and it seemed to go on forever. You just sat there stunned and powerless as they hurled horrible abuse at each other. Your whole world seemed to shift on its axis and your body shook with the trauma of it. You were crying uncontrollably and obviously distressed but they didn't seem to care, or notice, how upset you were. Eventually, your father stormed out of the house, slamming the door behind him and your mother crumpled back into her chair and sobbed. After a few minutes, she pulled herself together, looked at you and said, *'stop crying and eat your dinner, mummy's just going to the bathroom'* and you were left by yourself, immobilised in the high chair, with no one to comfort or soothe you.

So the Event is the argument at the dinner table, the Emotions attached to this event could include sadness, terror, anxiety, confusion and despair.

The Beliefs you may have been programmed with as a result of this experience could include, 'I am invisible', 'I am powerless', 'Eating brings an end to arguments', 'I'm not enough', 'Money is more important than love', 'money causes arguments', 'I'm safe when I eat', 'I must eat up and be quiet to keep the peace'... and more. Any of these beliefs could be a reason for holding onto excess weight as an adult. For example, if you have a subconscious belief that you're invisible, then having a much larger body may make you feel more visible—this would be the Benefit, or secondary gain, of having the excess weight. Conversely though, people also use excess weight to hide behind so completely opposing beliefs can all manifest as excess weight.

That's why finding your reasons for holding onto weight is a process that is unique to you. It is a journey only you can go on although, if you wish, you can use the skills of healers and therapists along the way to support you on this exploration into yourself.

My invitation to you, therefore, is to begin the investigation into all the benefits you have for keeping extra weight on your body. Play with the idea that maybe there is a lot more to the fat you have on your body than meets the eye.

CHAPTER 7
SPEAKING THE LANGUAGE OF
BODY FAT

"Symptoms are words trapped in the body."
French psychoanalyst Jacques Lacan (1901-1981)

"Every symptom is the way the body communicates; it is like a word or a message," Deb Shapiro, author of Your Body Speaks Your Mind. @edanddebshapiro

YOUR BODY HAS its own language and it's talking to you all the time. Somewhere along the way though, we've forgotten how to 'speak body'.

Happily though, this ability is our birthright so, if you choose, you can re-learn body talk. The first step is to know that, what shows up in and on your body, and how well your body functions, is speaking to you all the time as well as reflecting everything that's going on in your life and how you feel about it.

Why? Because your body is a living organism. It is not just a skin bag full of pieces like organs and bones. Your body is alive and conscious and it is profoundly interconnected with the mind, the emotions, and the spirit.

In fact, your body is also deeply interconnected to and communicating with every other consciousness in existence because ultimately you are connected with everything in the universe, including every other sentient being on this planet—and the planet herself.

Mother Earth is also a living organism.

Your body is always offering information about everything to do with you and your life and learning to once again speak this language will profoundly change your life.

BODY LANGUAGE

Our body-brain uses pain, inflammation, skin rashes, and the myriad of other physical symptoms, to communicate with us. However, instead of listening and paying attention, we stick our fingers in our ears and sing 'la la la la' while shovelling down whatever pharmaceutical drug or substance is available, or rubbing in whatever cream we've been prescribed, to drown out, or suppress, our body's way of speaking to us. In doing so, we are basically ignoring ourselves, which is a form of neglect and self-abuse. We will never see less abuse and neglect in our external world until we first address the abuse we direct internally in all the subtle and culturally-approved ways that we do.

If a baby cries because it needs sleep, nourishment, or simply a reassuring and loving touch, should the parents ignore these cries because they've read a book by some so-called expert that states the baby must be forced to follow a pattern or structure determined by someone else? Should the father say, *'no, you've had three cuddles already today, that's enough, you greedy baby. You need to toughen up so you're better prepared for this harsh and loveless world you've been born into...'*

That's a rhetorical question. I would suggest that the correct and obvious answer to anyone with a warm heart beating in their chest is 'no'. The baby knows what it wants and needs better than anyone. And primarily this baby, all babies, need an unlimited abundance of love and affection (with a few nappy changes thrown in the mix).

This, though, is an example of how a belief learned as a baby impacts the rest of our life. Let's say this baby did in fact absorb the belief from its cuddle-rationing parents that it had been born into a harsh and loveless world. What if the baby did grow up believing that love and affection was a limited resource that would be often denied to them when they reached out for it. How might this corrupted definition of love effect this person?

It could result in a number of scenarios. For example, this person's primal need and desire for more love and affection could unfold as sexual promiscuity as an adult. Or it could show up as gluttony because this person subconsciously gets a dopamine hit from the pleasure of

71

food as a poor substitute for feeling loved and cherished.

It could place a black cloud over this person's head so they go through life with a default attitude of negativity and pessimism from a subconscious belief that love will always be denied to them, and their various needs never met, no matter what they do. Alternatively, it could lead to low self-worth that manifests as depression, anger and violence.

If it's not addressed, this kind of belief may eventually show up on the body as disease. Perhaps a heart-related disorder as the heart remains the organ most associated with love. However, it's not only the heart that can be impacted by corrupted beliefs about love. A myriad of other heath dis-orders also have this as their root cause. The answer is finding and uprooting these limiting beliefs and replacing them with supportive and life-affirming ones.

FOOD IS LOVE... AND HATE

While we can use food to offer love and nourishment to ourselves, we can also use food as a weapon for self-abuse and neglect, anger and defiance.

So, there can be a rebellion aspect to being fat. For some overweight people, there is a 'screw you' aspect to it. With their bodies, they are essential saying, *'How dare you make me feel I need to jump through your hoops in order to be acceptable. I will not follow your rules about how I should look and I do not accept your stupid criteria for judging me and my appearance'*.

For this reason, over-eating can be an act of defiance. As soon as someone says 'you shouldn't eat that' or 'you're not allowed to eat that', the impulse to eat whatever it is becomes very strong. As well, an encounter like this can form a link between that particular food and rebellion. That might be why, decades later, when you're resentful of your boss making you finish some unnecessary work before you go can home, you end up eating a whole packet of a particular type of biscuit.

In a somewhat dysfunctional way, you're reclaiming ownership of your body, your independence and free will. Of course, this is not a particularly healthy coping mechanism. Ideally you will uproot this old programming and replace it with something more empowering but understanding the urge behind the behaviour is the first step to changing it.

Among the many subconscious reasons I had for holding onto excess body fat, one of the deepest and most pervasive was defiant rage.

My body fat was basically expressing my defiance to a world, and to parents and guardians, who told me that, as a female human, I was obligated to behave, look and speak in a certain way. I was also not permitted to behave, look and speak in other ways due to the social expectations placed on people of my gender.

On the outside I was doing and saying, and even thinking, all the right things as required by society of women. Things like, *'oh, I must lose weight, I'm not the right size, I should be thinner, I must do everything I can to be thinner, I must be on a diet, I must exercise, I must rein in my appetites, I must be smaller, I must be lesser, I must not eat this/that..., I've been so good today because all I've eaten is..., I'm too fat to be attractive to that man I like, I need to get thinner to be more attractive to that man I like...'* etc, ad nauseum.

But the fat jiggling about on my body told a different story. Like a man who insists he is not at all aroused while his penis is clearly engorged, my body was shouting my authentic truth in the most obvious way—via the excess fat on my body.

While I was sticking yet another diet plan to the fridge door, my body was yelling, *"Screw you world! Screw you and the stupid limitations you're trying to put on me! Screw you and the ridiculous, narrow box you're trying to make me fit into.*

"Screw you for dictating how I should look and sound. Screw you for dictating what size my body should be.

"Screw you for denying my divinity. Screw you for ignoring and belittling all the amazing gifts and talents I have to offer. Screw you for suggesting my only value lies in my physical appearance.

"Screw your misogyny. Screw you for suggesting I am lesser. Screw you for silencing me. Screw you for limiting my choices and opportunities. Screw you for undervaluing my contribution.

"Screw you for minimising me in every way, including physically. I reject all your stupid labels and boxes and decrees and values and limitations... and I will display this rejection of these things on my physical body. I refuse to conform to your narrow and miserable standards. I refuse to tow your line. I will not fit myself into your cookie cutter. I will write my defiance on my body, on my belly, on my thighs, on all the parts of my body where I hold the fat that you say is so profoundly unacceptable.

"SCREW YOU WORLD! I love my belly fat because it speaks my rage and defiance!"

I don't know about you but when I think of it like this, I think, *'Yeah! I totally love you, Fat! Go on, speak my truth!'*

The upshot is that, as long as you suppress, and do not express, your core authentic truth, your body will do it for you.

In fact, neuroscientist and author Dr. Joe Dispenza says "your body is your subconscious mind".

"Your subconscious is actually nowhere near as hidden as you might think," Dispenza says. "Your subconscious is speaking to you loud and clear all the time. To 'hear' what it's saying, all you have to do is notice what's going on in your body."

There are myriad behaviours and symptoms that the body-mind can use to express our truth. The body-mind uses these behaviours and symptoms as 'words' from the language spoken by our bodies—which I'm going to call 'Bodlish'.

Some of these 'words' are ones we would consciously prefer to avoid. For example, unconscious communication, or body talk, can be anything from nail-biting to teeth-grinding, a skin rash, nervous twitch, eye tic, or lip chewing all the way to the other extreme that includes self-harming with razors, anorexia nervosa and panic attacks. The amount of body fat we carry, and where we carry it, are words in the vocabulary of Bodlish that are used to express our truth.

SKIN DEEP

I remember, as a teenager aged about 15, being told by a doctor that what I ate had no connection with the condition of my skin.

My severe acne, I was told, was completely detached from what was going on in my life and the state of my diet. The doctor said the problem was that I had just too much testosterone (like it was my fault somehow). There was no rhyme nor reason for why I had this excess hormone, he said, it was just my lot. I would probably grow out of it, he said, but in the meantime, he could give me a drastic treatment involving chemicals that would permanently dry up my sebaceous glands. Yes, there would be regrettable side effects but hopefully my skin would be clear. Dried out but clear.

Thankfully, some little voice in my head told the teenage me that this was not the way forward so I declined the treatment. Yes, acne is a hormonal condition but our hormones are impacted by a number of factors including nutrition, stress and emotions.

So I didn't grow out of it, I still had acne well into my forties and it really flared up when I ate a lot of dairy foods and sugars. It still does if I unleash myself on the cheese board at someone's wedding, or eat a whole bar of chocolate, followed by a tub of ice-cream, in one sitting.

As well as being an inflammatory response to too many sugars, my ongoing acne was also connected to a very sluggish digestive system that was itself the result of an under active thyroid. The thyroid condition was in part triggered by the stress caused by the trauma of my parents' divorce, then many years of living in an environment of constant low-level hostility with my mother's new partner. The stress triggered my body-brain's famine response and I was soon using food to numb my emotions, to rebel and defy this new authoritarian figure in my life, to soothe my body-brain's panic that I was starving... which is an example of how unravelling the excess weight mystery can be a chicken-and-egg situation.

When my body was attempting to get rid of waste products and my struggling digestive system and sluggish bowels simply couldn't cope with it all, my body used other exit doors, namely my skin. So, just like my weight, the condition of my skin wasn't the problem, it was a symptom of underlying issues and slathering myself in topical acne creams was never going to be the solution.

In fact, to take it a little deeper, my skin issues were also reflecting my feelings about not being comfortable in my own skin and feeling insecure about my appearance. So ultimately it is these issues that need resolving as well as action that needs taking in the physical realm, such as avoiding sugars and dairy.

CUT AND RUN

A typical western doctor's approach to, say, an organ that isn't functioning properly, such as the thyroid, can be to surgically remove it if all other attempted treatments fail—as though the diseased organ is like a rotten apple in a bag of apples rather than a beautiful strand in an incredible and intrinsically inter-connected spider's web.

This 'rotten apple' theory means that we go under the knife to have these 'bad' bits of our body cut out. What happens then? Almost certainly this unleashes a domino effect of unanticipated and often disastrous side effects and we're told we'll need to take medication for the rest of our lives. Ironically, this medication brings its own set of nasty side effects and before you know it you're trapped in a downward spiral of pill-popping. You're taking pills for the side effects of the pills for the side effects of the pills... This scenario is what we're calling 'health care'.

The mainstream western approach to health and healing is essentially analytical and linear. Instead of an intelligent living organism and eco system, the body is viewed as a kind of machine and this is where we in the west have gone so horribly wrong. While this approach is revelatory in some respects, for example, in terms of understanding the structure and function of the human body, it comes with some weaknesses. This is why western medicine practitioners are brilliant to have around when you've had an accident and need patching up but when it comes to chronic disease and mental health, the success rate is woeful.

In many ways, modern western medicine is a 'one size fits all' method. It approaches the body as basically a collection of parts and one part will often be treated as though it exists in isolation to all the other parts.

In addition, modern medicine pays little to no attention to the mental and emotional components that make up a human being. This attitude is changing thanks to wonderful new branches of health care like functional medicine but it still persists.

This is why when you go to your regular doctor in the hope she or he can do something to eliminate the physical pain, or discomfort, that's showing up in your body, they often overlook or disregard the emotional component and focus only on the presenting symptoms with a view to suppressing them. So for a skin rash like eczema you may be given a topical cream but you probably won't be asked if you're facing new stresses or challenges. Happily the allopathic western medical approach to health is evolving quickly but in some circles they are still hanging on to some outmoded beliefs.

In summary, in order to change some of the less desirable ways our body-brain is choosing to express the truth that we are too fearful to do consciously, we must go on that journey of exploration into ourselves. We start by unpacking the symptom—which is whatever is showing up in the physical body—and follow the winding trail of breadcrumbs back to the root cause in your subconscious. What might you find there? Unexpressed pain or trauma, the burden of family secrets, the weight of an unpalatable truth, unexpressed feelings of shame, regret, rejection, abandonment, fear, etc.

As spiritual teacher Teal Swan explains in her YouTube video entitled 'How to find the root of any ailment[10]', there are aspects of you that you are aware of and aspects that you are not. There are aspects of yourself that you accept—like your efficiency, humour, intelligence— and aspects of yourself that you reject—your anger, ingratitude, and indecision.

It is the aspects that you are unaware of, or are rejecting and denying, that become a match to the physical illnesses and ailments that present in your body, including excess weight.

"It is not about something you've done 'wrong'," Swan says.

"If you've manifested an illness or accident in your life, this is a call to become aware of the subconscious processes within you, it's a call to awaken. You are being asked to make changes."

All ailments need approaching from all angles—an energetic, mental, and emotional standpoint, as well as a physical standpoint. Together, they create a clear picture of the ailment and also how to heal it.

"If you address ailments only on the physical level, you are only addressing the tip of the iceberg. Because your physical existence is just the tip of the iceberg," Swan says.

"If you are only addressing the tip of the iceberg, any physical step you take to cure an ailment will fall short. The ailment is likely to come right back because the blueprint for the ailment has not changed."

EXPRESS YOURSELF HEY HEY HEY HEY

The solution to all this non-conscious and undesirable self-expression? Madonna was right. You've got to consciously express yourself—fully, loudly, proudly. And there are limitless ways that you can do this, such as writing, music, building things, painting, poetry, drama, entrepreneurship, dance, yoga, film, cooking, racing cars, raising a child, repairing motorbikes, caring for animals, growing rhododendrons, baking, volunteering, picking up litter... whatever.

We are creative beings. We exist to create and to express through our creation. Moment by moment, we are constantly creating and recreating our world with our thoughts, words and deeds. Even the seemingly smallest decisions you make are expressing something about your truth. When you're in a shop buying a t-shirt and there are several colours to choose from, the fact that you choose the red one instead of the green one is an expression of something within you, although you may not be consciously aware of what. Perhaps you're not feeling very grounded and your root chakra needs support, maybe you're feeling sexy or wanting to be noticed, maybe the red reminds you of happy Christmases as a child, etc.

The treasure chest of your subconscious is full of wonders that are unique to you and they've made you who you are. Shine a light onto your inner world and watch how this reflects into your outer world and onto your body.

CHAPTER 8
GLOBAL OBESITY AND THE
WEIGHT OF THE WORLD

"At seventeen, I started to starve myself, I thought that love was a kind of emptiness. And at least I understood then the hunger I felt, and I didn't have to call it loneliness. We all have a hunger..."
— *lyrics from 'Hunger' by Florence + the Machine*

"Hang on one cotton-picking minute," I hear you cry.

"If being fat is actually stuck emotional pain and limiting beliefs, how come the whole world is suddenly getting so much fatter?" You ask indignantly.

"Tamara, are you really trying to convince me that, in the last 50 years, humans have just had massively more emotional pain than in the last 200,000 or so years? I'm not sure I buy that. Surely global obesity is simply the result of skyrocketing global sugar consumption and the fact that we're all sat glued to screens all day, rather than ploughing fields and chopping down trees with our bare hands, or whatever it was that our great, great, great grandparents did for fun?"

Excellent point well made my dear friend...

"Wait! I'm not finished," you cry. *"Are you seriously expecting me to swallow the idea that someone's fat because of some childhood emotional trauma that happened at the dinner table or in the school playground, or because of some past life as a sadistic priest or a promiscuous nun, or because they had an ancestor who lived through*

78

the potato famine? That sounds like a load of indulgent new age twaddle. Plus, it's a great big excuse for lazy 'poor me' fatties who can't stop eating cake because they're just too weak willed... not to mention that this 'pandering to the fatties' tactic is a great way for so-called 'spiritual healers' to get clients. Look, I'm just saying..."

That, my wise friend, is a valid question. And yes, on the surface it's a convincing argument. How can I bang on about unprocessed emotional trauma when we now have an estimated 41 million children under the age of five who are overweight or obese? Obese and diabetic five-year-olds.

How can I talk about the universe and channelling messages from a bunch of spirit beings when, throughout the world, it's estimated that, every 30 seconds, someone's leg is amputated due to diabetes?

In 2018, in America alone, 80,000 people will have their leg or foot amputated because they can't manage the food they're putting in their mouth and their type 2 diabetes is totally out of control.

In the UK, that annual figure is about 7,000 people. But rising frighteningly fast.

At the same time, treatment for type 2 diabetes now absorbs 10 per cent of the annual health budget for England and Wales.[10] This equates to over £25,000 being spent on diabetes every minute. In other words, £1.5 million every hour.

In total, an estimated £14 billion pounds is spent a year on treating diabetes and its complications in the UK and that figure is estimated to increase significantly.

The prevalence of diabetes[11] in the UK is estimated to rise to five million people by 2025. In 1996, that figure was 1.4 million. In the UK, 135 lower limb amputations[12] are undertaken each week on diabetic patients, while, annually, 1280 people become blind due to diabetes-related complications. Diabetes is related to 11.6 per cent of all deaths in the UK population. It is estimated that as many as one million UK citizens who have diabetes are unaware of their condition (UK

---

[10] http://www.lse.ac.uk/business-and-consultancy/consulting/assets/documents/diabetes-expenditure-burden-of-disease-and-management-in-5-eu-countries.pdf

[11] https://www.diabetes.co.uk/diabetes-prevalence.html

[12] https://www.diabetes.org.uk/about_us/news/more-than-135-diabetes-amputations-every-week

Parliament 2010).[13] In the US, nearly 26 million Americans have diabetes, while 79 million have pre-diabetes. That's 25 per cent of the population and most don't know they're at risk.

SUGAR RUSH

Type 2 diabetes is an inability to handle glucose. It is a major cause of blindness, kidney failure, heart attacks, stroke, Alzheimer's and dementia, and lower limb amputation. Type 2 diabetes comes hand in hand with obesity.

Yet what are we doing to our bodies every single day in the so-called first world? Many of us start the day by dumping a huge load of sugars into it via a bowl of cornflakes and a piece of toast slathered in jam or marmalade, washed down with orange juice. We follow that with a lactose-loaded latte mid-morning—and we double the sugar content for asking that it be 'skinny'. We have a sandwich at lunchtime with a can of cola, a muffin mid-afternoon, and rice or pasta or pizza in the evenings. Massive and pancreas-crippling amounts of sugar. It's no wonder the pancreas is waving the white flag of surrender and just basically giving up, which is when we're told we have type 2 diabetes, or non-alcohol fatty liver, and are offered a life-time on medication as a 'solution'.

In the 19th Century, diabetes was virtually unknown. It started presenting more commonly in the 1950s and by 1985, there were about 30 million people diagnosed with type 2 diabetes. Still though, even when I was a child in the 70s, we all thought diabetes was something only old people got. Not so anymore. In parts of the UK, 10 per cent of four and five-year-old children are already obese and on their way to diabetes.

These patterns are seen repeated in countries across the globe. The first World Health Organisation (WHO) Global report on diabetes,[14] published in 2016, revealed that the number of adults living with diabetes worldwide has almost quadrupled since 1980.

In 2015, a staggering 415 million people had diabetes and if we keep going the way we are, 642 million people globally will have the disease by the year 2040, according to the International Diabetes Federation (IDF). At which point, diabetes-related health expenditure across the

---

13 http://www.lse.ac.uk/business-and-consultancy/consulting/assets/documents/diabetes-expenditure-burden-of-disease-and-management-in-5-eu-countries.pdf

14 http://www.who.int/diabetes/global-report/en/

globe will exceed US$802 billion.

It's not just the treatment costs of diabetes, however, that are crippling the health and social systems of countries like the UK. It's the knock-on costs as well. In 2013/14, the annual costs resulting from diabetes in the UK included £8.4 billion for absenteeism and £6.9 billion for early retirement.

THE COST OF OBESITY

In the UK, the national obesity and diabetes crisis is bringing the British health care and social welfare systems to their knees. About 700,000 Brits are super morbidly obese and in 2016, the demand for gastric bypass surgery on the National Health Service (NHS) rose 40 per cent. Over the last decade, demand for this surgery has risen ten-fold.

In 2014/2015, the NHS spent £6.1 billion on overweight and obesity-related ill-health. The annual spend on the treatment of obesity and diabetes is greater than the amount spent on the police, the fire service and the judicial system combined.

By 2050, the UK-wide NHS costs attributable to overweight and obesity are projected to reach £9.7 billion with wider costs to society estimated to reach £49.9 billion per year.[15]

Frankly, we can't afford these kinds of sums.

A huge chunk of the NHS budget is now being swallowed up by preventable obesity-related conditions. So while cheap sugary food and drink manufacturers are raking in billions, alongside the advertising industry hired to relentlessly promote them, the after effects of these fake foods—from obesity to litter and plastic pollution—are being borne by the general populace. You and me. As well as the marine life and animals that are choking on our garbage.

All signs now point to this simply getting worse and worse unless drastic action is taken. Why? Because we are now raising more fat and diabetic children than ever.

A study by Middlesex University, Imperial College London and the WHO, found that, if current trends continue, more children and adolescents will be obese than moderately or severely underweight in the next five years.

Published in 2017 in *The Lancet*[16] ahead of World Obesity Day (11

---

15 https://www.gov.uk/government/publications/health-matters-obesity-and-the-food-environment/health-matters-obesity-and-the-food-environment--2

16 www.thelancet.com/journals/lancet/article/PIIS0140-6736(17)32129-3/fulltext

October), the study paper analysed the weight and height measurements of nearly 130 million people—the largest number of participants ever involved in an epidemiological study.

The researchers, who found four in 10 children aged five to 19 are overweight, have warned of an "absolute crisis" in child heath including a greater future risk of heart disease, cancer and diabetes.

"The trend predicts a generation of children and adolescents growing up obese," said Majid Ezzati, the Imperial College professor who led the study[17] and who has called for better regulations and taxes to protect children from junk food.

Commenting on the study, Dr Fiona Bull from the WHO blamed politicians for failing to act after years of warnings.

"Obesity is a global health crisis today, and threatens to worsen in coming years unless we start taking action," said Bull.

"We are surrounded by environments that market unhealthy, high-fat, high-sugar, high-calorie food. That's what is on the TVs, that's what is promoted at bus stops."

DIET DEBACLE

How can all these children be holding onto subconscious beliefs or emotions from traumatic childhood events that cause them to be fat? How can I blame unresolved trauma for obesity when we have an army of obese children? Surely it's a preposterous notion and we just need to outlaw donuts and sugary fizzy drinks?

Well, yes, I would argue we should outlaw fake food, or tax it to the high heavens, but that's just part of the picture, albeit a big part. It's frighteningly clear that, as a species, we're doing something horrifically wrong. Despite fifty or so years of a mass cultural obsession with calorie counting and being thinner, we are in a pandemic of fatness and diseases prefaced with the word 'lifestyle', which almost makes them seem acceptable. They're not. The physical toll of being overweight is one thing, the emotional toll is another. Anyone who's ever lived in an overweight body knows the pain, shame and self-loathing that comes with it. We should not be doing this to our children. The issue runs much deeper than just eating too much sugar—although we are and, yes, we really, really, have to stop and, yes, this is a massive part of the problem. The question is, why are we eating so much sugar? Why have we shaped our societies towards high

---

17 https://www.thelancet.com/action/showPdf?pii=S0140-6736%2817%2932129-3

processed sugar and grains consumption? Why do we spend so much time sat at screens in high stress jobs?

Who convinced us that we needed to chain ourselves to the financial industry for 25 years through a mortgage?

Why have we built car culture cities in which it's actually difficult to find pavements to walk on? (Could petro-chemical companies have had any influence on government town planning decisions? If only bicycle companies had as much sway.)

Why did we pave paradise and put up a parking lot?

Why do we apparently see nothing wrong with some corporations making billions, even trillions, from manufacturing products that are making us fat and sick?

And why don't we hold these corporations accountable for also producing oceans of plastic and chemical pollutants that are poisoning the earth and the seas and all other species?

Why are we not more outraged at pharmaceutical companies rubbing their hands in glee at rising rates of disease like diabetes, dementia (which is being called type 3 diabetes), and cancers because of the huge profit potential in selling drugs that will mask-but-not-heal the condition?

Why is economic growth and bottom-line profit viewed as the ultimate get-out-of-jail clause? *('Destroying the Amazon rainforest? Yes we are. Soz! But it's okay because there's money to be made...')*

Why do we let the powers who run our nations carry on as if it doesn't matter how much environmental damage is wreaked as long as there is a profit margin for some billion-dollar corporation?

Why is it okay to sell weapons of mass destruction in unstable regions run by dictators and then leave the women and children of those countries to fend for themselves when war breaks out?

Why do we have such a narrow definition of what something 'costs'?

Our global pandemics of ill health and obesity are indicators of much deeper problems with the way we are running our world and to what we are giving priority and importance.

The history of processed sugar production is an example of this.

FAT CHANCE

For about 200,000 years, humans did not have a global obesity pandemic. We didn't even have much of an obesity problem in 1972 when, according to WHO, there were 2.7 per cent of females overweight and the same for men in the UK.

Fast forward from the 1970s to today and those numbers have

skyrocketed. This pattern is repeated across the world. Today, almost half the population is overweight and a quarter are obese. Today, there are 1.4 billion overweight adults in the world and 500 million obese ones. British people are on average three stone (19 kg) heavier than they were in the 1960s.

What the hell happened!?

On the surface, processed carbohydrates are what happened and fat-phobic hysteria is what happened.

The question is *why* did they happen?

Why did processed carbohydrates and fat-phobic hysteria happen? Because we're in a war between the health of our minds and bodies and the profits made on the back of modern accessibility to fast, cheaply-made, and processed food.

In the 2012 BBC documentary, *The Men Who Made Us Fat*[18], reporter Jacques Peretti investigated the men responsible for the transformation in our eating habits; how business changed the shape of a nation, as well as how the food industry choreographs temptation.

A major turning point was in 1971 when US President Richard Nixon appointed a man named Earl Butz as Secretary of Agriculture. Nixon needed huge supplies of cheap food to keep voters happy so he could stay in power.

To make food production as cheap as possible, Butz had a vision to merge the country's army of small farmlets into enormous, industrial farms of unprecedented output.

'Get big or get out' was Butz's motto and his plan was to grow more corn than ever before, in order to keep food prices cheap and housewives happy, which would help get his party voted back into government. The thousands of small family farms, where the farmers had a relationship with their crops and animals, were eaten up by Big Agriculture and factory farming was born. Any thought of welfare for the animals involved, or caring properly for the soil and the insects that are part of nature's cycle, went out the window.

'Bah! Who cares if we kill a few bees? Who cares if chickens and pigs are kept in cages that don't have enough room for them to turn around? It's shareholder dividends and our annual bonuses we need to worry about! Not to mention getting voted back in for another few years...'

Soon, these new, larger harvests of corn became feed for the cheap

---

18   https://www.theguardian.com/business/2012/jun/11/why-our-food-is-making-us-fat

beef flooding the supermarkets and huge surpluses of corn were being created—this was soon turned into a brand new 'food' thanks to some Japanese scientists, it was a cheap industrial sweetener called High Fructose Corn Syrup (HFCS). This cheap corn sweetener has ended up in just about every processed food imaginable—take for example the typical American fast food meal of a burger, fries with tomato sauce and a Coke; the beef is from cows fed on corn; the Coke and tomato sauce are sweetened with corn syrup; the bread for the bun is made with corn syrup, and the fries are cooked in corn oil.

One of the biggest health impacts, though, was when HFCS replaced sugar in fizzy drinks like Coke and Pepsi in 1984. The reason was a no brainer—HFCS was a third cheaper than sugar. In two decades, fizzy drink consumption in the US has gone from 350 cans per person per year to 600 cans per year.

The damaging difference between regular processed sugar and HFCS is how it affects the body. There's something very specific about fructose that accelerates obesity, namely, the effect of fructose on the liver.

Fructose is easily converted to fat in the body, and scientists have found that it also suppresses the action of the vital hormone leptin. When the liver is overloaded with sugars, leptin simply stops working, and as a result the body doesn't know when it's full. Your brain thinks you're starving and you end up in a vicious cycle of consumption, disease and addiction.

SUGAR JUNKIES

Why is it that we just can't seem to get enough sugar? Because it is literally physiologically addictive. Sugar takes the brain prisoner by activating the same circuitry that is activated in addictions.

The havoc that processed sugars have wreaked on global health and obesity is now being more widely studied and accepted but this is a recent change. For the last 50 years, accepted wisdom was that we were all getting fatter, quicker, because of fat. It was the late American scientist, Ancel Keys, who convinced the developed world that dietary fat, particularly animal fat, was to blame for everything from heart disease to cancer, diabetes, obesity, etc.

'Stop eating fat because it will make you fat and clog up your arteries,' we were told. *'Don't worry about sugar though, it's harmless, just a source of nutritionally-empty calories but your body will burn those up for energy.'*

Remember when we all believed that? We were all like, *'Oh! Right, fat makes you fat, that makes so much sense...'* and so we all hopped on the fat-phobic band wagon.

One scientist who disagreed with Keys' anti-fat stance was the late UK Professor, John Yudkin. In 1972, Yudkin wrote a book called *Pure, White and Deadly*, which outlined how the rise in heart disease correlated to the rise in the consumption of sugar. This was not a popular argument with the influential sugar lobby however and Yudkin was basically black-listed and discredited by powerful sugar-funded opponents. As a result, the case against sugar was forgotten and the low-fat obsession took hold.

ABSOLUTELY FATUOUS

We were told that dietary fat was the devil incarnate, a demon that had to be avoided. We were told eggs would give us heart disease; we were told saturated fats in meat would clog our arteries, we were told to shun everything with fat in it.

And we did. We did what we were told. Since the beginning of the low-fat misinformation we've done exactly what all the experts told us to do. We avoided dietary fat like the plague and forced down masses of skinless boiled chicken and egg whites. In the 1980s, eating butter in public would draw gasps of horror from onlookers and feeding it to your children was akin to physical abuse.

Sure enough, we slashed our fat consumption but guess what else we did? We sent our refined carbohydrate and sugar consumption sky high. What else has gone sky high? Our levels of obesity, diabetes, mental illness, auto-immune conditions, dementia, heart disease, cancers, and more.

It took us a while but at last we're waking up. The judge and jury that had found fat guilty had got it wrong. They were presented with flawed evidence. Dietary fat wasn't the killer. It was that dastardly villain sugar, along with its processed carbohydrate cronies, that was— and is—doing all the damage.

When dietary fat became public health enemy number one, the food industry spied an opportunity and before long our supermarket shelves were swamped with low fat products, everything from yogurts to mayonnaise, biscuits and desserts. The low-fat industry boomed. The things that we were calling 'food' got ridiculous, such as fat-free cream.

Think about that for a minute—fat-free cream!

Fat was taken out of everything and sugar was put in.

The result? Profits for the food industry have soared and so has

86

obesity. The UK consumes around 2.25m tonnes of sugar each year, 75 per cent of which is sold direct to the food industry. From 1990 to 2015, the amount of sugar consumed in Britain increased by 31 per cent largely because of the 'invisible' sugar added to products like tomato sauce, soft-drinks, yogurt, baked beans, etc. The vast amounts of processed sugars we consume is beating us up from all sides. Because sugars aren't just harmless, empty calories. Sugar calories are deadly, toxic calories. All this sugar is making us morbidly obese, it's feeding cancer cells in our body, and is laying down the foundations of all the disease epidemics the world is now facing.

FAT BLAME SHIFTING

"Do you think Mother Nature is trying to kill you?" asks Dr Zoe Harcombe.

"Because this is what it boils down to. We've been eating red meat and animal products for three and a half million years. Do you think we would have survived this far if all the vitamins and all the minerals we need to survive are in the same foods that are allegedly trying to kill us?"

What's more likely to be the problem, asks Harcombe, the natural foods that we've been eating for millions of years, or the consumption of processed sugars that have increased 20-fold for the last 50 years?

We know now, beyond any shadow of a doubt, that our insane consumption of refined sugars and fake food is causing an unprecedented health crisis, immeasurable human and animal suffering, and environmental damage.

So why don't we just tax fake food to the high heavens? Why don't we ban it completely? Why don't we subsidise organic and biodynamic farming? Why don't we teach school children how to grow their own food?

Why are we allowing companies to peddle toxic white death to our children via cutesy animals and puppets instead of educating our children on what real food is as well as how to cook and prepare it? Not to mention value and respect it.

Why do we allow companies like McDonald's and Nestle to fill our public institutions, our hospitals, schools and universities, with fake food and vending machines full of sugary drinks, chocolate bars and crisps?

Why is it nigh on impossible to buy anything other than fast, junk food in our shopping malls and motorway services?

Why is it that when I'm driving the motorways of the UK, there is nothing to buy at the motorway services stops apart from highly processed junk from fast food chains? (With the notable exception of the excellent Gloucester Services, a haven of organic, ethical and locally grown food. I love this motorway services so much, I detour on long journeys to stop there.)

And don't get me started on the planet-choking amounts of plastic and non-biodegradable packaging we've created for these toxic fake foods.

What's happened to us? We've allowed consumerism and materialism to become our religion. Profit is our ultimate priority and the ends by which all means are justified.

So animal cruelty through factory farming is justified in the name of profit and economic growth. Barely liveable minimum wages are justified in the name of profit and economic growth. Feeding sugar to school children is justified in the name of profit and economic growth. Child labour in third-world countries is justified in the name of profit and economic growth. Poisoning our seas and soils is justified in the name of profit and economic growth. Polluting the air is justified in the name of profit and economic growth. Spending the biggest chunk of our lives away from our families doing jobs that don't fulfill us is justified in the name of profit and economic growth.

When making a profit at all costs is more important than the health of the planet and the welfare of people and animals, we are a species that's sick and out of balance with our natural selves.

Both individually and collectively, we are out of alignment and out of harmony with the rhythms of the Earth.

We think we are separate from each other and we're pretending that we are not an intrinsic part of this planet. This mass collective sickness and imbalance is being expressed through the range of physical and mental disease epidemics now sweeping the globe.

It will take a massive grass-roots movement to change direction and get off the highway to ill-health that we're currently speeding down. It starts with each of us taking responsibility for our role, however small. It starts with no longer buying the products of companies that peddle high sugar, nutritionally empty products that come in single-use plastic. It starts with choosing instead to buy the organic produce and products grown and made locally by people who care for their land, their animals, their ingredients. It starts with throwing out governments and rulers who do not prioritise the environment. It starts with loving yourself enough to deeply care about the quality of food, water and air you're offering to your body and brain.

CHAPTER 9
SUGAR ADDICTION AS A
SPIRITUAL ISSUE

"You are hooked - a junkie mainlining some of the worst, deadliest drugs on the planet: sugar and anything that turns to sugar in your body."
— Mark Hyman, author and MD @drmarkhyman

"The body is a projection of the soul."
— Teal Swan, author and spiritual teacher @realtealswan

IS THERE ANYONE left on Earth who hasn't heard the news of how we've been killing ourselves with processed sugars and refined carbohydrates?

Can there be anybody who still hasn't heard the story about how profoundly addictive and damaging these processed sugars and carbohydrates are to the human body? Surely everyone by now has heard about the studies that proved sugar is as addictive as cocaine?

I feel like no one can pretend not to know this anymore.

Unless you've been in a coma for 10 years, how can you not have read about the studies that revealed how refined sugar is more addictive than recreational drugs? So you must know that, just like alcohol, cocaine, and cigarettes, sugar takes the brain prisoner by activating the same circuitry that is activated in addictions. Namely, your pleasure and reward zone.

Is there anyone left who hasn't heard how sugar causes insulin resistance, high triglycerides, as well as the inflammation we now know is at the root of heart disease, dementias, and cancer?

If you've made it this far into this book, you've also read about the men who made us fat by feeding us all these processed sugars.

So come on, we know this! We know that sugar is the baddie!

I bet you've picked up a packet, or tin, in the supermarket and checked the sugar content. I bet you've told friends that you're trying to cut down on sugar. I bet you've read a book called something like *Quit Sugar*, or *Sugar Blues*, or *Pure White and Deadly,* or *Wheat Belly*... that kind of thing.

Too many really clever people have been trying to shake us awake about sugar for too long for us to not be finally getting the message. So many wonderful books and movies, documentaries, blogs and magazine articles have been shouting from the rooftops about how very, desperately wrong, we have been about sugar versus fat.

'Quit sugar because it's actually killing you!' we've been told again and again. So surely most of us now know that we've been victims of a major con job. Surely we now know that dietary fat is the innocent one that took the rap for global obesity while refined sugars went off to live in the Bahamas with its partner in crime, High Fructose Corn Syrup.

However, if this is really news to you, let me give you a quick rundown. Oh, and welcome back from that desert island you've been marooned on for the past few years.

Thanks to all the fake, processed and sugary 'food' we're consuming, we have obese children with diabetes, sleep apnea and an unprecedented dental disease epidemic. We have epidemics of cancer, heart disease, auto immune disorders, obesity, digestive disorders, muscular neural conditions, ADHD, ADD, Alzheimer's, Parkinson's, dementia... the list goes on. Sugar is the leading cause of liver failure in America.

All signs are now pointing to our unnatural diet being the biggest culprit. There are other factors contributing to this mess, such as our determination to wrap the world in plastic, fill the oceans with chemicals and spray the soils with poisons but let's just focus on sugars for the moment.

One would think that a diagnosis of type 2 diabetes, dementia, and the threat of impending blindness or a foot amputation would be enough to convince someone, everyone, to stop eating sugar.

However, for 105,000 people in the United States in 2018, the knowledge that they're about to go blind or have a foot amputated won't be enough. They'll keep eating and drinking sugar, and they will go blind or have their foot amputated. Tragically, some of these people won't even realise that changing their diet could save their life, sight and limbs because the only information source they have is a doctor who tells them the lie that 'diabetes is incurable' and prescribes more pharmaceutical drugs to manage their symptoms.

So yes, sugar is bad. We get it. And yet... unbelievably, incredibly, we are still eating mountains and mountains of processed sugars and carbohydrates. How can that be?

A few reasons. Actually quite a lot of reasons. None of them good.

SICKLY SWEET

Why can't we stop eating the sugar and processed junk masquerading as 'food' that's literally killing us?

The number one reason is because we are physiologically and psychologically addicted to the sweet toxin. We are sugar junkies. How? Because sugar activates the reward centre in the brain, energising you and making you feel fabulous, happy, and care-free.

"You are hooked," writes Dr Mark Hyman in his book *The Blood Solution 10 Day Detox Diet*. "A junkie mainlining some of the worst, deadliest drugs on the planet: sugar and anything that turns to sugar in your body."

In his book, Hyman states that we're all sugar addicts and the $1 trillion industrial food system is the biggest drug dealer around, contributing to tens of millions of deaths every year.

A hit of sugar to the brain releases feel-good hormones like dopamine and chemicals like beta endorphins, which relax us if we're stressed, dull our pain, soothe us if we feel hurt or sad, comfort us if we feel lonely or worthless.

So you eat more. Why wouldn't you!? It feels so nice when that drug hits your system that of course you want more of that feel-good dopamine and those pain-killing beta endorphins.

This is why, even though you were only going to have one chocolate or biscuit or slice of bread, you end up eating the whole box or packet. But even as the last mouthful is still heading down your oesophagus, the shame, guilt and self-loathing start stirring in your belly as they wake from the short slumber they took while you were at your private sugar party.

Just like cigarettes for a smoker, or a shot of vodka for an alcoholic, sugar in its many forms feels like our friend. We've had these neural pathways programmed into our brains from a very early age. Like any addiction, coming off sugar will mean enduring a period of withdrawal. You'll feel awful, you'll crave that sweet hit from the sugar drug but you do need to kick the habit if you want to transform your health and your weight.

SNOW JOB

The second reason we can't quit sugar is because we've been deeply, subconsciously brainwashed through relentless advertising and media imagery to associate processed foods and sugary drinks with happiness, fun, youth, good looks, and health.

McDonald's has its 'happy meals' aimed at children while our impressionable youth are told that *'Coke is Life'* and *'I'm lovin' it'* via commercials of gorgeous, adventurous, and exciting, young people who look like they're winning at life against a pop music soundtrack.

Processed sugary foods have done a quite staggeringly brilliant job of selling themselves as your cool friend, your happy-go-lucky companion, your personal cheerleader who says things like *'You're great! You're awesome! Have a chocolate sundae because you deserve a treat! Go on, do it, you're a rebel who breaks all the diet rules! You're just like Che Guevara, only cooler, braver, and more revolutionary...'*

We are force-fed this messaging day and night via every media platform available. Why do big food corporations do product placement in movies and music videos? Because it works. They're obviously not going to tell you the truth, which is *'hey, we're selling you a bottle of overpriced, sickly sweet, brown fizzy water that can rot your teeth and trigger your body into storing masses of fat'*. That pitch wouldn't get past many marketing teams. No, they're selling you a feeling, emotions, and the promise of a lifestyle. They're selling you a sense of belonging and self-worth. They're feeding your ego.

So adorable, cherubic children are shown on our screens eating chocolate eggs with toys in them.

Bronzed, muscular men with perfect teeth and gorgeous smiles slug back sugary caffeinated drinks with ridiculous labels like 'power drinks' or 'fuel for men'.

Beautiful, thin women gaze seductively at us from our screens eating chocolate, yogurt, ice-cream, rice pudding, or whatever, as though it's giving them an orgasm. The secondary message we're lapping up is that these attractive women are eating this stuff because they're liberated and independent. *'I'm doing this for me because I'm a modern woman of style and sophistication'* is the subtext message. Happily, in 2018, the UK government announced plans to make it illegal to advertise high sugar foods to children using cartoon characters. It is a step in the right direction but it's not enough. This is like chucking a bucket of water at a forest fire.

Thirdly, too many very powerful corporations, that have a strong vested interest in making sure we keep shovelling down their cheap-to-make sugary fake food, have the ear of governments and food and health authorities. These powerful fake food corporations put their money into sports teams and fitness events, they fund studies into nutrition and diet that always seem to show how their products have no directly proven detrimental effect on health *when consumed in moderation as part of a balanced diet...*' yada yada. They get their products into schools, hospitals, motorway services and education facilities, they get their names associated with worthy charities, sports events and community causes, and of course they pour fortunes into advertising and marketing. Then, when their cheap, addictive food-like substances result in obesity, they mumble something about each person being responsible for their own calorific and nutritional intake.

Fourthly, we are already hardwired at a primal level to associate sweetness with love and nurturing—this used to be a good thing for our survival as a species but we've screwed it up.

We're born with the urge to seek sweetness programmed into our genetic material as a survival driver at conception. This was reinforced in our brain's neural pathways by the sweetness of our mother's breast milk. We would be fed by breast or bottle, drinking in the sweet liquid while gazing into our mother's adoring face and we felt unconditionally loved. We were hooked.

As we grew up though, this 'love is sweet' message got skewed. Sources of sweet nourishment moved out of the natural world and into the industrialised world of processed sugars. Our parents would offer us chocolate or bright, artificially coloured sweeties, lollies and candy as a reward or bribe if we were 'good'. The insidious underlying message in this casual bribe being that we weren't 'good' by default.

This may explain why we call people we love names like 'sweetie', 'sweetheart', 'sugar' and 'honey'. It makes us feel all warm and melting inside.

So when we crave sweet substances, it is a sign that what we are really craving is more love in our lives. We feel unloved and unlovable so we eat sugars to compensate. Why do we feel that love is missing in our lives? Because we've lost touch with who we really are and with our natural selves. We are mistakenly seeing ourselves as separate and alone. We feel detached, hopeless, despairing, lost, empty, invisible, lacking, and worthless. We eat sugars to escape these feelings in just the same way as an alcoholic drowns their sorrows in alcohol. It's self-medication. All of these substances are used to alter the chemical balance in our brains in order to feel better.

We want to feel loved and comforted, so we eat sugar. We want to feel pleasure, so we eat sugar. We want to feel popular and fun, so we eat sugar. We want to feel desirable, so we eat sugar. Why do we need this fake pleasure? Because we've created a harsh and competitive world that sucks the joy out of being alive. We've swapped community for capitalism. Instead of letting our children grow and learn through play, we lock them in rooms and stress them out about sitting exams. And we give them sugar to make it all a little better.

Like a junkie, we use our drug of choice to take our minds off our worries and to blur the edges on life's unpleasant parts. We use sugar to treat and reward ourselves. We offer ourselves a poor substitute for love through sugar.

What does this mean? You can boil our toxic relationship with sugar down to this: Looking for love in all the wrong places.

It is not, in fact, the sugar that is the problem, it is the factors that are driving us to consume it; factors including isolation, disconnection, loneliness, low self-worth, and hopelessness.

THE RAT PART EXPERIMENT

A famous study by Canadian psychologist Bruce K. Alexander in 1978 aimed to prove that psychology—a person's mental, emotional, and psychosocial states—was the largest cause of addiction, not the drug itself.

Called the Rat Park Experiment[19], Alexander wanted to refute other studies that connected opiate addiction in laboratory rats to addictive properties within the drug itself. No, said Alexander, drugs do not cause addiction, rather it's caused by a person's living conditions.

Previous opiate addiction studies had been done on rats placed in tiny, isolated cages that were starved for hours on end. These rats had no room to move and no interaction with other rats.

Apart from just being inhumanely cruel, this method ignored the fact that rats by nature are social, industrious creatures that thrive on contact and communication with other rats. Putting a rat in solitary confinement does the same thing it would do to a human, it drives them insane. If humans in solitary confinement had the option to take mind-numbing narcotics, they likely would. (Our prison systems overrun with drugs, anyone?)

Alexander did the same opiate tests on 16-20 female and male rats who lived in a spacious Rat Park where the rats had wheels and balls

---

19   https://www.serenityatsummit.com/news/overview-rat-park-addiction-study/

for play, plenty of food and space for mating and mingling with one another. What happened? These happy rats not only did not get addicted, they consistently shunned the drug and chose plain water over morphine water.

The Rat Park study team concluded that drugs themselves do not cause addictions. In fact, it is a person's environment that feeds an addiction. Feelings of isolation, loneliness, hopelessness, and lack of control based on unsatisfactory living conditions make a person dependent on substances that temporarily relieve these unpleasant feelings. Under happy, supportive and fulfilling living conditions, people resist drug and alcohol addiction.

MAN, I COULD MURDER A PLATE OF KALE

So sugar isn't love and it doesn't have our back. Worse than that though, it wreaks havoc on our health and our life. It's like the manipulative and abusive partner from whom you just can't find the strength to break free. You wake up one morning and tell yourself, *'Enough! No more. It's over. I don't need this in my life, it's destroying me...'* but a couple of days later you're back for more. Because, Lord knows, when he's being sweet, no one can make you feel like they do.

That's right, your relationship with sugar is abusive.

It's our thoughts and emotions that are the key. It is not about willpower. It's about the effect of comfort foods on our brain chemistry.

Have you ever found yourself wandering into the kitchen just because you feel like eating 'something' but you're not sure what? I bet that 'something' isn't steamed broccoli, is it? That 'something' is going to be melted cheese on toast, or ice-cream, or cake, chocolates, or biscuits. Hormones and neurotransmitters in the brain affect your behaviour and make it almost impossible not to reach for comfort foods, especially after a period of reduced calories.

Then, when you do 'give in', you beat yourself up for being 'weak'. It's the same as shaming yourself for being weak because you can't fight the urge to breathe.

Physical hunger is almost never the reason we reach for a chocolate bar or cupcake. We reach for refined sugars and carbs because they are soothing and comforting. We're yearning for meaning, fulfillment, connection, feeling worthy, pleasure... and when we don't have them in our lives, we substitute them with something else—sugar, alcohol, cigarettes, so-called reality TV, porn, gambling, shopping, social media...

So, yes, chances are you do need to drastically cut your sugar intake and I know you have every intention of doing that. You're convinced that sugar is toxic poison and you vow to resist its sweet temptations. You vow to cut it out of your diet! You forbid yourself to ever eat sugars again!

Does that kind of thinking sound familiar?

That's right, we're back in the territory of the dieting mentality again. Deprive, restrict, deny... resist.

By itself, this approach won't work because it's too much like punishment. Instead, we need to address the reasons why we're using sugar as a love substitute and why we're turning to it for comfort, soothing, de-stressing, and that hit of pleasure.

We do this by loving ourselves more and showing that love to ourselves in a variety of new, non-food ways.

We do this by loving ourselves enough to properly reconnect with and nourish our bodies.

We do this by loving ourselves enough to fill our days with things that give us pleasure and enjoyment.

We do this by working on the underlying issues and subconscious beliefs that have us believing lies such as *'I'm not good enough'*, *'I'm not valued'*, *'I'm not worthy'*.

When we love ourselves enough, this love will naturally spread out into the world and we will no longer be able to sit by and do nothing as our planet is systematically destroyed by those who seek wealth and power (to fill their own emptiness).

Heading down this road is what this book is all about.

CHAPTER 10
DIETING, DISCONNECTION
AND DOMINATION

"Here we are, one consciousness embodied in seven billion different forms."
— Panache Desai, author and spiritual teacher. @PanacheDesai

"The hardest prisons to break out of are the ones we build ourselves."
— Ashley Dunn-Bratcher, age 27, weight 672lbs, featured on reality TV show My 600lb Life

"If you make sure you're connected,
The writing's on the wall,
But if your mind's neglected,
Stumble you might fall..."
— 'Connected' by the Stereo MCs

THE GLOBAL EPIDEMIC of obesity and lifestyle diseases is a red herring. The real epidemic facing the human species is disconnection, isolation, despair, and loneliness through separation from our spiritual selves.

Excess body fat is the physical manifestation of emotional and psychological baggage on both an individual level as well as a collective species level. It reflects our individual separation from our natural and spiritual selves as well as our collective consciousness separation.

When we release our emotional baggage and get connected back to who we really are, the extra physical weight will resolve itself. This is true at both the individual level and the collective group consciousness level. When you lighten the load on your soul, this is reflected in your physical body. When we lighten up emotionally, we lighten up physically. When we connect to our spiritual selves, we enlighten. We let light in. We get lighter in all senses of the word.

Instead, we've bought into the lie that life on this planet is about struggling to get ahead, working hard and 'making something of yourself'. That it's about being 'successful', which we've defined as being able to parade the education, the money, the spouse, the children, the big house, the fancy car...

As we go through life, we feel powerless and fearful when in fact we are infinitely powerful and brilliant co-creators with God. We have all these fears... fear that we won't find a partner to love us, fear we won't have enough money, fear we'll lose our jobs, fear our loved ones will be hurt, fear of being homeless, fear of being sick, fear of not being liked, fear of being judged, jailed or killed, fear of being alone and unloved. All fears are rooted in the fear of being rejected, unloved and alone. We've developed societies where these fears flourish—every man for himself—instead of creating supportive communities.

We've forgotten that we are born worthy and successful with nothing to prove. We have become disconnected from who we really are, which is divine sparks of the Creator Energy that is often called God. We've forgotten that we are powerful co-creators in partnership with this intelligent energy, or consciousness. This intelligent consciousness flows through every cell of our body. It is our life force, our spirit.

For me, the situation we now find ourselves in is the collective physical symptoms of a spiritual and emotional disconnection from who we really are. This disconnection from our spiritual and natural selves, on both an individual and a species level, is contributing to the many forms of pain and suffering now manifesting on Earth.

If we believe ourselves to be separate from each other, as well as separate from our home planet, Mother Earth, and the rhythms of nature, then, on the face of it, losing excess weight should be a simple mathematical equation. But we are not simple bio-mechanical machines. We have energetic bodies as well as physical bodies. We have a global collective consciousness and we are all connected at an energetic and spiritual level. We are multi-dimensional. So when, as a species, we become disconnected from our Mother Earth, who is herself a conscious being with a soul; when we lose our connection with Divine Spirit and when we lose sight of who we really are then, as a species and as spirit beings, we will reflect this collective spiritual and emotional pain and disconnection through pandemics of disease—like obesity and diabetes, cancer, heart disease, autoimmune disorders, dementia, etc.

DECIMATION DECIDER

How have we become disconnected from who we really are? It's been a gradual process lead by the ideologies of consumerism, capitalism, conquest, domination, competition, and industrialisation—all of which are underpinned by a drive to seek control, which is ultimately fuelled by fear.

It's happened through our arrogant and ignorant efforts to think we can make Mother Nature play by our rules. We have gone out to show that we can 'improve' on what God and Mother Nature provided. So we do things like build huge steel warehouses where we force crops to grow in artificial light all through the year, not realising that the sun's rays carry frequencies of health and healing and knowledge that are then transferred to us through their consumption. You cannot substitute the energy of the sun, or the benefits of sunlight, with artificial UV lighting.

We have saturated our soils with pesticides and herbicides and then we've been scratching our heads with surprise when populations of bees die off in their billions due to Colony Collapse Disorder.

'Insectageddon?' We ask in surprise. *'But why are all the insects of the Earth dying off in their trillions?*

Because the poor creatures unfortunately share their planetary home with short-sighted human morons who are killing them.

Just like homicide and suicide, anything with 'icide' at the end of it means death. Pesticides are designed to kill life. That's their purpose: killing life. And yet we spray them liberally all over our food and our planet, does that sound like a clever thing to be doing? And just so you know, if we did manage to wipe out all our pollinating insects, the human species would also be extinct about four years later.[20]

Not content with poisoning the soils and decimating rainforests, as well as choking the oceans with plastic and sewage, to ensure we do as

---

[20] https://www.express.co.uk/news/world/982361/disappearing-bee-population-result-death-four-years-louvre-beehives

much harm as humanly possible to marine life as well, we also treat the animals of this planet like our own personal slaves.

Under anaesthetising terms like 'the agricultural industry', we have made animals suffer unspeakable and shameful cruelties so we can have cheap meat and dairy products. Much of which we throw away.

If everything is energy (and it is), including emotions (energy in motion = emotions), then by consuming the flesh of these suffering and sad animals we are also consuming the pain, grief, worthlessness, and despair that sits in the cells of their bodies and the tissue of their muscles and organs. We are integrating these emotions into our physical and energetic bodies with every bite.

Then we wonder why we feel so low and undervalued for reasons we can't put our finger on. So to try and make ourselves feel better, we turn to substances that will numb these feelings. We robotically and mindlessly reach for a cheap sugar hit via a packet of biscuits or a box of donuts because we have been well trained and brain-washed by the advertising sector to believe happiness lies in that brand of fizzy drink, or in that bucketful of thigh muscle on bone that's been fried in cheap oil and sliced by machine off the body of a chicken that lived its whole life in a cage and was injected with growth hormones. We call these thighs 'drumsticks' to forget what they represent, which is the white-washed cruelty of animals used in the fast food industry. If you want to eat chicken, choose organic meat from birds who lived free-range on grass. No cages and no barns.

As long as we go on blindly consuming so-called 'foods' that God and the Earth played little part in producing and, as long as we go on pretending that what happens out there in the mass factory farms and agricultural industry has nothing to do with us, then the more we become disconnected from our Spirit, from the Earth and from who we really are (which is multi-dimensional, spiritual beings, in case you were wondering).

Ultimately, the pain we suffer as a result, both individually and collectively, goes deeper and deeper. Consequently, we get sicker and sicker. But instead of reconnecting with nature and with our inner wisdom, which knows that the way we are behaving is insane, we push ahead with this charade and turn to pharmaceutical drugs. We pump ourselves full of prescription drugs. Because companies are queuing up to sell you a pill or cream for whatever ails you. And then there are pills to manage the side effects of those pills. We see no irony in taking 20 different pills a day in order to barely function and calling this 'healthcare'.

HONOUR THE BODY TEMPLE

What can we do about it? We can learn to start loving and honouring ourselves more. If we truly honoured ourselves, we would respect and care for the physical vessel in which our soul resides. In turn, we would honour the planet we call home.

Just like the way a mother feels towards her baby, the unconditional love she has for the new life drives her to want to give the child the very best nourishment, she naturally protects and nurtures this new born, anticipating and meeting all the baby's needs—from clothes to keep warm and dry to bathing, nappy changing, cuddling and affection.

When we love ourselves unconditionally, we provide a platform for loving and caring for others. Eventually this would extend to the whole world, the earth, the forests, the oceans, the marine life, the air, the animal and insect kingdoms.

Instead, the abuse and violence that we see in our external world is a reflection of abuse we direct at ourselves. Dieting is a form of self-abuse because it comes from a premise of judgment, criticism and punishment. It orders you to think *'there's something wrong with me' and 'I'm not good enough as I am'*. It has you directing hateful thoughts to yourself like, *'I hate my belly'* or *'my thighs are disgusting'* or *'I'm pathetic and hopeless because of this weight'*. Such thoughts are not loving and do not honour the staggeringly complex and intelligently designed physical vessels we call our bodies.

When we are kind and compassionate to ourselves, it provides a platform for also being kind and compassionate to others. To start with, this will be those close to us friends, family, and pets. From there it can swell into the community and eventually we can transform the world around us through love and compassion. Just as the most powerful way to transform ourselves is through self-love and self-compassion. When we truly love something, or someone, else we want only the best for it. And in the case of a human, 'the best' is optimal health and happiness.

Does forcing down chemically flavoured diet shakes, instead of nourishing your body with an abundance of colourful fruit and vegetables, feel like loving yourself? (Rhetorical question. That would be a 'no'.)

When we love ourselves enough, we don't need a diet book written by a reality TV show 'celebrity' to tell us how many grams of protein and carbohydrate to eat before 9am. Instead, we tune into our bodies and instinctively choose whole foods that nourish and heal our bodies and we do this from a place of self-care.

When we love ourselves enough, we don't force ourselves onto a treadmill for 30 minutes, every day as part of a regime. Instead we naturally run, dance, and play because it feels good for our bodies to move in that way, or because it feels good to be part of a team or social group, or because it feels good to run on grass or on a beach with our dog, or because it feels good to take deep breaths as our lungs pump harder and our hearts beat faster, pushing toxins from our bodies. Just like a baby, or child, who moves their body because it feels good and natural, if left to find our natural rhythm, we would also eat and move in a way that nourishes and heals our bodies, minds and spirits.

GET YOURSELF CONNECTED

When we get connected back to who we really are and to the rhythms of Mother Earth, and when we find a sense of meaning and purpose, get happy, and release our layers of emotional baggage, then we will naturally come back into balance in the emotional, mental and spiritual, at which point the extra physical weight will resolve itself. Because the extra weight is a reflection of imbalance in ourselves and our lives.

Unfortunately, from the dominating culture's overly materialistic, left-brained perspective, the physical side of the weight-loss equation has traditionally been the first and only part of the equation that we consider in the modern world (as you and I well know, my fellow recovering dieter).

The idea is that, the way to manipulate and control the amount of fat we have on our bodies, is by focusing obsessively on what we put in our mouths, by weighing and measuring food portions, recording what we eat, writing menu plans for the week ahead with everything carefully calculated based on calories, fat grams, protein, carbs, etc.

As we've already explored, this is a flawed theory that has been proven incorrect countless times in the worldwide laboratory that is the bodies of millions of real people. But it's also been proved flawed in actual laboratories of bespectacled sciencey types in white coats, so why on earth this theory is still being pushed by everyone from government ministries of health to giant weight-loss corporations is beyond me. Although I kind of know why. As long as we're all flailing around, blaming calories for the obesity crisis, then sugar gets off the hook a bit longer, which means manufacturers of high sugar fake foods can continue pushing their toxic products at us via advertisements using beautiful, thin people and super cute cartoons. *'How can this be bad for me when that adorable bear, wearing a baseball cap backwards, is eating it?'*

I know that some people like the counting approach, be it calories, grams of sugar or fat, syns or points, etc. It makes them feel that they are in control, they believe they know where they are with their lists and calculations. If that's you, good luck to you, but for me it smacks too much of traditional calorie counting and that just has too many bad memories and negative associations.

I've spent years and years filling hundreds of notebooks with lists of what I'd eaten each day with the calories totted up in a column on the right-hand side of the page. It can be helpful but it can also become another compulsive, controlling behaviour.

If, as a child, your life was cracked apart as a result of parents divorcing, neglect, pressure, bullying, or other trauma, then maybe what you put in your mouth was quite literally the only thing you felt you had any control over. This is how conditions like anorexia nervosa can take hold.

But my issues with this meticulous, eagle-eyed, always-on-guard approach goes deeper than this. I see this as an attitude born out of the domination and control mentality of the power structure we live in. It's an attempt for the mind and intellect (masculine) to control the body and nature (feminine). Rather than reconnecting with the rhythms of the body; and listening to the appetites and needs of the body, it instead relies on imposing an '*I know what's best for you*' set of rules on the body. By dieting, we are essentially bullying, or bulldozing, ourselves. Oftentimes, this is just mirroring the kind of bulldozing we received from others, usually parents or caregivers.

An example from my own life is a time I remember in particular when I was made to sit for hours at the breakfast table (it felt like hours, maybe it wasn't). I was forbidden from leaving the table until all of the cereal in my bowl was eaten. What is this telling the child? Among other things, it's telling them that they are not allowed to decide when they are hungry or that they are allowed to choose the foods they prefer.

Another example, a child is crying after being smacked by its mother for some childish transgression. The distressed child continues to cry until the mother threatens, '*stop that crying right now or I'll really give you something to cry about'*. The child learns that they are not allowed to express their feelings and that if they do express feelings that are unacceptable to the authority figure, harsh punishment will be meted out.

Instead of taking a broader view of nourishment and considering that our physical appetites are intertwined with our need for emotional and spiritual nourishment, we continue to treat the body as if it is ours to impose our will upon, to control, to manipulate, to dominate until we get it to do what we want—the problem is that what we want it to do is based on false beliefs of worthlessness seeded in the patriarchal soils of female inferiority and powerlessness.

This mindset *of 'I own you'* is the same mindset that created a world in which we feel it is our right to snatch birds and animals from out of their natural habitat—most of which we've stolen anyway—and imprison them inside glass boxes or behind bars and insist they live out their lives in these prisons for our convenience and entertainment.

It's the same mindset that spawned civilisations where financial profit is the ultimate goal and so justifies any means—including the unsustainable pillaging of Mother Earth for her resources. It's this mindset that justifies the systemised mass cruelty that are our factory farming agricultural processes. Humans have derived huge power and wealth from controlling the reproduction of the female of the species—whether that be hens, cows, sheep, deer, pigs, or women. Male creatures that can't be used in this way are destroyed as 'waste products'.

For the sake of our individual happiness, as well as for the sake of the happiness of the whole human race, it's imperative to bring a stop to this relentless need to control, dominate, and impose ideological rules upon one another.

When you impose the rules of dieting upon yourself, you're essentially saying, *'Shut up body! I'm not listening to you! I've read a book by an Instagram influencer and I know how to force you to shed this fat that I hate so much, so I'm going to deprive you and punish you with arduous exercise until you do what I want you to...'*

Let me, then, suggest another way to approach your body and its appetites. Your body is divine. It contains an intelligence so profound and so interconnected with the Earth and the Universe, as well as with your soul, that your attempts to control this innate intelligence with calorie calculations and food diaries are absurd.

Would it not be a better idea to align yourself with this intelligence? To partner with it? Does it not seem like it might be a better idea to tune in and listen to the whisperings of your soul through your body?

Instead of imposing the same rules and silencing on your body that so many have experienced from being at the pointy end of a heterosexual, white, patriarchal system for centuries, let's break this cycle. I do not believe we will succeed in transforming the power imbalances in the world until we cease transform the power imbalance in the relationships we have with our own bodies.

The violence and abuse we direct at ourselves through the culture of dieting—which essentially claims we are not good enough as we are—is reflected in the external world. We all want world peace but that's not going to come until we find peace in our own hearts and minds.

CHAPTER 11
OK HIPPIE CHICK, BUT WHAT
DO I ACTUALLY EAT?

"Civilised man is the only chronically sick animal on the planet. There is no NHS in the jungle. There are no GP surgeries, no giraffes queuing up to be treated for chronic conditions. We make our pets sick and fat, we can give elephants type 2 diabetes21 when we put them in captivity. Civilized man is the only animal clever enough to manufacture its own food, and the only animal stupid enough to eat it."
— *Dr Barry Groves (1936-2013), author of Eat Fat Get Thin!*

JUST BEFORE WE get to the 16 steps, let's talk about food for a moment. This is the part of the weight-loss puzzle you've probably already spent years trying to figure out.

That is understandable. On the surface, it seems like the physical body is the obvious and natural place to start. It's where every authority figure has told you to focus.

And it seems like common sense. After all, if you want to shed some excess fat from your body, it seems obvious that you need to look at what you're eating and how you're exercising in order to do that.

This calories-based approach has seen you spending thousands of hours pondering and monitoring what you're eating, and what combinations you're eating it in. Like whether to avoid carbs and proteins in the same meal, whether you have food intolerances, what time of the day you're eating, how many times of the day you're eating, or whether some foods are better eaten in the mornings and

---

21 https://www.tandfonline.com/doi/full/10.1080/01652176.2011.585793

others in the evenings. Do you need to stop eating by 6.25pm in the evening? Should you be vegan, keto, LCHF, raw vegan, pescetarian, paleo, gluten-free, dairy-free, sugar-free, vegetarian, fruit-free, VLCD, macrobiotic, FODMAPS?

You've probably gathered by now that I don't believe this is the road to success and happiness nor to sustainable weight-loss. However, I'm not saying that what you eat and drink is not important. What you put in your body is profoundly important—it's just not important for the reasons that the diet industry has led you to believe. We need to switch focus from weight-loss to healing the diet damage.

This is because all those years of dieting, as well as just living in these modern times of chronic stress, our unrestrained pill-popping approach to medication like antibiotics and antacids, as well as being exposed to an unprecedented amount of environmental toxins and heavy metals, means that your system is likely damaged in some way that is preventing you from shedding fat.

For the purpose of healing and reversing the physical damage that's been done to your body over the years, we need to use food and movement as medicine. At the same time, we remember that our struggles with weight reflect energetic imbalances. So while addressing our issues from an emotional, mental and spiritual perspective is essential, our healing journey also requires changes made in the physical realm.

THE HEALING PATH

I know you want to have all this excess weight gone from your body, like, yesterday! But it's essential that you now switch your focus from weight-loss to healing your body.

Just like the dog's tail that wags when you stroke its head, ultimately, weight-loss will be the effortless by-product of healing your body's struggling systems and releasing your emotional baggage. This process takes time though, depending on how much damage needs sorting out—the longer you've been persisting with dieting and denying your emotional stresses, the more damage you've probably got to heal.

As well as giving it time, this also involves some effort on your part in ensuring you nourish yourself with the medicinal foods that will reverse the damage of years of dieting. This is your chance to cultivate patience, self-forgiveness and self-compassion.

Because here's what's happened. Your years of on and off deprivation dieting means you've now got a metabolism that is wired to pack weight on at every opportunity and to jealously guard these precious fat stores. What else have you picked up along the way? This could be hormonal imbalances, an almighty sugars addiction, systemic inflammation, leaky gut, insulin and leptin resistance, and an under functioning thyroid gland, thrown in for good measure. It takes time to turn all this around. There are no hacks. It's like trying to do a U-turn with a super tanker.

POLITICS OF FOOD

Before we go any further into this topic, the last thing I want to do is get into the realm of telling you specifically what to eat. That's just dieting repackaged under a new banner (although I do offer guidelines and suggestions). Unless I know you personally, how on earth can I advise you on what's best for your body?

Having said that, let's talk about food. Food is energy. Food is spiritual.

We modern day humans have managed to make eating very complicated but maybe it doesn't need to be. No one has to tell a wild animal what, when, or how much to eat. For animals in the wild, diseases like obesity and diabetes are unknown. It's only when these wild animals are fed by humans that they start developing these diseases.

So what diet should you follow? What should you eat?

There is one main food guideline on the How To Heal Your Weight programme. It is, *'Did Mother Earth make it?'*

For me, the important question is not whether a particular food is a protein, a carbohydrate or fat, the important question is, *'did Mother Earth make it and does it still resemble what it looked like when she did?'*

The path back to healing, balance and aligning back to your natural optimum body weight is through reconnecting with your natural self. Eat real foods. In other words, the low HI and high MEM diet, which is low Human Involvement and high Mother Earth Made. Buy fresh ingredients and do your own cooking.

As a guideline, were there five steps or fewer between taking the ingredient from the earth and getting it to your plate? Is your food alive? Does it contain life force? Is it full of enzymes, sunshine and gut-friendly microbes? Or is it dead?

Take, for example, pasta and potatoes.

In mainstream weight-loss wisdom, these foods are bundled together under the label of starches. They are treated as basically the same from a weight-loss perspective but these foods are not the same.

Pasta is a processed food made by humans and potatoes are made by Mother Nature. Potatoes are full of essential vitamins and minerals. Pasta is often made of processed flour denuded of the nutrients it once contained. You can pull a potato from out of the ground where it grew from exposure to sunlight and rain. You cannot reach into the ground and pull out a sheet of pasta. The rain and sun didn't make a packet of dried pasta grow.

So primarily, I believe we should eat the foods that nature provides. I don't care if you're a vegan, paleo, keto, high fat, low carb, vegetarian, pescetarian, flexitarian, pegan, gluten-free, raw vegan, carnivore... We could argue about the rights and wrongs of meat-eating ad nauseum. For me, the most important factor is love and care and a commitment to reduce suffering of all beings. We need to be responsible and thankful about the way our food is grown, which means it needs to be organic and sustainable. Is it grown or bred with love and respect? If it's an animal bred for food, is that animal, and its sacrifice, treated with honour and dignity? Is it afforded a happy life before slaughter?

If you're a meat and dairy eater, then animal welfare should be the prime concern. If animals are bred for food, they must be treated with kindness and compassion, they must live in something similar to their natural environments and be encouraged and enabled to enjoy their lives. They must be looked after properly with love and gratitude, and given foods appropriate to their systems.

Ideally, we wouldn't farm animals in the barbaric 'modern' way at all. Animals would be able to roam wild and free because the human race hadn't stolen every last bit of land on the planet and destroyed their natural habitats to put up endless rows of high-rise apartments, shopping malls and parking lots.

However, when we do farm animals for food, they must be killed with as little suffering and pain as possible. This is not just for the sake of the animals, although that is paramount, it is also for our sakes. The sake of the people consuming the flesh of these animals. Because everything is energy. Every cell that comprises the flesh we eat is encoded with the energy and emotions of that animal. If that animal felt hopeless, imprisoned, despairing, violated, vulnerable, enslaved, etc. then that is the energy you're taking on when you consume that meat.

So what do we do? Here are a few suggestions you could be getting on with as a starting point. Take these and run with them but also come up with your own:

1. Eat food. Real food. Not fake food

Ask yourself this, who made it? A machine in a factory switched on by some guy wearing protective gear from head to toe, or planet Earth? Make it your mission to eat masses of colourful fresh, organic, locally-grown vegetables in all shapes and sizes. Eat huge salads dressed in quality cold-pressed oils, lemon juice and vinegars. Make soups; roast, steam and bake vegetables; prepare bone or vegetable broths... there are some amazing 'food as medicine' books out there so start cooking and preparing your own food. When we remove ourselves from the process of preparing and cooking our own food, we again disconnect from Mother Earth and our natural selves.

2. Eat good-sized meals three times a day

Don't snack, says Dr Zoe Harcombe, unless you're a cow or want to be the size of a cow. If you eat throughout the day, you're drip-feeding yourself glucose, which means you're in fat storage mode. Leave four or so hours between meals and eat enough plant fibre, protein, and fat at each meal so it's easy to do that.

3. See food as medicine

Harness the healing properties of food... turmeric reduces inflammation, lemon juice cleanses the liver, coconut oil and garlic combats candida, asparagus flushes out excess fluid and salt as well as protects the urinary tract, carrots enhance vision... and so much more. This subject alone fills hundreds of books. Get yourself copies of brilliant books like *Foods That Heal* by the Medical Medium Anthony Williams (Hay House) and *Cooking For Hormone Balance* by Magdalena Wszelaki (Harper One).

4. Natural world remedies

Learn about herbal remedies, herbal teas and essential oils, and incorporate them into your life. These are powerful tools so don't underestimate them. We've been brainwashed to believe that medicine is only what comes in a tablet made by Proctor & Gamble. Big pharma medication too often just disguises the symptoms. This is 'disease symptom management'. It is not healthcare. Natural remedies and therapies, by contrast, can heal the underlying issue.

5. Shun processed foods

Treat all processed foods like the demon misery monsters that they are. If it doesn't look like something that Mother Nature created, don't eat it. A 'sausage' made from something called Textured Vegetable Protein and packed with preservatives is not real food.

6. Reduce sugars drastically!
You know this. We all know this. Refined sugar is toxic death. So why are we still eating it? For a whole host of reasons, convenience, denial, apathy, comfort... it's a drug, remember. Lay off refined sugars in their many and varied guises. As well, reduce anything that the body views as sugars. I'm looking at you, white flour.

7. Eat good fats
Seeds, nuts, cold-pressed oils, eggs, avocados, oily fish (ideally small ones like sardines, herring, mackerel... avoid the big species like tuna and salmon because they're probably farmed and may be full of mercury).

8. Give your system a break
Give your body an extended nightly fast of 12 to 16 hours break between your last meal in the evening and first meal in the morning. This is known as intermittent fasting and will trigger a process called autophagy, your body's natural self-cleansing, detox system.

WHAT ABOUT EXERCISE?
I don't like the word 'exercise'. It's loaded with connotations about punitive regimes, forcing yourself to the gym, doing it because you 'should' rather than doing it because it feels good.

I prefer to talk about 'moving your body' and no, I am not talking about the need for hours and hours of jogging. Lordy, no. I wasted years on that. Ironically, that kind of high intensity cardiac activity can actually increase the stress hormones in the body, cause leaky gut, and trigger powerful urges to eat. Plus, if years of dieting and stress have left your adrenals in a state of exhaustion, then high intensity exercise is the last thing you, or your poor adrenals, need. If your adrenals are chronically fatigued, what you need is to basically sleep for about three months; *not* join the gym and drag yourself off to a Boxercise class.

If you're an overweight, recovering dieter, who's dragging yourself through the day on sugars and caffeine, then intense high cardio exercise can be detrimental to your health and wellness. (If you're a lean, fit, whippet-like person, don't let me stop you... but, um, did you pick up the wrong book?)

That's not to say high intensity sports like basketball, rugby, sprinting, and so on aren't good. Of course they are, and the nature of these sports often mimics the 'chased by a tiger' pattern of *run like your life depends on it then stop, rest, get your breath back*' for which the human system is designed. But if you haven't held a ball since you were on the high school netball or volleyball team 25 years ago, then maybe don't worry too much about throwing yourself around a squash court like a maniac just yet.

My theory is that, if you have to force yourself to do something, don't bother. Ultimately, your body loves to move and wants to move. When you're healthy and full of vitality, you won't be able to stop moving because every fibre of your being will be compelled to dance, sway, stretch, run, jump.

In the same way that children move, moving our body is a way to express the joy of living.

Enjoy the pleasure of moving the body without needing to be beating yourself with the calorie whip. So if you really don't feel like getting to that gym class, don't go. Do you feel like just taking a walk in the garden instead? Maybe you want to put on your favourite album and dance around the lounge? Just get outside and walk.

Of course, all types of movement are wonderful—if your body is ready for them—so if you love the high cardio 'whoo yeah!' type activity, keep doing it because the benefits are wonderful, namely releasing stress and balancing hormones, building cardiovascular health, building muscle, social interaction, and a sense of personal achievement.

If though, you're an exhausted, chronic dieter whose body-brain is still set to fat storage mode due to long-term threat of dieting-induced famine, it's a whole other story.

The workouts that are powerful in triggering health and healing in the mind and body include activities like yin or restorative yoga, tai chi, qi gong, dancing, walking, gardening... yes, I know you've heard this kind of thing before but it's often still presented as being about calories. So you'll then get some kind of stupid chart that says something like *'one hour of gardening burns 215 calories...'*. This completely misses the point and misunderstands the value of this kind of activity.

Let's take gardening for example. Gardening connects you with the Earth at a primal level. The very act of putting your hands in soil, and of nurturing plants, shifts your brain waves into a deeper, more meditative state. At an unconscious level, our cells communicate with the cells of the soils. When we move into the slower brain waves like alpha and theta, we open up parts of our brain that we can't access when we're in the alert, multi-tasking, beta state. We become more in touch with our intuition, we feel grounded, connected, and peaceful, and we can more readily receive inspired guidance.

On a physical level, our hormones come into balance. Cortisol and adrenalin levels fall away while the 'feel good' neurotransmitters like serotonin and dopamine are increased. When this happens, our body knows it's safe to burn fat. So it does.

END OF PART ONE

HIGH FIVE! You've made it to the end of part one. You're now primed and ready to begin your own personal journey.

The second part of the book is a kind of workbook. You can work through each step by yourself, or you can work through the steps as part of a group. Why not get some others involved and start a weekly support group?

Take as long as you want on each step and use them in whatever way suits you. You might want to just read them all first then go back and start again to do all the exercises and tapping meditations.

The 16 steps are divided loosely into the four areas of your life that contribute to your weight, namely the mental, emotional, physical and spiritual aspects of your being. Remember though, this is not a '*lose 16lbs in 16 weeks*' or a '*six weeks to your best beach body*' type of plan.

We're playing the long game here. If you've spent the last two, five or 10 years failing to permanently shift your excess weight, I don't want you to be in the same position in another two, five, 10 or 20 years from now. It's time to stop tinkering with the carpets and curtains and get down to the replacing the very foundations of your house.

Step by step, we're going to start unravelling the beliefs and the resistance that are keeping your excess weight in place.

So, step one of the Heal Your Weight transformative journey is gently beginning the process of ceasing the resistance you have to your current weight and body, and moving the needle a little closer to self-acceptance. By doing so, you begin the process of allowing your mind, body and soul to heal. This allows your body to naturally realign itself to your ideal weight.

PART TWO

THE 16 STEPS

STEP 1
STOP WITH ALL THE
SELF-HATE

"We are led to believe that we are lazy, that we eat too much and don't exercise enough. These are not the cause of our health problems, they are the symptoms."
— *Tim Noakes, author of The Real Meal Revolution. @ProfTimNoakes*

A message from The Spirit Collective: The Scuba Diver

Dearest one,

You look at your body in the mirror and your ego mind judges and assesses the form of your flesh by the standards set by a variety of external sources including the media, the advertising industry, a patriarchal system that benefits from your lack of self-esteem in that it keeps you in 'your place'—a place that is most advantageous to the leaders of this societal structure.

Your soul does not measure and judge your body and its form by these same standards.

Your soul sees the body as its divine vehicle for operating in this sometimes hazardous, three-dimensional world.

To the soul, your body is like the scuba suit that is used by divers to explore the wonders of the underwater world. The diver is most concerned that the suit will keep them alive and safe – the appearance of the suit while she or he is moving about in this underwater world is of little concern to the diver.

The primary concern is whether this suit will keep the diver dry, safe and alive as she or he carries out their exploration of this incredible and exotic space. So would the diver refuse to carry the lead weights, or any other piece of equipment, that makes up part of the scuba kit and which are so necessary for reaching new depths while under the surface of the ocean?

Would the diver say: 'I don't like how this weight-belt looks on me. I'll leave it behind...'? No. The diver wears however many of the lead weights are required to get the best experience, as well as stay alive, whilst exploring under the water.

This is how your soul views the fat that is carried on your frame. The weight is there for a very good reason. Or reasons. Your soul does not judge the outward appearance of the fat by the measures dictated by the mainstream culture and media of your world. Media such as magazines are themselves products that aim to sell you other products via the subtle, persistent and erroneous message that you are not good enough. Such standards of physical acceptability are of zero importance to your soul and the work it wishes to carry out while having this human experience. We love you.

ISN'T IT CRAZY when one of the hardest things for us to do is to accept ourselves just as we are? Instead, we blame our unhappiness on our bodies and we think we'll be happy and able to love ourselves when we're thinner.

That is not true. Despite what mainstream media and the diet industry continue to insist. We've been led to believe that if we get thin, happiness will follow, but it's the other way around. Harmony and balance in the mind pave the way for harmony and balance in the body. Once you find peace with yourself, regardless of your weight, that's when everything begins to change. When you stop fighting and resisting the excess weight on your body, you create a space for it to begin releasing—because you're transforming the reason for it being held there in the first place.

Real positive transformation of your mind and body starts by accepting yourself where you are now. It begins by ditching the diet culture mentality so you can explore the real reasons for why your body and brain are so determined to keep the extra weight on your frame—that's assuming you actually have problematic levels of excess weight on your body and you're not just a normal woman who's been convinced that there's something wrong with her incredible body due to the relentless and misogynistic narrative of the mainstream patriarchal culture in which you've been steeped since birth... [*OMFG don't get me started*]

The exercises and ideas in this book are designed to begin transforming those deeply ingrained neural pathways in your brain that are keeping you stuck and fat in the obsessive world of dieting. This world generally involves self-criticism, fat shame, food guilt, deprivation, restrictive rules, punishment, despair and defeat, etc. but you persevere with all that because you think that you'll be happy, and finally able to love yourself, once you're thinner. Because here is the key point. A lack of self-love is learned behaviour. We learn it from the people around us during the first seven or so years of life. We do this through being shamed, being criticised or by absorbing the example set by those around us. The daughters of mothers who based their self-esteem on their weight and appearance will likely do the same.

How, though, do you stop fighting and resisting the excess weight on your body when this mindset is now second nature to you? The diet mentality is your default mode. It's so ingrained in your programming that you do it automatically without even realising. It's become automatic to judge every food that comes your way as 'good' or 'bad', 'should' or 'shouldn't'. It's become automatic to pull your top down over your 'shameful' belly. It's become automatic to dress in a way that hides your 'flaws'. It's become automatic to praise yourself for not eating much and to scold yourself for eating too much. This is all learned behaviour, which means it is connections in the brain, and it can all be rewired at any age.

The first step on any journey is to assess the direction you've been going in and, if that's not getting you to where you want to be, stop moving in that direction and head off in a new direction. When it comes to this weight-love plan, the first steps are about understanding the extent of the profound damage that dieting and the dieting mentality has wreaked on your body and mind. It's about understanding that the premise of dieting is based on flawed and misapplied science and understanding that you can never arrive at a place of health and self-love via the path of deprivation and self-criticism.

'If only I can deprive and whip myself long enough, I'll be able to love myself...'

It doesn't work that way and we need to change that record, my beautiful friend. Your first task therefore is the cessation of self-judgment and self-criticism. We need you to move the needle away from self-loathing and start moving it in the direction of self-acceptance. This starts with pressing 'stop' on the self-criticism tape looping in your head.

If you're anything like me, this will be one of the hardest steps in this whole process. I spent a good 40 years berating myself for not being... enough (thin enough, good enough, pretty enough, clever enough, successful enough, and so on... soooo freaking boring). And I held onto this habit and this mindset because I thought it was a good thing. I believed that constantly being on my own back like this was 'good for me' because it 'kept me motivated and focused on striving to better myself...'.

'All this self-whipping keeps me on my toes,' I told myself. *'How will I ever achieve anything if I don't drive myself relentlessly with a spiel of harsh self-criticism?'*

That's not exactly how I sold it to myself but it was along those lines. Like the abusive teacher who whips you with a belt behind closed doors, then tells you it's for your own good, or that you made them do it.

The *'self-criticism motivates me'* stuff is all absolute bollocks. Love is the greatest motivator.

But turning the tide on all that is not so easy simply because it's ingrained behaviour and you've been doing it so long.

CHANGING TACK

The challenge is that when you've been pedalling in one direction for so long there is a comfortable familiarity that comes with it. You've built up all the muscles in your body and mind to now do this pedalling with ease. You know every inch of this road. You can't imagine not cycling this road. You don't know the other road, it's scary and you don't know where it leads! This old road is the one you know and pedalling on this road is what people expect of you now. They understand that this is 'you'—and you understand that this is 'you'. You're not sure who you are without this air of self-deprecation and undercurrent of apology for any inconvenience that your existence may be causing.

Shifting all this takes a commitment to the process because it needs

119

to be gradual and gentle and compassionate.

When you start transforming though, subtle things start to shift, your energy changes and people notice—usually at a subconscious level. You stop apologising for yourself. You start making choices. When someone asks, *'what movie do you want to see'* or *'what do you feel like eating?'* you stop saying, *'I don't mind, what do you want to do?'* and you start considering what you would really prefer.

You stop saying those stock phrases that have been a regular part of your vernacular like, *'oh silly me'* or *'I've never been good with...'* or *'I could never do that...'* or *'God, I hate these freckles/ wrinkles/ grey hairs...'* or *'I'm such an idiot', 'how could I be so stupid...', 'when will I ever learn?', 'why can't I get this right...', 'my clothes are tighter', 'my belly seems bigger today', 'I shouldn't have eaten that cake yesterday'...*

When you stop, or slow down, the constant stream of low-grade self-abuse, some people won't like it. Some may attempt to push you back into the familiar box of self-criticism—even people you love and who love you. They'll do this by pushing those buttons that have always had the desired effect in the past. Others may just gravitate out of your life. Be patient and loving with all these people though, it's normal for people to feel unstable when the status quo starts to shift. Understand that they are, in a way, doing you a favour by pressing your buttons because they are showing you where these buttons are—once you have identified a button, you can begin the work of unpacking and dissolving it. No one can press a button that you don't have.

To start with though, all you need to do is be aware that subtle yet powerful energetic shifts will be underway once you start changing your internal language. Observe yourself and others through this process.

So how do you start? You start by noticing all the ways you criticise yourself and replace these thoughts with ones of self-praise and acceptance.

Why is it so important to check on the things you say to yourself? Because these thoughts are the building blocks of your entire reality, including your physical form.

Deepak Chopra, in his book, *Quantum Healing*, described it by saying every single cell in your body is bathed in neurotransmitters. So every single cell in your body is eavesdropping on your internal dialogue. What this means to you is that every single cell in your body knows what you are thinking (consciously and subconsciously) and is reacting accordingly. Each of these cells is also a point of attraction in a universe that's run on the Law of Attraction so when you're constantly saying to yourself, *'Uh, I'm so fat, wah, boo hoo...'* this becomes your vibration and all of your cells respond by creating that reality.

As well as noticing what you say to yourself, you're also going to start noticing negative self-talk in others. When you attune your ear to it, you'll find that this kind of low-level and socially acceptable self-abuse peppers the speech of most people, particularly women. Make the decision that you will also no longer support your friends and loved ones in abusing themselves in that way.

Do not allow them to pull you into their self-hating narrative either. This is a common way for a woman who's feeling down on herself to make herself feel better by pulling others into her miserable pit of self-loathing as well. This kind of thing can seem quite innocuous, for example, your friend might say, *'Did you see the Grammys last night? Didn't Taylor Swift look amazing, wouldn't it be nice to look that good...'* the subtext being the suggestion that neither you nor your friend look good. This is what I call 'swallowing comparison poison'.

How do you respond to your friend? You can say something along the lines of *'Taylor Swift is beautiful, absolutely, but so are you Darling... and I sure as hell know that I'm gorgeous.'*

When you start to tune your ear to it, you'll realise our mass media is flooded with casual misogyny and we echo this in our day to day lives and interactions with each other. Start noticing when people around you make comments on a woman's body or age. Notice too if you're colluding with this. Don't judge yourself for it, you're simply a product of your culture and you're doing the best you can to belong by 'following the rules'. Be aware though that the trillions of casual comments thrown daily into the collective consciousness are perpetuating a culture where women are kept controlled by putting the onus on them to criticise themselves.

In other words, we've been taught to keep ourselves in check. We've been programmed to devalue ourselves and we've learned these lessons so well that the patriarchy barely has to lift a finger now to keep us down—we're doing so much of the heavy lifting for them. Keeping ourselves in the background and making sure other women are kept low and in check as well.

Thank goodness, there are signs of this changing. More women are stepping into their power but the change is slow and when you look around the world at who is ruling and making laws... (Putin, Trump, Jong-Un, Netanyahu, Assad...) it is apparent that we are still on dangerous ground.

What has the Russian President got to do with your failed efforts to lose weight? Ah yes, good question. That might seem like a bit of a stretch. Let me explain, Putin is the product of a nation and world run on toxic masculine values of the patriarchy. [*As opposed to the many positive masculine values that the wonderful men on the planet have to offer—power instead of force, support instead of suppress...*]

The patriarchy runs riot when it controls and dominates the feminine. By aligning with the cultural suggestion that the female is lesser and that there is something innately wrong with your female body and that you cannot rest till you 'fix' yourself (although you'll never be fixed because you can always be younger, thinner, more attractive), you leave the way clear for these values to run the show.

How do you start breaking out of this trap? By putting down that whip you've been beating yourself up with. By switching focus from what's wrong with you and your body to what's right about you and your body. By opening the door—even by just a crack—to the idea that you are perfectly divine exactly as you are, and that joy is your birthright.

Maybe that's too much of a leap just yet, don't worry so much about being divine just yet, we'll get to that later. For now, just stop beating yourself up. At least be aware of it. You may need to clear some beliefs that perceive a benefit in beating yourself up so, unfortunately, you're not going to stop until you stop seeing a benefit in it.

As Marianne Williamson wrote in her brilliant book *Return To Love*, you do not serve yourself or the world by dimming your light. So this process begins with simply noticing when you are dimming your light in the hundreds of supposedly small (but in fact hugely important) ways every day. From the way you speak to yourself, to the conversations you're having, to the media you choose to consume. If you're buying those magazines that fat-shame famous women and show grainy, long-distance photos of a celebrity's cellulite on a beach holiday, Sister, you need to ask yourself some hard questions about what your brain is consuming as much as what your stomach is consuming. You don't want to be a match to the energy of these mags.

Ultimately, the big question about what you do, think, or say—about anything—is, does it come from a place of love? Or a place of hate and fear?

That is the important part. It's not so much the action you take but the motivation behind it. Let's go back to a metaphor with which we're all so very familiar. Cake.

As a binge-eater, are you going to slowly eat that big slice of cake, taking your time to savour the flavours, because it's delicious and you appreciate the efforts of the baker and the love and care they've put into it? Or are you shoving that cake down your gob in fistfuls without tasting it because you're trying to suppress your inner pain and self-loathing with a moment of sugar-induced calm? In both situations, you consume the cake but the effects in the mind and body are poles apart.

What we're doing on this 16-step plan is beginning the process of rewiring your brain, changing your perceptions, making space for new solutions, and laying the foundations for your mental, emotional, physical and spiritual transformation so that you can stop fighting your fat, make peace with yourself, and start allowing any extra weight to just leave of its own accord because you've shifted the reasons it was there in the first place.

That is why this first step is about introducing you to the idea that it's possible to accept and have peace with, even love, your body exactly as it is right now. We want to introduce your body and brain to the idea that there is never any reason to feel ashamed of yourself for how you eat or look or behave.

How do you go about putting down that self-loathing whip? Surprisingly, you start by giving it full voice, which is what we'll do in your first EFT Tapping meditation, up next.

TAPPING SCRIPT: 'I CAN'T ACCEPT MYSELF WHILE I'M THIS FAT'

IF YOU'VE NO idea what EFT, or tapping, is then head to the back of this book for the *How To Fat Tap* guide. Otherwise, limber up your tapping fingers and let's get started. You're going to tap your way through the following script.

Feel free to adapt the script to use whatever words feel more real, raw, truthful and relevant to you. The more specific you can be about your situation and feelings, the more powerful the healing will be. Feeling is healing so what we're looking for is an emotional response. For example, when I'm doing this and the script reads something like, '*I am carrying more weight than I want to...*' I might change that to, '*I* *f**king hate all this f**king ugly fat wobbling on my f**king belly...'.*

Me, I like to add in swear words. I'm a bit of a potty mouth. I've toned them down for this book but there's still the odd one here and there and I don't always use asterisks to soften them. If you like swear words as well, add them back into this script. If you're offended by them, forgive me and change them in your head to 'fork' and 'frock'.

Okay, let's get on with the tapping. Ideally, you want to be alone and undisturbed for at least 20 minutes. And it's better to say the words out loud (sometimes I yell them at the top of my voice) but if you're somewhere that you can't speak out loud, say the words in your head.

Now, using a scale from zero to 10, decide how intensely you are fighting this battle with your weight; how intensely you feel you cannot accept yourself while you weigh what you presently weigh, 10 being the strongest. We want to tap on this until this number gets somewhere from zero to three. Even if you don't get it all the way to zero today, you may find that the remaining energetic residue works its way out after a sleep cycle. Otherwise, you've got more tapping to do till your number shifts downwards.

The tapping points are the karate chop point of either hand, the eyebrow (EB), side corner of the eye (SE), under the eye (UE), under the nose (UN), chin crease (CH), the lower end of one or both collarbones (CB), under an arm about three inches below the armpit (UA), and top of the head (TH).

Once you have your number, start tapping on the karate chop point on the side of your hand and say the following set-up statement out loud three times...

Even though I can't stand being this fat, and I feel like I can never accept myself while I look like this, I accept that these are my feelings and I am open to the possibility of loving myself anyway.

Even though I really don't like what I see in the mirror and it feels impossible to accept the way I look or ever love my body while it looks like this, I accept and respect that I have these feelings.

Even though there's a part of me that hates myself for having this fat on my body, and I beat myself up for letting myself get this way, I deeply accept that I have these feelings, these feelings are valid and they're true and they're mine.

Pause, take a deep breath and continue tapping around your face and body, starting with the point at the start of one or both eyebrows...

EB: I hate being this size
SE: I hate having all this fat on my body
UE: I feel so fat and big and blubbery
UN: I don't like my body like this
CH: I can't accept myself
CB: How can I accept myself like this?
UA: I do not like what I see in the mirror
TH: I'm ashamed of all the fat on my body

EB: I feel so fat and my clothes feel tight
SE: No matter what I do I seem to get fatter and fatter
UE: It makes me feel so low and depressed
UN: I feel hopeless about all this fat
CH: It colours every part of my life
CB: I see the world through these fat glasses
UA: My whole life gets viewed through my fat lens
TH: I just want to climb out of all this fat

EB: I wish I could just wipe it off my body
SE: I hate this fat
UE: I can't bear having all this fat on my body
UN: And I don't know how to get rid of it
CH: I'm so desperate to find a solution
CB: I'm so angry that nothing I've tried so far has worked
UA: What is all this fat doing on my body?
TH: Why is it sticking to me so stubbornly?

EB: I hate feeling like this and I hate this fat
SE: I don't know how to shake this feeling
UE: It consumes and envelops me
UN: I don't know how to take off my fat-coloured glasses
CH: It's exhausting thinking about this all the time
CB: It's exhausting putting so much mental energy into these feelings
UA: If I didn't think about this all the time I could do more with my life
TH: This obsession with my weight is stealing my life from me

Pause for a moment. Close your eyes and take a long, deep breath. Consider anything that came up for you while we were tapping. Any old memories, grudges, emotions, realisations... just tap on anything else for as long as you need to and then continue...

125

EB: I'm so tired of being stuck in this dieting loop of despair, frustration and self-hate

SE: I'm so tired of being unhappy

UE: Could I just stop all this self-judgment and self-criticism?

UN: Could I give myself a break from all that?

CH: Do I really have to beat myself up so much all the time?

CB: What if I could be just a little kinder to myself?

UA: Even if I can't accept my size, maybe I can accept other things about myself

TH: Or maybe I can just stop obsessing about my weight – even for just a short time

EB: But I've been criticizing myself for so long now

SE: That I don't know how else to operate

UE: When did I first learn to criticize myself?

UN: Who did I learn that from?

CH: Maybe it's time to unlearn it

CB: Because frankly, this approach isn't working!

UA: All this self-criticism isn't getting me the results I want

TH: It's time to see my body in new way

EB: What if I could let myself off the hate hook?

SE: Wow, imagine not having to hate myself anymore!

UE: Imagine finding things to like about my body

UN: Maybe I can start by being grateful for all the things my body does

CH: Maybe it's time to thank my body for the incredible things it does

CB: I've been taking my amazing body for granted for too long

UA: And I've been focused on only what I see as 'wrong' with my body

TH: But what about what's 'right' with it!

EB: Thank you for my heart that has pumped every second or so from the day I was born

SE: Thank you for the lungs that keep clean oxygen flowing through me

UE: Thank you for my hard-working liver, kidneys, and pancreas

UN: Thank you for my skin

CH: Thank you for the feet that take me wherever I want to go

CB: Thank you for my incredible hands that never stop working, creating, expressing

UA: Thank you for my bones that give me support and structure

TH: Thank you for my eyes and ears

EB: Thank you for my nose and mouth

SE: Thank you for my throat and neck
UE: Thank you for my reproductive organs and genitals
UN: Thank you for my stomach and digestive system
CH: Thank you for my amazing brain
CB: This brain that filters two billion units of information per second...
UA: ... deciding what I need to notice and what I don't
TH: I know there is so much more to my beautiful body than all this...

EB: I've barely touched the surface
SE: Thank you for every last molecule that forms my body
UE: This body that enables my soul to experience this world
UN: I know I am blessed to have this body
CH: Body, I love you
CB: Body, thank you, I love you
UA: Body, thank you, I love you
TH: I love you my beautiful, incredible body

Pause for a moment. Close your eyes and take a long, slow inhale and exhale. If you feel called to continue tapping positive statements, take some time to do that until you feel finished. A good sign of being finished is when you naturally want to take some extra deep breaths or if you yawn.

Then, go back to the number you had at the start of the session and see if it has shifted downwards. If not, keep tapping on whatever came up for you, especially any memories, emotions or 'aha' moments. If you feel called to do so, repeat this script as often as you feel is helpful over the next few days. Ideally, we want you to feel like you can accept your body as you are today so that number needs to be edging closer to zero.

When you're bringing the session to an end, cross your hands over your chest, take a deep breath and say 'transform'.

In your mind's eye, imagine this new knowledge of how to accept your body as it is today is pouring into every cell of your physical and energetic bodies until your whole being vibrates with this frequency.

Take the time to visualise this happening. Watch as every cell of your body absorbs and reflects this new information. Watch your cells release the old patterns and witness the new choices being encoded into your DNA.

Mindfully open your eyes onto a whole new world in which you are beginning to accept and appreciate your body.

EXERCISE:
CHANGE THE SELF-HATE TUNE

FOR YOUR FIRST exercise, I want you to start consciously noticing all the ways you subtly criticise yourself. I invite you to be on the look-out for, and hyper aware of, your habitual low level self-abuse.

As well, I invite you to cease all that self-criticism and self-judgment and to cease all comparison with others. If you can't stop it then at least notice and observe it. Notice how you speak to yourself. Notice what that voice in your head is telling you about yourself.

You can do this exercise all in one day or spread it out over as many days as you wish.

First though, I want you to get yourself a new notebook, writing journal or diary. This is going to be your Weight-Love journal and it will be your partner on this process. Choose one you really like, or decorate a plain one. This journal is where you will do the exercises and actions in the 16 steps and where you'll diary about how you're feeling and what happened in your day. This is a place to log what you tapped on and how you felt about the tapping. It's a place to note down small shifts in your patterns of thought and behaviour. It's a place to note down your big and little realisations. For example, *'OMG I eat things I don't really want to please other people! I'm not going to do that anymore.'*

1. SPOT THE SELF-CRITICISM

In your brand, new, Weight-Love journal, note down the criticisms you throw at yourself. Be on alert for the language you use with yourself, both in your own head and in conversation with others. Write down any negative phrase you find yourself telling yourself and note it down when you find yourself thinking or saying it.

A red flag for this kind of subtle self-abuse is when you use words like 'should' and 'shouldn't' or 'have to'. Sentences like, *'I really shouldn't eat that...'* or *'I should have done that differently/better...'Just notice when you think to yourself things like 'ugh look at my stomach', 'is that another wrinkle?', 'I wish I had a waist like* [insert name of envied person here]*', 'darn, I promised myself I'd be good this afternoon but I had that chocolate', 'what's wrong with me, why did I* [insert terrible, horrific, unforgivable deed like eating cheesecake here]*?', 'I'm not clever enough to ...', 'I'm so* *stupid for forgetting to post that letter/send that email/buy milk on the way home...'* etc.

This includes noting the ways you give yourself dysfunctional praise, such as, *'I've been so good today, I didn't eat that cookie...'*

2. DELETE THAT THOUGHT

When you do notice these reflex-action, self-abuse phrases popping out, stop them in their tracks.

Think, *'stop'*.

Take a deep inhale. Hold your breath for a moment.

Let out a long, slow exhale and think *'delete and cancel that thought'*.

Take another inhale and imagine exhaling that toxic thought out. Say to yourself, *'I replace that criticism with self-acceptance'*.

3. BAN THE INNER CRITIC

Then, have a little chat with these thoughts. You may want to say something along the lines of, 'Well, hello! I hear you inner critic! Gosh, we've been together a long time now, haven't we? But here's the thing, I'm breaking up with you because you've been lying to me and, frankly, you're really boring. I've decided to like myself as I am so you can go bother someone else with your negative drivel. I say that with love, obviously.'

After you've had this kind of conversation with your inner critic, you can shorten your reaction. Every time you notice a self-criticism pop in, say something like, *'cancel, clear, delete and replace with 'I choose to love myself as I am'*.

4. TAP ON IT

Whatever you're beating yourself up about, tap on it to get it into perspective. Ideally, make fun of it. As soon as you can laugh about something, it's lost its power over you. For example, tapping on the karate chop point of either hand:

Even though, I'm beating myself up for the terrible crime of forgetting to pick milk up on the way home from work, I choose to relax and forgive myself...

Even though, my heinous, milk-related negligence may spark the end of the world as we know it, I choose to relax about it...

Even though, I'm not sure I'll ever be able to buy milk again after this missed opportunity, I am ready to put it behind me...

Continue tapping around the face and body saying whatever comes to mind about how you feel about forgetting the milk.

5. PROGRAM THE POSITIVE

Next, replace the self-abuse with self-love and write these positive substitutes next to the original negative ones you've written in your Weight-Love notebook.

Take whatever type of insult you almost threw at yourself and replace it with something appropriate. If we stick with the 'forgetting to buy milk' incident, let's call it milkgate, you might think and/or tap, *'Bah! Who cares about the milk! What about all the things I did so well today! That brilliantly worded email, that joke I told, the delicious lunch I made, my excellent report...'*

If you were down on yourself about your appearance, say something like *'I love this colour on me', 'Look at my beautiful eyes/hands/nails/hair/smile...'*

If you've questioned your ability at work, tell yourself, *'I'm better than I give myself credit for.'*

If you've got 'bad parent' guilt, remind yourself that there's no such thing as the perfect parent, you're doing your best. *'I'm a great parent, my kids know they're loved and that's the best thing I can ever do for them.'*

Other positive replacements could be, *'I love the way I feel when I dance', 'I was always good at art/music/maths...', 'I'm a great listener'. 'There must be something wonderful about me because I have such great friends'...* etc.

As for any 'shoulds' and 'shouldn'ts' that pop up, swap them out for 'prefer' and 'choose'. 'I should' is disempowering while 'I choose' is empowering. So, instead of *'I should really go to the gym today'* replace it with *'I choose to go to the gym today'*. Or *'I choose to eat that...', 'or 'I choose to not go to the gym today because I'd prefer to stay in and watch Netflix.'*

ACTION AND AFFIRMATION

Action: Body love

Open your Weight-Love journal and at the top of a page write:

'I love my body because...'

Then write at least five ways to finish that sentence. For example:

... my heart hasn't stopped beating for every second I've been alive.
... of the delicious foods my tongue allows me to taste.
... my feet have taken me all over the world.
... my hands allow me to make, create and earn a living.
... a hot shower every morning feels so nice on my skin.
... it birthed my amazing children.
... my skin lets me feel the wind and the sunshine.
... my ears let me hear the music I love so much.
... my eyes let me see the face of my beloved.
... my arms let me hug my loved ones.

Affirmation

Write the following affirmation on a post-it note and stick it somewhere you see it every day, like your bathroom mirror when you're brushing your teeth. For most effect, say it while looking in your own eyes in the mirror. Say this affirmation as many times a day as you can. Aim for 100 times.

'I am now walking the path of self-love and acceptance. I forgive myself if I stumble.'

STEP 2
SHAKE OFF THE FAT SHAME

"We as women don't have the luxury of tearing each other down; there are enough barriers out there. There are enough people out there ready to tear us down. Our job is to lift each other up, so we have to start practising now... That is one thing we can do better as women, we can take better care of each other."
Michelle Obama, former first lady of the USA @MichelleObama

A message from the Spirit Collective: Fat scapegoat
Dearest one,
The fat on your body that you view as excess has not held you back in your life. It has given you an excuse to hold yourself back in life.
You create the excess weight so it can take the blame for your failures.
By persisting in your determination to lay the blame for life's disappointments at the feet of your weight, you successfully avoid looking for the real reasons you are, deliberately, holding yourself back in life.
These reasons, ultimately, come down to fear. We say, know thyself. When you know who you truly are, there is no fear.
We love you.

I KNOW WHAT you're thinking.
You bought this book because you wanted to lose a few pounds,

maybe fit back into your old jeans. You didn't ask for a thesis on the patriarchy and you're not sure you can really blame Russian president Vladimir Putin for the fact that your jeans feel too tight. (Lord knows that man has a lot to answer for but your muffin top as well? Hmmm...)

And, frankly, as much as I keep telling you you're a divine Goddess who must love herself, the truth is that you don't feel like a Goddess, the laundry needs hanging out, the cat has just thrown up on the faux Persian rug, and you're sorry but, if you're being honest, you really do hate your belly flab and your bingo wings.

I hear you, I do.

Fair enough. This is where we're going to get honest about all that. No more doing pretend self-love because that's what you know you're supposed to do. This step is about taking stock of where you are now and being absolutely truthful about how you feel about your body and yourself right now.

We want to bring all that self-judgment out into the open, shine a big light on it and take a good long look at it.

WEIGHT IS A SHAME REFLECTION

Many of the people who've come to me with help for weight-loss have said that they feel embarrassed and foolish about being concerned about their weight. They say it feels 'superficial' and 'trivial'. Which is another thing they can use to beat themselves up and deny their right to own and express their feelings.

Caring about the amount of weight that our frame has to support, and that our organs and bodily systems must cope with, is not trivial, it is crucial.

What we weigh is central to how we feel about ourselves and how we present ourselves to the world. Weight is intimately related to our sense of wellbeing, the health of our relationships, our careers, our friendships, our satisfaction with our lives, and our self-esteem.

I don't mean, though, that being overweight lowers our self-esteem; I mean that having underlying self-esteem issues is a root cause contributor to weight gain. The weight is the reflection in the mirror, not the cause.

Here's something to consider though. Feeling ashamed about your body fat is a red herring. You think that you're ashamed of being fat when, in fact, the fat is generously giving you a scapegoat on which to project your shame about something else in your life.

Fat shame is masking deeper layers of shame that have nothing to do with your weight. But the stuff that we really feel shame about is so painful that we take all that shame and repackage it as fat shame. This is another reason why some people keep the weight. It means they've got something to 'blame' the shame on without having to look at the real issues because 'going there' seems so painful. Keeping the excess weight means you don't have to look deeper for reasons to explain those intrinsic feelings of shame and low self-worth. Awareness of that is the first step to bringing it into the light.

Here's the dilemma though, how do we change our physicality without dieting and shame? If restricting food is not the answer, what is?

The answer, my gorgeous friend, is in changing the relationship we have with ourselves, our bodies and with food (and with the planet and Universe as well but, again, that might be too big a leap for right now, don't stress yourself about needing to become enlightened just at the minute).

When you love yourself enough, when you comprehend your true worth and appreciate your amazing body, you won't need to threaten and punish and bribe yourself to eat the right foods; you will be naturally motivated to want to nourish yourself properly because you love and respect yourself and your body. You will care for your body's wellbeing so you will prefer the organic wholefoods on which you know it thrives.

For the same reasons, you will avoid the processed fake foods that do such profound harm to your body and brain. You want to keep yourself safe and well. You will no longer want to feed yourself processed fake food that comes in single-use plastic packaging.

As you shift your mindset from one of negativity and criticism to one of love and acceptance, you raise your energetic vibration. I mean that literally. That is not some philosophical metaphor. I mean you, your being, your energy, will literally vibrate at a higher frequency and as a result, you will naturally gravitate towards foods that match this new frequency; foods that also vibrate at a higher frequency.

Surprise, surprise, this means more natural plant-based foods and fewer (ideally, none) refined and processed foods. (We both know that deep-fried ice-cream and cheesey fries are not the foods of spiritual enlightenment.)

You won't need to 'try' to do this. You will not need effort or willpower because you will be increasingly repelled by chemical-laden, fast foods.

Low vibration emotions, like depression, guilt, and shame, are a match to low vibration foods. That's why, when we get romantically jilted or rejected, the subsequent depressive period sees us hit our sofas with a giant tub of ice-cream, bag of Maltesers, bottle of sauvignon blanc, and packet of cigarettes for a box-set binge on zombie rom-coms. (Just me again?)

That's why you don't ever hear anyone saying anything like, *'Oh no, the love of my life has ripped out my heart, thrown it on the floor and stomped on it so I really feel like numbing my pain with a bucket of spinach salad and big pot of Oolong tea...'*

STOP THE INSANITY

The issue we have is that we've been so successfully indoctrinated with the messages of the diet, beauty, food and fashion industries that accepting ourselves as we are is inconceivably difficult.

Judging and disliking our bodies, and thinking we are 'good' if we restrict and deprive ourselves, has become our default mode. Self-criticism is second nature. This is no accident. Many trillions of dollars are at stake by perpetuating the idea that we have a problem that some corporation can fix or that we can be improved on in some way—billions of tonnes of everything from acne lotion to blue hair dye, vaginal wash, mascara, and aftershave have been peddled on this premise.

There is a wonderful quote attributed to artist Caroline Caldwell: *"In a society that profits from your self-doubt, liking yourself is a rebellious act."*

It is a piece of breathtaking, evil genius to have actually convinced people to be ashamed about a normal and unavoidable part of being human, you know, like getting older, or having body hair.

Think about that for a minute. We've been brainwashed to battle aging. If there is anything that is inevitable in this world, it is getting older. Yet women have bought into the lie that there is something wrong with it. How would they sell us all those anti-wrinkle creams if we didn't?

Because that's the other piece of astounding, evil genius. First, we've been brainwashed to view the process of aging as something to be ashamed of and fought against, then we've been convinced that various corporations can sell us some potion or 'weapon' that will 'fight' this process. Just think of all the industries that would crumble if we all decided that aging was in fact a really desirable and wonderful process and that human life got more satisfying and richer with the wisdom and perspective accrued over the years.

135

Consider too all the industries that would go out of business if 3.5 billion women decided they didn't hate their faces and bodies. Think about how much plastic packaging wouldn't end up in our oceans and soils.

Ponder too the 'amazing coincidence' in how the so-called 'flaws' and 'problems' that women in one country have are always mysteriously what comes naturally to them. So in Asia, women are slathering on expensive skin-whitening creams, and having their eyes re-shaped, because there is something 'wrong' with their brown skin and beautiful eyes. In the west, women are paying to lay on tanning beds of UV light because there is something 'wrong' with their paler skin.

Consider the profound change that would take place in the world if 3.5 billion women shifted all the energy they'd been putting into weight-loss and so-called anti-aging, and instead focused all that energy and creativity and determination on creating sustainable, compassionate societies where people lived as part of Mother Earth, in harmony with her cycles and rhythms.

What do we do instead? Fight against this natural order at every opportunity to pretend we're somehow in control of Mother Earth and above her influence. So we ignore the natural sunrise and sunset and live our lives with electric lights and alarm clocks. The corresponding harm this does to our circadian rhythms is managed with pills and caffeine. We sit in chairs all day when our bodies are designed to stand and move. We cover the soles of our feet with rubber so the energy of Mother Earth is blocked from entering our systems where it can rebalance our bodies and reconnect us back to the planet.

THE WRONG ROAD TO HAPPY

On the surface, why do you want to lose weight? In order to be happier. Most of us would like to be happier, there's nothing wrong with that. However, you cannot get to happiness city by plodding along *'I hate myself'* street. Going down that road takes you in completely the wrong direction. It takes you to fat and miserable city. To put it another way, it is a violation of one of the laws that runs this universe to expect happiness and health to be the fruit reaped from the tree of deprivation and self-criticism. It is a universal law that, what you give your attention to, or fight against, grows stronger. In other words, what you resist, persists. This includes being resistant to having excess fat on your body.

One of my favourite spiritual teachers, Teal Swan, sums it up in her

YouTube video on weight-loss[22]:

"Resist the weight and it will stay there," says Swan. "Focus on all the things that don't work, all the things you've tried, and on the fat you do have and you will get more of it.

"Resistance is the reason that most diet plans don't work well. You're not doing things from the standpoint of allowing and joy, instead you're fighting against the fat.

"You put yourself on diets that don't feel good to do, that are hard to do. You're depriving yourself so you're pointing yourself in the opposite direction of joy. You simply can't maintain that. It nullifies the whole entire prerogative of weight loss," Swan says.

"The only reason you want to lose weight is because you think it will make you happier if you lose weight. So, if what you're doing to lose weight makes you less happy, you're pulled in the opposite direction of both weight-loss and happiness.

"When it comes to weight-loss, the harder you try to lose weight, the worse everything will get," Swan says.

To sum up, the harder you resist your excess weight, the more it will stay there. The good news then is that, when you release resistance to your current weight and accept yourself as you are, you begin the process of allowing the body to heal and to naturally realign itself to your ideal body weight.

Did you get that?

Weight-loss lies in weight-love.

Losing excess weight is about giving up the diet fight and finding any way you can to fall in love with yourself as you are.

This is massively good news, right! Isn't it?

Well, kind of but it's not so straight forward. Turns out it's not so easy to just turn off the joy-choking dieting tap when you've been letting it flow for years and years. It's going to take some effort to uproot this programming.

We've been so effectively brainwashed that we cannot say, *'I love and accept myself as I am regardless of my weight!'* and be anywhere close to meaning it.

Who would have thought just deciding to accept yourself as you are would be so hard?

Who would have thought that it's you, yourself, who fights hardest against your own self-acceptance? That it's you (and, in my case, me)

---

22 https://youtu.be/wzJiMp-P_IY

who resists so defiantly the idea that perhaps you're fine as you are; enough as you are, worthy as you are, acceptable as you are.

'Nooo! I'm not good enough as I am!' your ego cries. *'How on earth can I ever like or approve of myself with all this... this...* [you grab at your fat rolls] *this disgusting fat!'*

Despite being aware on one hand that emotions like self-judgment, shame, self-directed anger and frustration are contributing to the type of *'I'm not good enough'* subconscious beliefs that are keeping the excess weight in place on our bodies, it can still be monumentally hard to shake off the shame and embrace self-love and acceptance.

We cannot imagine living our lives without thinking in terms of calories, diets, 'good' and 'bad' foods nor without endlessly worrying about our weight, finding fault with our bodies.

That's why this book is about rewiring our brains through the deletion of the files and programs we're carrying about dieting and weight and create some new neural pathways.

EXERCISE:
WHAT DOES THE WEIGHT
REPRESENT?

THIS EXERCISE IS about exploring what the excess weight represents to you, thereby looking for clues for why it persists in appearing on your body.

In your Weight-Love journal, start a new page and write at the top:

'What does this excess weight represent for me?'

Then start writing. Don't stop writing for at least 10 minutes. Set an alarm. Don't take your pen off the paper. Write everything that comes to mind. Even if you initially write something like, *'what a dumb question! This weight represents nothing more than 12 years of too many late night bowls of double chocolate fudge ice-cream...'*

As an example, here is what I wrote when I did this exercise...

"This weight represents a lifetime of struggle and failure. A never-ending battle. A war I can't seem to win. A war that will be with me for life. I've got the skirmish under control but if I take my eye off the battlefield, the enemy will rush me and defeat me—the enemy being fat. I can't stop struggling to keep it at bay. I can't give up the fight and surrender or I'll be held prisoner forever—I may be at war but at least I'm not their prisoner. Free to keep on fighting, that's what I believe. And there is some honour in this battle... I will not quit! I am not a quitter!

"But what if my choice to always be fighting something means I have to create 'an enemy'? Maybe my excess fat is serving me by acting as 'the enemy' that I must be locked in battle with.

"Why must I be locked in battle? Because if I don't fight I'll be taken over, consumed, annihilated. This reminds me of how I felt growing up. Living in an environment where I felt under constant attack. I was constantly on alert, constantly anxious and trying to predict the next thing that might get me attacked so I could head it off at the pass.

"What if I'm determined to keep fighting because, if I stop fighting, it means I've let him win? Is there a part of me that believes that? Have I simply switched my battle with him into a battle with my weight? So,

he IS my weight. And I f@#king hated and resented him. And I wanted rid of him as well. I wanted him out of my life but I never got what I wanted. He stayed. I couldn't get rid of him just like I can't get rid of my fat.

"Wow. My weight represents him and my battle with him. He is the weight I'm carrying. The burden I'm carrying. He is the emotional pain I'm carrying.

"Now that I know that, can I let this battle cease? Can I finally stop fighting and recreating him as fat that must be constantly battled? Is this fat the body armour that keeps him at a distance? What is the benefit of holding onto this battle? It makes me feel like he hasn't won. I cannot let him win. But what if there are no winners and losers? What if the only one losing out is me... by keeping the weight on. What if he's winning by keeping me in this miserable battle?

"What's the subconscious belief? 'I'm stuck with this situation, there's nothing I can do about it, no one is listening to what I want...'

"But what if that's not true? What if I'm not stuck with it? Maybe this is a false belief that I no longer need? And maybe I can let it go."

When you've finished writing everything that comes to mind, take some quiet time to ponder any subconscious beliefs that were revealed in the process and say to yourself, 'What if that's not true? Maybe this is a false and limiting belief and I can now let it go...'

Then spend a few moments, visualising these false beliefs floating up and out of your mind, brain and body, leaving your system permanently.

TAPPIG SCRIPT: SHAKING OFF THE FAT SHAME

USING A SCALE from zero to 10, pick a number that matches how intensely you feel angry, or ashamed, or frustrated, about being overweight, 10 being the strongest.

Once you have your number, start by tapping on the karate chop point on the side of your hand and say the following set-up statement out loud...

Even though, part of me still hates being this size and hates myself for letting myself get to this size, I accept that these are my feelings and I have every right to feel this way.

Even though I'm ashamed to admit that I still wish I wasn't fat and I can't completely accept myself while I'm this heavy, I'm open to the possibility that I can 100 per cent love and accept myself anyway.

Even though I'm ashamed of myself for not accepting myself, and I'm judging myself for judging myself and I'm beating myself up for beating myself up, I choose to relax and forgive myself.

Pause, take a deep breath and continue tapping around the face and body, starting with the point at the start of one or both eyebrows...

EB: I wish I could say that I've given up fighting my weight
SE: But if I'm being honest, I haven't
UE: I still wish I was thinner
UN: I still hate weighing this much
CH: I still can't accept myself at this weight
CB: And I can't stop resisting this weight on my body
UA: I don't want it on me
TH: I want it gone

EB: And the urge to keep fighting it is strong
SE: I don't accept myself like this
UE: But resisting my weight, ensures it persists
UN: And I understand that emotions like shame and unworthiness...
CH: ...are the building blocks of excess body fat
CB: But I can't shake these feelings and negative thoughts
UA: So now I'm annoyed with myself for judging myself
TH: Which means I'm judging myself for judging myself

EB: Giving myself another thing to feel anxious and guilty about
SE: I'm scolding the part of me that won't accept myself as I am
UE: If the key is self-acceptance
UN: I'm getting worse!
CH: And I'm judging myself for that too
CB: So many reasons for beating myself up
UA: Beating myself up for not loving myself enough
TH: Beating myself up for beating myself up

EB: How on earth do I break out of this ridiculous circle?

SE: How on earth do I love myself if I still hate the excess fat on my body?

UE: Part of me refuses to approve of myself...

UN: ...until I've earned that approval...

CH: ...by being thinner

CB: Ah yes, that familiar old pattern of having love withheld from me...

UA: ... until I've earned it by being thin enough, pretty enough, smart enough... yada yada

TH: Where did I first learn this pattern?

EB: When did I realise that love was conditional?

SE: Who taught me that I had to earn this conditional love?

UE: Whose love am I really trying to earn by being thinner?

UN: I've spent years cracking the whip over myself

CH: Telling myself to work harder, do more, be more, do better...

CB: No accomplishment is ever quite enough

UA: No achievement is ever quite enough

TH: So I drive myself—striving, pushing, punishing, forcing myself to be good enough

EB: Good enough by who's measuring stick?

SE: I've been whipping myself like a slave master for years

UE: That's got me to where I am today

UN: Unhappy, overweight, frustrated, desperate...

CH: So maybe it's time to try a new approach

CB: At least be open to the possibility of loving myself as I am

UA: Even if it is a process, a journey

TH: Even if the way back to self-acceptance is a journey

Pause for a moment, close your eyes and take a long deep inhale, then exhale, through the nose. Give yourself a couple of seconds to consider anything that came up for you while we were tapping. Any old memories, grudges, emotions... tap on anything else for as long as you need to and then continue...

EB: Unconditionally loving myself isn't so easy

SE: I've beaten myself up for so long that's it's hard to stop

UE: But I am open to the possibility of loving myself as I am

UN: I choose to release all the old patterns of negative thoughts about myself

CH: And even if I stumble back into old habits along the way

CB: I'll forgive myself for it
UA: Because these old patterns are deeply ingrained
TH: So when I fall back into them for a moment

EB: By having a negative thought about myself or my body
SE: I'll forgive myself and love myself for recognizing it
UE: I'll re-affirm my efforts and my decision to love myself
UN: Maybe I can stop judging myself by someone else's measuring stick
CH: Maybe I can grab that measuring stick and break it into tiny pieces
CB: Ok fine
UA: But how do I like my body in this moment
TH: How do I live with myself right now?

EB: Because I'm so hideously, shockingly fat right now!
SE: But am I really?
UE: Is that really true?
UN: Am I really so hideous?
CH: Is it really so unbearable to be me as I am right now?
CB: I've managed so far without imploding from hideousness
UA: Maybe I can cut myself some slack on the continual self-bashing
TH: Maybe – just maybe – I can even think of some things to like about myself

Take another pause here for a deep breath before continuing. Close your eyes and take several long slow breaths before continuing.

EB: Maybe a little reality check is in order
SE: Sure I've got more fat on my body than I would prefer
UE: But so what?
UN: So freaking what?
CH: What if I just stopped being that bothered
CB: Would it be so terrible to not mind so much what I weigh?
UA: Instead to turn my attention to finding fun in life?
TH: This constant worrying about my weight is boring

EB: It's a buzz killer
SE: And a joy thief
UE: Screw it, I'm done with the self-bashing
UN: I'm done with the fat shaming
CH: It's a dead-end road
CB: A dead-end dieting road

UA: Surely there's more to life than this
TH: More to life than obsessing about my weight

EB: I'd have so much more time, energy and money without this battle in my life
SE: This battle that goes on in my own head
UE: More time and space for volunteering at an animal charity, running for local government, writing blogs, learning sofa upholstery, writing a best-selling erotic novel about vampire ghosts and zombie witches, studying yoga in India, learning cheese-making in France [you get the idea, insert own dreams and ambitions...]
UN: If only I emptied my head of this weight-worry nonsense
CH: Made space for really living life
CB: Maybe I can gently let those old negative patterns go
UA: Gently untangle myself from the sticky vines of fat shame
TH: This is my body

EB: It's the only one I've got
SE: And I choose to love it
UE: I choose to honour it
UN: I choose to be grateful that I have such a wonderful body
CH: I choose to respect my body
CB: To nourish it with whole foods
UA: Foods made by Mother Nature
TH: I choose to begin walking the path of self-love and acceptance

EB: Taking the first steps down this new path
SE: And forgiving myself if I stumble
UE: Maybe it's not so hard to love myself
UN: Maybe I'm not so bad after all
CH: Maybe I'm actually awesome
CB: I AM awesome
UA: Maybe I am worthy of unconditional love
TH: I am worthy of unconditional love

Pause for a moment, close your eyes and take a long, slow inhale and exhale. If you feel called to continue tapping positive statements, take some time to do that until you feel finished. A good sign of being finished is when you naturally want to take some extra deep breaths or if you yawn.

When you're bringing the session to an end, cross your hands over your chest, take a deep breath and say 'transform'.

In your mind's eye, imagine this new knowledge of how to live your day to day life without shaming yourself for being fat pouring into every cell of your physical and energetic bodies until your whole being vibrates with this new frequency.

Take the time to visualise this happening. Watch as every cell of your body absorbs and reflects this new information. Watch your cells release the old patterns and witness the new choices being encoded into your DNA.

Slowly open your eyes onto a world in which you no longer shame yourself for being fat.

Go back to the number you had at the start of the session and see if it has shifted. If not, keep tapping on whatever came up for you. If you feel called to do so, repeat this script as often as you feel is helpful and tap on anything that comes up as result, especially any memories, emotions or 'aha' moments. This is a huge topic though, you may need to revisit this issue from a variety of different angles before you can sincerely say, *I love myself as I am regardless of my weight'*.

ACTION AND AFFIRMATION

Action: Self-love Ritual

For this action, you'll be spending an evening on self-pampering. Do this an hour or so before bedtime so you can go straight to sleep afterwards. (Don't skip this if you're a bloke, I'm talking to you, too, tough guy, go run that bubble bath and prepare to get sudsy.)

1. Prep up

Some of the things you might like to have on hand: Soothing music; candles; essential oils; big soft towels; organic soap; organic body lotion or oil; a loofah or flannel; an ink pen, henna, or something else you can use to write on your skin, and an erotic novel.

2. Create your home spa

Run a hot bath and, while it's filling, dim the lights, light some candles and put some soothing music on. Put some essential oils into the bath and then soak. If you don't have a bath, turn your shower into a place of pampering.

3. Lather up

Using a soft sponge or loofah, gently rub your whole body, taking the time to admire your limbs, your skin, the shape and curves of your body. Tell every part of your body that it is beautiful and thank it for everything it does for you - your feet, your eyes, your hands, your skin, your hair, your belly, your genitals, and so on.

For example, massage your toes one by one and tell them they are beautiful, thank them for connecting you to the earth, thank them for letting you walk and move your body. When you've finished thanking every part of your body that you can see, go inside and thank all the parts of your body that are beneath the skin, your heart, lungs, liver, pancreas, spleen, bones, muscles, veins, arteries, kidneys, lymph, fascia, ligaments, tendons, blood, colon, intestines, brain, stomach... be aware of and acknowledge to your body that even if you thank every part of your body you can think of, there are still trillions more cells, hormones, chemicals, enzymes... countless other parts of you that are working tirelessly to serve you.

4. Relax

When you're out of the bath (or shower), wrap yourself, and maybe your hair, in a towel and just lie on your bed listening to soothing music.

5. Written on the body

When you're ready, take up your pen or your henna and write '*I love you*' on your belly. Add anything else you want, such as a shape like a love heart or flower. You might want to write more words, *'My body is beautiful, 'I am enough',* and so on. If you don't want to write anything that will be visible, write these words in body lotion or body oil and then rub them in. Lie back and relax again. If you feel like it, take some time for self-pleasuring (this is where the erotic novel may come in).

Drift off to sleep.

Affirmation

Write the following affirmation on a postcard or post-it note and stick it where you'll see it at least once a day. Repeat as often as possible.

'I am open to the possibility that I can love and accept myself regardless of my body's size.'

STEP 3
UNPACK YOUR FAT BAGGAGE

"When our psychology changes; our biology changes. There is no mind-body split. It's only in the 20th Century that this illusion has arisen that's caused us to try and treat people's bodies as independent from their minds. Our minds and bodies function on a continuum."

Dawson Church, EFT tapping authority, health researcher and writer @dawsonchurch

"Anything that is not true creates pain,"
Luis Angel Diaz, author of Memory in the Cells @CMRbyLuisDiaz

A message from the Spirit Collective:
The language of body fat
Dearest one
In both animals and humans, the body is a vehicle of expression. The physical body is the 'voice' through which your species expresses the soul and the inner most thoughts and emotions.
Some forms of bodily expression are more obvious and easily interpreted than others. A person can express emotions like joy, happiness and sensuality through dance. A person can release anxiety through physical exertion such as running or boxing.
It is through the gestures, postures, behaviours and facial expressions known as body language that a person will intentionally and unintentionally reveal their prejudices, moods,

neuroses, beliefs, likes and dislikes, and more.

Every human is constantly revealing their inner most selves through the language of their physical body. This expression of self through the physical form extends to what you choose to put on your body and to how you choose to dress yourself. It is revelatory what colours you choose to wear, how you style your hair and adorn yourself with jewellery, beauty products, tattoos and piercings. A person also reveals their inner self on the outside through such choices as cosmetic surgery and self-harm. All of these practices are different tools of self-expression however it goes much deeper and is more complex.

The human species uses every part of the physical body to express and manifest its energetic form. This includes the bones, the organs, the skin, as well as the fat that is stored on the body. When a part of the physical body manifests a disorder, it is expressing an emotional component of the person's psyche.

There are no exceptions to this.

Body fat has its own consciousness. Every fat cell on a person's body has its own consciousness whilst also being part of the collective fat consciousness. Body fat cells operate individually as well as collectively. They can be thought of as similar to a colony of worker bees or ants. Each bee carries out its own work as instructed for the health and survival of the hive.

Like the bees and ants working for the survival of the colony, the primary concern of your fat cells is your survival. Your fat cells respond to physical as well as emotional and mental threats. When heavy metals such as mercury, lead and fluoride enter your system, perhaps through your food or water supply, they are quarantined within your fat cells. These metals are rendered inert and prevented from harming your delicate internal organs by being stored within a cushion of fat. As the human species exposes itself to more and more toxins, the more the body must protect itself by storing these contaminants within fat cells. For weight-loss purposes, detoxing the body of heavy metals and other contaminants will help aid the reduction of fat cells.

Your body fat speaks your truth. In fact it is obligated to reflect your truth. If you do not express your thoughts and feelings with your voice, or another creative channel, then these thoughts and feelings will be expressed through your body in another way. This energy must be expressed; it is a law of the universe. One of these tools of expression is body fat. The fat on your body is a reflection of your fears and insecurities; of your loves and sadness, and of your belief system.

When a person wraps their body or internal organs in fat they are doing so for a reason. This fat may be acting as a shield, or body armour. This is not just a metaphorical construct. The physical properties of body fat can deflect or scramble certain harmful frequencies—this includes negative thought forms from other people as well as the myriad of frequencies humans are now exposed to from wireless internet, telephones, satellites, microwaves and radio waves.

Our point is that body fat serves many uses but ultimately its reason for existing is your protection and safety. Your aim in reducing the amount of body fat you are carrying is not served by disliking the appearance of the fat or viewing it as the enemy.

We love you.

WE HAVE LOOKED at the idea that you have the amount of adipose tissue (fat) on your body that you do because your body-brain perceives that this is exactly the right amount of this tissue for your optimal safety and survival.

So why might your body-brain think holding onto all this extra fat is the best thing for your survival in the world?

This is where the fun begins because there are oh so many and varied good reasons you may have for holding onto excess adipose tissue and these reasons are unique to your experiences in this life, in your past lives, as well as to the experiences of your ancestors from whom you have inherited your genetic coding.

Having said that, the human experience and condition does have many commonalities. All of us have families, friends, and relationships; we all want to be loved and we all navigate the choppy seas of growing up and finding our way in the world.

So maybe some of your reasons for being fat are similar to the ones I had, maybe some of them are completely opposite.

You and I may both be holding onto body fat as the result of a childhood trauma or event but the specifics of what happened to you are different to what happened to me so the beliefs we formed as a result of our experiences may be different—but they may be similar.

Much of what is supposedly 'wrong' with us comes down to Love. Or, or more specifically a corrupted view of Love or a perceived lack of Love. In fact, I'd argue that all of it, everything, comes down to Love. I'm not talking about the notions of romantic love expressed in red heart-shaped Valentine's Day cards and pop songs. I'm talking about a divine, unconditional, profound and all encompassing Love of ourselves, of others, of life.

Many of us have formed beliefs that we are not good enough, that we don't deserve to be happy, that we are worthless, unloved, unheard, unimportant and invisible. These are all subconscious beliefs so on the surface you may think, *'well, that's not me, I don't have any beliefs about not being good enough...'* But I've worked with so very many wonderful people, living admirable lives, who harbour these kinds of beliefs running in the background of their operating system that I've reached the conclusion that the programmes running your operating system often seem outlandish and ridiculous to your conscious mind.

From what I've observed, that there are some common universal beliefs and programmes that typically contribute to someone holding onto excess body fat. I've divided them into six main themes, which are listed below:

Fat as love:
This is when you have wonderful memories of eating food with people who love you and who nurtured you so you turn to food to feel loved and nurtured. Food is how you nurture yourself, how you treat yourself and how you reward yourself. Trouble is, the resulting excess fat is also seen by the body-mind as love and comfort so you hold onto it to feel loved. In a similar way, we may use food to treat or reward ourselves. This can be a pattern formed in childhood when a parent promised a treat like ice cream or a trip to a fast food restaurant in return for 'being good'. This pattern gets set in our programming and, as adults, we subconsciously give ourselves a 'reward fix' when we have that cookie. It sets off a chemical cocktail in our brains that makes us feel happy, loved and deserving of something sweet because we are good.

Or you might have had a grandmother who showered you with love and affection and you have some deep memories of her soft fat belly or her large shelf of a bosom. You equate this big belly and bosom to feeling completely safe, nurtured and loved. At some level, your own soft fat belly reminds you of her and that feeling of being completely enveloped in her unconditional love and doting. Of course you're going to want to be reminded of that! And if you can carry this love with you always simply by having a big soft belly, who would blame you? In a similar way, I had one client who realised she wanted to be a big, cuddly, mum who gave her kids great hugs. This, to her, was the idea of a good mother. Subconsciously she was keeping the weight on to be a "cuddly mum".

Consciously, though, you don't want that 'unsightly' belly so you deny yourself the foods that comfort you and make you feel loved. This is when the trouble starts because, when you do this, at some level it feels like abuse from a critical and unloving parental figure, even rejection. So eventually you'll rebel against that 'punishment' and go on a binge-eating session of these foods as both rebellion and defiance as well as for comfort.

When we subconsciously believe that there is a lack of love in our lives, we crave carbs and sugar because the chemical fix of sugars gives us a hit of the 'love' neurotransmitters[23], which include dopamine and serotonin. When we reach for sugar, what we're really reaching for is love.

To put it another way, when we eat that gorgeously, gooey piece of caramel chocolate we are in one sense making love to ourselves. This might go some way to explain all those chocolate bar TV advertisements in which the woman (it's always a woman) seems to be having some sort of orgasmic reaction to the sugary sweet. It's food masturbation.

One of the problems though is that long-term stimulation of the brain's pleasure center drives physical addiction to the substance in question—be it sugar, nicotine, alcohol or cocaine—and the overconsumption of sugar brings with it an avalanche of diseases and disorders ranging from obesity to cancer and heart disease.

Fat as protection:
This is when people use body fat to avoid unwanted sexual attention or to act as a buffer against emotional abuse. Subconsciously, people make themselves unattractive to avoid the wrong kind of attention. This is tragically common in those who have experienced sexual abuse.

---

[23] http://www.bbc.co.uk/science/hottopics/love/

The extra weight literally puts more distance between them and the abuser. This can be emotional or mental abuse as well as physical, a bullying boss for example. The body uses weight and fat to help define the boundaries of a person who finds it hard to stand up to others. Extra weight makes them literally harder to push over.

Similarly, when you don't trust people—again due to beliefs formed in childhood—then excess fat literally keeps other people further away.

However, the concept of protection is much broader than this. Fat as protection can also be about protecting yourself from the very real harm of heavy metals and environmental toxins. If at some point in your life, or over time, you were exposed to heavy metals such as fluoride, mercury or lead, the body may be protecting your delicate internal organs and brain from these substances by basically locking them away in your fat cells as a kind of quarantine. The issue for people living on earth today is that we are being bombarded with a lethal cocktail of toxic substances that is unprecedented in human history. Never before have we surrounded ourselves with so many toxins. From the pesticides sprayed on our food, to the plastics we wrap everything in, to the toxins pumped into the air from factories and cars, and to the chemicals that are added to everything from shampoo to cosmetics, carpets and cleaning products.

On an individual level, we can redress the damage in part through a regular practise of cellular detoxification with, say, green juices and spirulina, coupled with working on releasing the beliefs that keep some part of you resonating with the frequency of these toxic substances.

However, until we as a species address the profoundly sickening way we are choosing to live with regard to how we treat this planet and the priorities of our societies and communities, our individual attempts to detox our individual bodies can only do so much.

Fat as safety:
There are countless ways that excess weight can make us feel safer. For example, some people gain weight when they get married as a way to avoid being unfaithful. It's like putting up a sign that says *'sorry, I'm off the market'*.

Or they feel safer with, literally, some extra weight to back them up and support them. The subconscious belief and benefit could be something like, *'that bully can't push me around if I'm heavy'*.

For some of us, we essentially create a suit of armour with body fat. We surround ourselves in fat so that other people can't get close to us.

We believe we are keeping ourselves safe by doing so.

Alternatively, if someone was taught that everyone in their family is overweight and, in order to belong in the family they must be overweight as well, then holding onto excess fat allows them to perpetuate this belief and remain in the family unit where they feel safe and accepted. Or maybe you've picked up beliefs from your parents that *'life is a struggle'* and *'nothing worthwhile comes without struggle'* so you are subconsciously ensuring that you keep struggling by having excess weight to struggle and battle against in order to feel worthy and accepted, and therefore safe.

Fat as self-sabotage:

This is similar to 'fat as safety' in that we tend to sabotage ourselves under the idea that we're safer. At its root, self-sabotage is misguided self-protection.

So excess weight gives us a great excuse for not doing something we're afraid to do. For example, *'I'll start dating/ travel/ go skydiving / learn to swim / get a new job... when I lose weight.'* Why do we procrastinate? Usually out of fear; fear of change, fear of failure, even fear of success. Say you succeed in getting that amazing new job or promotion, will that mean longer hours, harder work, no life-work balance, more competition...? And will that ruin your marriage and impact your health? Better not risk it!

Fat as survival:

If someone has financial or job worries, or if their ancestors experienced famine or starvation and that experience is now coded in their DNA, this can result in holding onto excess weight.

According to our lizard brain, we are more likely to survive the winter, or a famine, if we have extra fat. It's a primal survival strategy. The thing is, our lizard brain doesn't see a difference between 21st century anxiety about how to pay the mortgage triggers and Neanderthal man's anxiety about dying of starvation. Both trigger the same stress response. Solution? Build up the precious fat stores. It's like money in the bank saved for a rainy day.

The tentacles of this subconscious fear of famine go deeper, however. The last 50 or so years of our calorie-reduced, low-fat dieting, and processed foods culture has triggered our lizard brain famine response to a massive and chronic extent. Because how does the body-brain know a famine situation is looming? It clocks the reduced number of calories we're consuming. What does it do in response? Triggers the hormonal changes required to shift from a fat-burning to a fat-storing metabolism. It also shifts to sugar-burning for fuel, instead of fat burning. This means your body-brain prefers to break down muscle mass for fuel rather than dip into your fat stores. As well, it incites a raging desire for high sugar foods. From there, it's a hormonal meltdown into insulin and leptin resistance and, frankly, once you're in this vicious cycle, then obesity is guaranteed.

Fat as distraction:
Remember as a child when you fell down and hurt yourself? Or maybe you were angry about something and having a tantrum. In this kind of situation, did your parent attempt to deflect you from your emotions by distracting you with food? Did he or she try (understandably) to stop the tantrum, or the tears, by offering you your favourite chocolate or a piece of pizza or an ice-cream? What this can do is teach the body-mind that pain is numbed with food. This can be physical, emotional or mental pain. We're taught that everything is made better by eating or drinking something. The downsides to this technique is that the emotion is not left to run its course so can get stuck in our energy fields as unprocessed trauma. It also teaches us to avoid feeling our feelings. *'Shhh, there, there, stop crying...'* we're told. *'If you dry those tears I'll give you a lovely piece of chocolate...'* And so we grow up into people who use food to avoid and numb any uncomfortable feelings. As well as become people who believe there is something wrong with having and displaying a full spectrum of emotions. We feel ashamed for crying—despite the fact this is a normal and healthy function of our body, as natural as urinating and breathing.

These six fat themes contain just some of the many good reasons we have for holding onto excess body fat as padding for physical and emotional protection. We use excess weight to feel grounded, to define our boundaries, to provide a buffer between us and the world, and more.

Here's the other point to make. You will probably have more than one, if not all, of these belief themes all jumbled together, overlapping and interweaving...

So your mission is to go within and go deep; to uncover and uproot the reasons you have for keeping the excess weight as well as to take the steps to undo the damage caused by dieting and allow your body to really heal at a cellular level.

Then, when you no longer need the weight, it'll simply melt away of its own accord because you no longer have a job for it to do.

Let's start, then, finding some of the core beliefs you have that are keeping excess weight on your body.

EXERCISE: FIND YOUR CORE BELIEFS

ACCORDING TO VARIOUS spiritual philosophies, including the philosophy of yoga, a human being is made up of many energetic bodies or layers, kind of like an onion. The numbers of layers vary between spiritual philosophies. Some say we have three layers, some say five, some say seven, and so on. I believe they're all correct in their own way, it's just that some philosophies break things down in a different way to others. Generally speaking though, we can say we have physical, mental, and spiritual layers, or bodies.

The outermost layer in this onion analogy is the physical body. The layer beneath this is our mind or mental and emotional layer, which comprises our thoughts, feelings, beliefs, and emotions.

The innermost layer is our spiritual layer, the home of our soul. Just like the fruit that rots from the inside and eventually shows up on the skin, whatever happens at our spiritual and mental layers is eventually reflected in our physical layer. So whatever manifests on the body as a physical issue—be that excess weight, a skin rash or even a broken bone—starts out in the spiritual or mental layers as energy, perhaps in the form of a belief or emotion, or an inherited programme.

Let's look at a simple example. Imagine you're in a classroom and your attention has wandered when, suddenly, you realise the teacher is asking you a direct question. You feel caught out and embarrassed, your body heats up and blood rushes to your face turning it red, you find it hard to speak and find yourself stammering an apology.

In this scenario, you have a belief about the situation, which could be something like *'it's wrong to daydream during class'*. This elicits a thought like *'oh no, I've been caught doing something wrong, I'm in trouble and I'll be punished'*.

This triggers a feeling followed by your body's physical response— aka symptom.

Let's say you do not have a subconscious belief that daydreaming during class is wrong. Perhaps your belief is, *'If I daydream in class then it's the teacher's fault for being dull.'* In that case, the belief would elicit a different thought, a different feeling and a different physical response.

Let's take another example.

You're at your desk when an email pings through from your boss. *'Please step into my office now to discuss the project,'* it reads. You have a subconscious belief formed in childhood that your best is never good enough so your first thought is *'oh no, she hates my work, I'm in big trouble over something...'*. This thought manifests in the physical body as anxiety, creating a knot in your stomach and a feeling of nausea. You start breathing faster and you may even get teary. You walk into her office red-faced, fearful and defensive.

What if, though, your subconscious belief was *'I'm really good at what I do'*. In which case, your first thought would be, *'Oh great, the boss wants an update, it'll be good to get her feedback on it...'*. You would calmly and happily walk into her office with a smile.

So the pattern starts with a belief, that leads to a thought, that elicits a feeling, which triggers a physical response, aka symptom.

Belief — thought — feeling — physical symptom.

So if the 'symptom' is excess fat on your body, we work this pattern backwards to find the belief, or beliefs, that is, or are, perpetuating the weight.

Physical symptom — feeling — thought — belief.

Using this pattern on excess weight, it could look something like this:

Excess weight — shame — I'm so weak-willed and unattractive — I'm a failure.

Or

Excess weight — hopelessness — nothing that I try to lose weight ever works — I'm powerless.

UPROOTING CORE BELIEFS
For this exercise, we're going to be hunting down some of the

subconscious beliefs and programmes you're holding onto that are part of why your body-mind is using body fat to serve you in some way.

To find your core beliefs, also called your root or bottom beliefs, we simply start at the top and dig down.

Here is an edited version of a process I went through to find a couple of my (oh so many!) beliefs and benefits around staying overweight. For me, one of the 'benefits' of the extra weight was ensuring I didn't get too excited or too happy because part of me held a belief that it wasn't safe to be too happy. Somewhere in my childhood, I'd learned that some people didn't like seeing me happy so would do something mean to make me sad. This was why and how I learned that it wasn't safe to be too happy; you invite sabotage.

I call this the 'interviewing myself' or 'Q&A with myself' exercise. You take a pen and paper, write down a question to yourself and then answer yourself with your first thoughts.

The trick is to write whatever comes to mind, no matter how silly it might seem. Don't take the pen off the page, don't edit your writing and don't re-read it until you've spent at least five minutes just downloading your thoughts from your brain and onto the page. If you can't think of what to write, then write *'I can't think of what else to write...'* over and over again until something comes up—just keep that hand moving!

This is called Stream-of-Consciousness writing. Try it yourself. The question to keep going back to is, *'what's the best thing about that?'*

Alternatively, ask yourself, *'if I lost all my excess weight, what would be the worst thing about that?'* Or *'why is part of me afraid of being thin?'*

To give you an idea, here is an example that I wrote when I asked myself what was most bothering me about my weight:

Q. What's bothering you most about your weight?
'I just hate being fat, I absolutely hate it and I don't know how to get rid of this fat. I've tried everything I can think of but it just won't budge, it's like my body wants to be fat! I despair I'll ever be able to solve this puzzle and I can't ever be really happy until I lose all this extra weight.'

Q. What's the best thing about never being really happy?
'What?! Jeeze, there's nothing good limiting my happiness!'

Q. Calm down, close your eyes and think. What's the best thing about not letting yourself be truly happy?

'[Sigh.] Ok I'll play your dumb game. If I was truly happy, I wouldn't need to worry about anything and if I didn't worry, then maybe I wouldn't get anything done because I'd have no motivation to achieve anything if I was happy as I was.'

Q. Good. What else?

'I guess if I don't get too happy about something then I can't have that happiness taken away. They say what goes up must come down so if I get really high with happiness, maybe I'm setting myself up for a big fall. Maybe it's safer to just stay on an even keel all the time, don't get too happy and don't get too sad.'

Q. You're doing really well. What's your first memory of being really happy and then having it taken away?

'I guess I was really happy as a three-year-old living in England and I was upset that I was taken away to live on the other side of the planet in New Zealand. So maybe I learned that something really bad happens when I get too happy.'

Q. Are any other memories surfacing?

'I remember being told off for getting too excited and laughing too loudly.'

Q. Okay, so being too happy gets you in trouble. What else?

'I remember my mum often got migraine headaches. Almost one every week. When she did, we had to be quiet. If we were too loud and boisterous, it made her headaches worse.'

Q. Right, so being too happy made your mum's headaches worse. What else?

'I remember someone used to tell me not to get too excited. The phrase 'don't get too excited' is one that I heard a lot, it was like a warning. I can't remember from whom but the suggestion was that, if I got too excited, I'd only be disappointed. I was taught that getting too excited is like tempting fate, it's better not to have too many expectations that way you won't be disappointed and you'll be content to settle with what you do get even if it's not much.'

Great! So the 'benefit' of staying overweight is regulating your happiness levels in line with subconscious beliefs such as *'it's not safe to be happy'*, *'my excess weight limits my happiness to keep me safe from disappointment'* and *'getting too excited and happy is just tempting fate to take it away'*.

Beliefs like this are a great place to start rewiring the subconscious programming to accept new replacement beliefs such as *'it's safe for me to happy'*. Such beliefs, when brought into the light of day and consciously questioned, immediately start to shift and transform.

Ask yourself, *'When did I learn this belief? Who taught me this? When was the first time I felt like a failure?'* and see what memories arise, the earlier in your life the better.

Take your time, sit in stillness and let the memories rise to the surface, bringing the attached emotions with them—rage, hurt, sadness, betrayal, loneliness, fear, etc. Allow yourself to feel all these emotions. Let them rise and pass.

This process of exploring your memories and emotions for limiting beliefs is something you can work on every day. It's a process of examining your life and noticing patterns that keep repeating. Noticing phrases that continually pop out of your mouth. Noticing if you're attracting the same situations and people into your life, and examining it all as clues for finding limiting, subconscious core beliefs.

If you need help with this process, seek out a healing practitioner who offers a modality such as EFT Tapping, hypnotherapy, ThetaHealing, The Work by Byron Katie, The Completion Process by Teal Swan, or any other technique that gets to the roots of subconscious emotional drivers and clears them—essentially you're reprogramming negative thought patterns by deleting and replacing files in your brain/computer.

TAPPING SCRIPT: FEELING SAFE TO CHANGE OLD BELIEFS

FOR THIS TAPPING meditation, we acknowledge that some subconscious part of us perceives benefits in holding onto the excess weight while beginning the process of releasing the beliefs that are keeping the weight in place.

Using a scale from zero to 10, pick a number that matches how strong you feel these old beliefs are that are rooting the weight in place, 10 being the strongest. Say the set-up statement three times while tapping on the karate chop point of either hand:

Even though part of me has really good reasons for holding onto this excess weight, I relax about it and forgive myself.

Even though there's a part of me that believes holding onto this excess body fat is in my best interests, I choose to love and accept myself and my body.

Even though I have these subconscious beliefs about the benefits of keeping this extra body fat, I honour myself and my subconscious motives.

Take a deep breath before using two or three fingers to tap around the points on the face and torso:

EB: *Part of me believes...*
SE: *This extra weight is protecting me*
UE: *Part of me believes...*
UN: *This extra weight is keeping me safe*
CH: *Part of me believes...*
CB: *It's not safe to release this excess weight*
UA: *My body and brain want this weight*
TH: *They believe the weight is serving me somehow*

EB: *A subconscious part of me...*
SE: *Has really good reasons for keeping this weight*
UE: *That subconscious part of me...*
UN: *Believes keeping this body fat is in my best interests*
CH: *At sometime in my life...*
CB: *I've decided that the best way to survive...*
UA: *Was with this extra fat as protection*
TH: *This body fat was my armour*

EB: *This body fat was my shield*
SE: *This fat was protecting me*

160

UE: Loving me
UN: Taking care of me
CH: That's what part of me believes
CB: And maybe that was true at one time
UA: Maybe this body fat armour...
TH: Was a great protector

EB: It was my body fat fairy godmother
SE: Always looking out for me
UE: But maybe I've outgrown this suit of armour
UN: Maybe it no longer serves me so well
CH: Because my needs have changed
CB: Maybe the armour that once protected me
UA: Is now a hindrance
TH: It's weighing me down

EB: It's holding me back
SE: Slowing me down
UE: Pulling me under
UN: It's gone from protecting me
CH: To drowning me
CB: I am so grateful to my body fat
UA: For looking after me when I needed it
TH: But my needs have changed

Pause and take several deep breaths before continuing:

EB: With the greatest of respect and gratitude
SE: To my faithful old suit of body fat armour
UE: I am ready to transform now
UN: I am ready to rise like the phoenix
CH: Emerge like a butterfly from its chrysalis
CB: This suit of body fat armour doesn't fit me anymore
UA: It's no longer fit for purpose
TH: It can be recycled into something new and beautiful

EB: I have change and evolved
SE: I have better ways of keeping myself safe
UE: I choose to know that...
UN: I am safe without the extra weight
CH: I choose to understand that...

CB: I am protected without the extra weight
UA: I choose to believe that...
TH: My best interests are no longer served by this extra weight

EB: So I now release all the subconscious beliefs
SE: That view this weight as a benefit
UE: I now delete, cancel and uproot
UN: All the subconscious beliefs
CH: That are keeping this excess body fat in place
CB: I release all these limiting subconscious beliefs
UA: From every cell of my physical and energetic bodies
TH: I replace these old beliefs

EB: With the following new beliefs
SE: I know how to be safe without the extra weight
UE: I know that I am safe without the extra weight
UN: I know how to be safe in a lean and healthy body
CH: I know that I am safe in a lean and healthy body
CB: I know what it feels like to be unconditionally loved
UA: I know that I am unconditionally loved
TH: And so it is.

Continue tapping positive statements around the body until you feel finished. A good sign is when you naturally want to take some big deep breaths or you feel like yawning.

When you're bringing the session to an end, close your eyes, cross your hands over your chest, take a deep breath and say 'transform'.

In your mind's eye, imagine this new knowledge of how to be safe without the extra weight pouring into every cell of your physical and energetic bodies until your whole being vibrates with this new frequency of unconditional love.

Take the time to visualise this happening. Watch as every cell of your body absorbs and reflects this new information. Watch your cells release the old patterns and witness the new choices being encoded into your DNA.

Mindfully open your eyes onto a whole new world in which you no longer believe that extra body fat is a benefit.

ACTION AND AFFIRMATION

Action: Wardrobe detox

Go through your wardrobe and pull out everything that doesn't fit you properly, or that reminds you of something you want to let go (for me it was a dress I bought to go on a date with a guy who turned out to be emotionally abusive). Put it in a bag for charity. Buy yourself a new outfit that does fit you properly.

Affirmation

Write the following affirmation on a postcard or post-it note and stick it where you'll see it at least once a day, like the bathroom mirror or the back of your phone. When possible, look into your eyes and, using your own name, say this to yourself as many times as you can. Aim for 100 times a day and every time you see your reflection.

"[Name], *I love you. You are brilliant, bold and beautiful. I really, really love you.*"

STEP 4
THE BENEFITS OF BEING FAT

"I stay fat because it just wouldn't be fair to all the thin people if I were this good-looking, intelligent, funny and thin. It's a public service really. — Rebel Wilson, actress, writer and producer. @RebelWilson

THIS STEP IS called 'The Benefits of Being Fat' but I know what you're thinking. You're thinking, *'Whaaat? Sister, are you freakin' crazy? Having all this fat on my body is doing nothing that's of any benefit...'*

Believe me, I know it's difficult for a hardcore, long-term, committed dieter to accept that there's a part of them that wants all this fat hanging off their frame. But none of us are victims. Whatever you have in your life has a reason for being there, this includes your weight.

Just like the bear who chubs up to get through the winter hibernation, or the deep-sea diver who packs on a few pounds so as not to freeze in the North Sea, extra body fat has myriad of benefits. Some of them, however, might be a little dysfunctional because, bless us, we are complex, multi-dimensional creatures.

The beautiful thing about this way of looking at the world is that, if you've created this, you can recreate it. It's a very powerful position to be in. The only problem is that we often don't know how we created something and we don't know how to uncreate it.

Ultimately, you need to understand how it's serving you, what are the secondary gains, or the pay offs, of this situation? Then you offer yourself different options.

There are thousands of benefits and beliefs related to the amount of weight we carry on our bodies. It might be helpful to think of them as being all stacked on top of each other, like a Jenga tower, if you're familiar with that game, or a pyramid made out of playing cards.

The trick is to get to the bottom beliefs; the ones in the bottom of the pile. If you can pull out some of the really foundational beliefs underneath, then a lot of the ones higher up will come tumbling down with them—like pulling out the bottom piece in a game of Jenga.

THETA BRAIN BELIEF SPONGE

How do we get all these beliefs that form our reality? For the first seven or so years of our lives, our brain is in Theta brain wave, which means we are basically a sponge that unquestioningly sucks up everything that's presented to us. This is the imprint period where we're soaking up everything that goes on around us, absorbing the beliefs and values of our parents, culture, media, religion and environment. We absorb and accept the beliefs and values of those closest to us without analysing or judging them.

So if we're a little white boy born into a bigoted family in the deep south of America, in our first few years of life we take on the belief that black people are lazy and violent, gay people are an unnatural abomination, men are superior to women, that abortion is criminal and sinful, etc.

We accept these kinds of beliefs as easily and credulously as we accept beliefs like, *'my cat purrs when he is happy'*, *'bananas grow in Africa'*, *'broccoli is good for me'*, and *'we always have Sunday lunch at Grandma's after church'*.

Let's say that, on the same day that that little white boy was born in Texas, a little girl was born in Switzerland to a lesbian couple who run a dairy farm out in the country. This little girl grows up surrounded by women and gay men. She observes women doing everything from cooking to chopping wood and the idea that a person is incapable of doing something because she is female never enters her sphere of reality. By the time she is exposed to cultural and institutional sexism, the notion that women are lesser is so incomprehensible to her that it makes no impact on the neural pathways of her sense of identity and self-esteem. It simply does not compute. She grows up believing she can do or be anything, and so she does.

This is a small illustration of the astounding power of our childhood programming and the convincing nature of beliefs.

"A belief is a thought that is thought so often that it creates physical, tangible results, which then reinforces the original belief. And your beliefs form the rules that you run your life on," writes Carol Talbot in her book, *You The Divine Genius.*

Once we are programmed to hold a certain belief, our brains are constantly seeking evidence to support and perpetuate that belief. If, therefore, we believe black men are violent, or that blonde women are dumb, we will notice all the 'evidence' of this and, every time we do, that particular neural pathway in our brain gets a bit stronger and bigger. *'See!'* we cry, when a news headline supports our opinions, *'I told you!'*

At the same time as we're constantly finding reasons to maintain our status quo position, our brains are also busy filtering out the evidence that does not support this belief. We don't even notice the contradictory evidence. We feel safe in the knowledge that the world continues to spin as we expect it to, we know where we are and we remain smugly confident that our truth is THE truth.

In that first seven years, we are programmed with thousands upon thousands of unconscious beliefs that form the structure of our reality. Depending on the family and society that we're born into, this could be beliefs like *'our family is rich and Daddy can buy anything I want'* or it could beliefs such as *'life is a struggle', 'money doesn't come easily', 'I'm just not one of life's lucky people', 'nothing comes easily to me, I have to struggle for everything', 'it's not safe to speak up, I'll be punished for talking back to my dad'*... and so on.

Of course, we can evolve and change our beliefs once our critical thinking faculties develop. As we grow up and are exposed to new ideas and world views, we hopefully begin to question some of our basic assumptions. That's why travel broadens the mind. It's because you are exposed to ideas and ways of living that may call into question all your assumptions about right, wrong and 'normal'.

Questioning some of your basic assumptions about dieting, your weight and your body is what you and I are working on in this book. Because, make no mistake, you and I have been profoundly, deeply, programmed with the concepts that provide the foundation stones of the diet industry as well as with the misinformation about calories and weight-loss.

The powerful impact that these beliefs, instilled in childhood, have on the whole of our lives cannot be overstated. Fast food companies are all over this. They understand that what they're really selling us is a feeling, aka a squirt of oxytocin or dopamine—not a cheap bread bun with cheap, processed cheese slapped in the middle.

Is it any wonder then that this is the food we find ourselves reaching for when we want to reward ourselves or feel loved as adults? And this is not just a mental and emotional connection, it is a physiological one.

The taste of your McDonald's meal is recognised by your brain, this triggers those unconscious beliefs and then 'feel good' chemicals are spurted into your blood stream. You are, in effect, addicted to the chemicals your body releases on tasting this food.

DUBIOUS BENEFITS

When you start pulling back the layers of your subconscious beliefs, be prepared for uncovering some screwed up 'benefits' to these beliefs. Remember, your subconscious mind doesn't operate in the same way as your logical, conscious mind.

As an example, people who get sick all the time may have learned as a child that it's only when they're ill that they get love and attention from their mother or father, thus the subconscious belief is formed '*I must be sick to be loved*'. Who, then, can blame them for getting sick when it makes them feel cherished and loved?

In fact, I had a client recently, a woman in her thirties, who suffered with chronic rheumatoid arthritis. This condition was ruining her life but, in the process of unravelling the emotional roots underpinning her condition, she admitted that it was her "winning card". She said, "no one argues when I play the arthritis card". So part of her healing path was learning new ways to define her boundaries and new ways to feel loved.

For me, I had some very bizarre and often conflicting beliefs and secondary gains around my weight. I used food as both a rebellion against specific people as well as against society as a whole with its rules about how women must look, act and behave.

I also used dieting and weight to bond with my mother—it was the battle we fought together and some subconscious part of me believed it made us closer. And here's the thing. It did make us closer in a way but it wasn't healthy and there are many other more nourishing and loving ways I can be close to my mother without the disempowering codependence of either endlessly battling weight together or bonding over our rebellious acts of eating cake together. *'Oh go on,' we'd giggle, 'just one... let's be naughty. We'll start being good again tomorrow.'*

One of my biggest 'benefits' though was avoiding love relationships because of a belief that 'men abandon me' and 'people who love me, leave me' and 'it's not safe to be happy because people will try to take your happiness away...' I also had beliefs about the weight protecting me from sexual abuse. Yep! I had some issues! And I still have my issues, it's an ongoing process. The key is being able to love and accept yourself right now, as you are, complete with all the emotional baggage that is showing up on your physical body.

PLAYING THE PAY OFF GAME

What kind of pay off, or benefits, can be attached to carrying excess weight? To get you thinking, here are some examples of beliefs and benefits I've come across in my clients and myself...

'If I'm successful at losing weight, I'll have to be on a diet for the rest of my life to maintain it.'

'If I lose weight, I'll need to give up my favourite foods and there would be no pleasure in my life'

'If I lose the weight, I'll have no excuse for not pursuing my dream...'

'If I lose weight I'll be happy and I don't deserve to be happy.'

'If I lose weight I'll be happy and it's not safe to be happy.'

'If I lose weight and pursue my dream and fail, I can't blame the weight, it'll be all my fault... and I will fail because I'm a failure.'

'If I lose weight, I'll be giving into all the misogynist cultural and social pressures on women that I resent so much.'

'If I lose weight it'll be like admitting that arsehole was right and that I did need to lose weight.'

'If I lose weight, people will congratulate me and I'll feel like I'm towing the line.'

'If I lose weight, people will expect more of me.'

'If I lose weight, I'll be judged more harshly and I'll attract more jealous criticism.'

'If I lose weight, I can't have the foods that are all I have in life to make me feel loved and comforted.'

'If I lose weight, I'll be more attractive and might wreck my marriage by going back to my promiscuous ways...'

'If I lose weight, I won't have to struggle with it anymore and having struggle in my life gives me a purpose and motivation.'

'I'm a mum now, it's not right for me to be slim and sexy. Good mothers are not slim and sexy.'

'If I lose weight, I'll be gorgeous and the men at work will treat me differently, talk disrespectfully about me behind my back.'

'If I lose weight, I'll lose my government sickness payouts so I'll have to get a job and that's scary because I'm not sure what I could do for work...' and so on.

There are thousands of benefits and beliefs around being

overweight. These foundational beliefs are generally those that we picked up in the first seven to eight years of our life when our brains are like sponges, including in the womb when we spent nine months swimming in an embryonic soup of all the chemicals and hormones produced from our mother's emotions and thoughts.

There is no critical evaluation of the information at this age, it's all taken on board without judgment and forms the structure of a person's belief system.

So if we constantly hear our father saying, *'no, we can't afford that, money doesn't come easy'* we may form a belief about having to always struggle to earn money. This belief then sits in our energetic field vibrating at its own unique frequency and, like a magnet, it pulls situations, people and experiences into your life that match this resonance and validate this belief. This is the Law of Attraction, it also means we unconsciously attract people and situations that trigger our emotional wounds. It's why a person with rejection issues attracts commitment-phobes. This is not the universe punishing you, this is your Higher Self offering you every opportunity to heal by bringing your wounds to the forefront.

To shift your experiences in this life, you need to uproot the beliefs that are bringing in the experiences you don't want and replace them with beliefs that attract your desired reality.

EXERCISE:
FIND YOUR FAT BENEFITS

HOW DO YOU find some of your subconscious benefits to being overweight? Extra weight is used by the body to define our boundaries, as well as to protect us and keep us safe in a variety of ways. Consider, then, how your weight may be keeping you safer and more protected. What or who in your life has been perceived as a threat?

PART ONE: FIND YOUR FAT BENEFITS
Open your Weight-Love journal and work through the following questions using stream of consciousness writing. Set a timer for 10 minutes per question.

Q1. If I woke up tomorrow to find my body had miraculously transformed and I was at my ideal weight, what would be the worst thing about that? What challenges would it bring? How would friends and family react?

Q2. What was happening in your life the last time you weighed what you now see as your goal weight? What was going on in your life?

Q3. Think back to a time you felt you were at a healthy weight, just before you first started gaining weight, were you happy? How old were you? What was going on?

To give you an idea, here are some example answers:

Q1. If I woke up tomorrow to find my body had miraculously transformed and I was at my ideal weight, what would be the worst thing about that?

A. I'd have to buy a whole new wardrobe and I can't afford to do that. Money is always so tight! I wish we had more money. And if I were thin tomorrow, I wouldn't have the same motivation to eat properly and get to the gym—I might get lazy. And I might start getting more attention from the men at work, that always makes me feel uncomfortable and I worry that my work doesn't get taken seriously when sexual chemistry is a distraction. I also know that office affairs almost always end in disaster and I bet it would be me who would lose my job or lose out on promotion. It makes my skin crawl when a male boss looks at me in a leery way or says something suggestive. I feel vulnerable. I also feel angry because I'm there to do a good job not be some kind of pretty distraction. Plus I really need my job, I need the money...

For this person, the extra weight helps them feel safe from unwanted sexual attention that could jeopardise their job as well as making them feel valued for the quality of their work, as opposed to their physical appearance, something that's very important for many women. If this person has subconscious core beliefs about money always being tight, the extra weight makes them feel better able to survive a potential famine.

Q2. What was happening in your life the last time you weighed what you now see as your goal weight?

A. I hadn't been married that long and I got pregnant. I really don't want to get pregnant again... in fact, I really don't feel like having sex very much at all. I feel a little guilty about that because I know my husband wants sex and I love him very much but I'm just too tired...

This is a very common one for mothers. They don't want to have more children and so they lose interest in sex and pile on weight to make themselves unattractive. This is all subconscious behaviour. Plus they're tired and stressed from the demands of life, which triggers cravings for sweet and fatty foods.

Q3. Think back to a time you were at a healthy weight, just before you first started gaining weight, were you happy? How old were you? What was going on?

A. I was about seven years old, my parents were divorcing. They both had new partners and I didn't know what was going to happen to me or where I would live, who I would live with. It was all really awful. I remember feeling anxious all the time.

The body remembers everything. Let's say your goal weight is 64kgs (10 stone/140 pounds) but the last time you weighed this was a really tough and unpleasant time in your life. Your body-brain may associate that weight with being unhappy, vulnerable and unsafe. So it will resist being at that weight again.

PART TWO: 'WHAT'S IT GOING TO TAKE?'

When you've done Part One of this exercise and found some of the reasons you might have for holding onto excess weight, the next step is to question these 'benefits'. I call this the *'What's it going to take? Maybe it's possible...'* strategy. Your brain loves to have a job to do so when you put suggestions like this to your brain, it starts searching for answers and ways to provide these things. Again, write this down in your Weight-Love journal.

For example:

1. What's it going to take for me to feel like my work is valued? And that I'm respected for my work? Maybe it's possible for me to know I'm valued for my work without keeping this weight on. Maybe I can be attractive without being vulnerable. Maybe it's possible for me to be attractive without being vulnerable.

2. What's it going to take for me to know I can be slim without getting pregnant? Maybe it's possible to know I can be slim without being pregnant. What's it going to take for me to be slim without feeling I have to have sex? Maybe it's okay for me not to want to have sex for a while. Maybe it's okay for me to express my fears to my husband. Maybe it's normal for a person's sex drive to rise and fall. So maybe I can take the pressure off myself and cut myself some slack. Maybe I don't need to be the perfect mother and ever sexy wife. Maybe that's unrealistic.

3. What's it going to take for me to know I can be happy and safe at my goal weight? Maybe it's possible for me to be happy and safe at my goal weight. Maybe I can be at my goal weight without triggering the unhappiness from my childhood. Maybe it's possible for my body-brain to understand all that is over now. I'm grown up, I can look after myself. I'm no longer that vulnerable child.

PART THREE: DIGGING NEW NEURAL PATHWAYS

To really ramp up effectiveness of the 'what's it going to take...' statements, say them out loud while tapping on the meridian points on your face and torso.

For example:

EB: What's it going to take
SE: For me to know I can be happy and safe
UE: At my goal weight?
UN: Maybe it's possible
CH: For me to be happy and safe in a slim body
CB: Maybe it's possible for me to be slim
UA: Without triggering childhood trauma
TH: Maybe it's possible

EB: For my brain to disconnect the link
SE: Between unhappiness and my goal weight
UE: What's it going to take to break this
UN: Subconscious link with misery and my goal weight?
CH: What's it going to take to feel safe and happy at my goal weight?

CB: I'm all grown up now
UA: That's all in the past now
TH: I know what it feels like to be slim without triggering childhood trauma

When you've finished your *'what's it going to take?'* tapping, pause, breathe, sit quietly with your eyes closed and be assured that your brain has started the process of coming up with answers.

TAPPING SCRIPT: RELEASE RESISTANCE TO WEIGHT-LOSS

WE HAVE PROGRAMMING that tells us to behave in certain ways to keep ourselves in our comfort zone. So, even though it's not healthy to be overweight, some part of your subconscious mind believes that holding the excess weight is safest so we resist being at a weight that is outside of our comfort zone.

This might be because we have beliefs about how being healthier, being slimmer, might have negative consequence. For example, *'I'll be expected to do more...' 'I'll be attractive to the opposite sex and tempted to cheat...',* or *'if I'm slim and attractive, that handsome man over there might hit on me and then we'll date and I'll fall in love with him and he'll break my heart just like all men do so, no, it's best I go home now and eat a tub of ice-cream...'*

Subconsciously, you believe that it's not safe to change your physicality. Motivation and action naturally occurs in the absence of resistance with the things we want. EFT Tapping expert Brad Yates[24] gave the following example about motivation and resistance in an interview with Marna Thall of ThinWithin.com.

"Let's say you're thirsty and want a glass of water,' said Yates. "You don't need motivation to get up, find a glass and turn on the tap. If there's no resistance, you don't need to think, 'ok, I've got to get myself all revved up, I've got to think about how good that water's going to taste and somehow find the motivation to stand up and get that water...'

"There's no resistance so taking action is effortless. You just go and get the glass of water."

How can you tell if there's any resistance in your mind and body to releasing excess body fat? Yates says that one way to do this is to close your eyes and imagine looking at yourself in a full-length mirror. Imagine seeing yourself at your ideal weight with all your excess weight simply gone. You're standing there and you're as slim and toned as you've always wanted to be. Now, notice the thoughts and emotions that come up. Does it feel 100 per cent safe to have this

---

[24] Brad Yates at www.tapwithbrad.com

body? Rate your resistance on a scale from zero to 10. Zero being no resistance and 10 being completely panicked and negative about the idea.

The following tapping script is based on one given by Brad Yates. For more of his work, go to his website at www.tapwithbrad.com for a wealth of free instruction videos.

Say the set-up statement three times while tapping on the karate chop point of either hand:

Even though I may be resisting being thinner, I choose to love and accept myself.

Even though I may be resisting weight-loss, I accept my feelings and profoundly love myself anyway.

Even though I may be resisting being thinner, as crazy as that sounds, and as much as I may want to insist that I would never resist being thinner and losing weight, I may have to admit that some of my choices say otherwise. So even though I sometimes resist being thinner and healthier, I choose to deeply and completely love, honour and accept myself.

Take a deep breath and then continue tapping:

EB: All this resistance to being thinner
SE: All this resistance to reducing my weight
UE: But part of me is wondering
UN: Why would I resist being healthier and thinner?
CH: I don't even want to ask myself that question...
CB: Because it sounds so ridiculous
UA: But that is great!
TH: Because if I have hidden reasons for resisting weight-loss

EB: Then part of me doesn't want to question that
SE: So if I avoid asking myself that question
UE: I get to say safely in my comfort zone
UN: I may consciously say that that is not what I want
CH: Consciously I say I want a healthier and thinner body
CB: But my behaviour and choices often says otherwise
UA: I find a lack of motivation in making healthier choices
TH: Sometimes I just don't feel motivated

EB: To nourish myself in a better way
SE: Or to move my body
UE: Or to relax and rest when my body needs that
UN: And when I'm not feeling motivated
CH: That's because there's resistance
CB: It's not that I'm simply resisting being thinner and healthier
UA: Obviously I want to be thinner and healthier
TH: But because of past events

EB: I've had some misunderstandings
SE: About the possible consequences of being thinner
UE: Bad things might happen if I lose weight
UN: Or I might miss out on something
CH: I have all these ideas
CB: About the consequences of losing weight
UA: About how they would be unpleasant
TH: So it's not that I'm simply resisting being thinner

EB: I'm resisting the negative consequences that I'm afraid of
SE: But I choose to clear that fear now
UE: I choose to clear that resistance now
UN: What am I afraid might happen?
CH: Where did I get the idea that that might happen?
CB: What did I experience in my past?
UA: That suggested that being healthier
TH: Would be unfortunate?

EB: Would be uncomfortable?
SE: Might even lead to pain
UE: And given that I believe it would cause pain
UN: It's not stupid to be resisting weight-loss
CH: It's pretty brilliant
CB: If being thinner leads to pain
UA: I am a genius for resisting it!
TH: So instead of beating myself up for the choices I've been making

EB: I choose to love and appreciate myself
SE: And I also choose to acknowledge
UE: That part of me might be confused
UN: Allowing myself to know that I can be healthy
CH: And still take care of myself

CB: And then I can let go of all kinds of other pain
UA: I'm allowing myself to know it's safe to lose weight permanently
TH: I'm clearing all my doubts about that now

EB: I'm clearing those doubts and fears at a cellular level now
SE: Clearing them all the way back through my past
UE: Back through all the times I got that idea
UN: That the best way to take care of myself
CH: Was to resist being thinner
CB: I'm clearing those misunderstandings
UA: So I know that it's safe to be thinner
TH: And I'm creating that in body, mind and spirit

Close your eyes and take several deep breaths as you imagine this clearing taking place at a cellular level. Then, again in your mind's eye, see your ideal thinner body in a full-length mirror and see if you feel more comfortable with this image. Repeat this tapping meditation as often as you feel the need, changing the words as you hone in on your specific memories and experiences.

When you're bringing the session to an end, close your eyes, cross your hands over your chest, take a deep breath and say 'transform'.

In your mind's eye, imagine this new knowledge of how to live your day to day life without being resistant to weight-loss, pouring into every cell of your physical and energetic bodies until your whole being vibrates with this new frequency.

Take the time to visualise this happening. Watch as every cell of your body absorbs and reflects this new information. Watch your cells release the old patterns and witness the new choices being encoded into your DNA.

Slowly open your eyes onto a world in which you no longer resist releasing excess weight from your body.

ACTION AND AFFIRMATION

Action: Morning me-time

For at least five days, set your alarm 20 minutes earlier than normal and start the day with 10 minutes of silent meditation followed by 10 minutes of stretching. Doing several rounds of yoga sun salutations are fantastic for this, you'll use every muscle, bone, and joint in your body.

Affirmation

Write the following affirmation on a postcard or post-it note and stick it where you'll see it at least once a day. Repeat it out loud as often as possible, especially when you're looking at your reflection.

'I know what it feels like, and how to live my life, without needing excess body fat as protection.'

STEP 5
EMOTIONAL OBESITY

"Emotions are our body's reactions to our thoughts."
Eckhart Tolle, spiritual teacher and author @EckhartTolle

"The modern physician should know as much about emotions and thoughts as about disease symptoms and drugs. This approach would appear to hold more promise of cure than anything medicine has given us to date." — Hans Selye (1907-1982), endocrinologist and pioneer of stress research and its biological effects.

"I cannot fathom why people think I'm promoting obesity. If anything, I'm just promoting self-love, acceptance and happiness, right now, today, in this body, because it's the only one we have."
— Whitney Thore, star of reality TV show, My Big Fat Life, @whitneywaythore

A message from the Spirit Collective:
Weight is a mirror
Dearest One,
Weight is never about weight. Weight is a mirror.
Your weight is a reflection of your thoughts, beliefs, words, and actions. Attacking the weight is as effective as attacking your reflection in a mirror when you are unhappy with the way you perceive your external appearance.
First, the mirror is not an accurate reflection of you. You are so much more than your physical body.

Until you cease with limiting the worth of your being to the physical shell in which your soul resides, you will be blind to your true value and power.

However, we do not wish to denigrate your physical body. This shell is in fact a beautiful and divine and intelligent organism in its own right. However it is not the reason for your existence, rather, it is facilitating your existence.

A man may go to his office in an expensive and perfectly tailored suit but it is the work he does there that is important. His purpose is not to simply be seen wearing a suit, his purpose is in creating, loving, serving, experiencing, contributing, providing. The suit looks wonderful, without question, we do not wish to detract from the beauty of the suit, its cloth and the craftship, but the suit is not the man's raison d'etre. It is an expression of him.

The suit, just like the weight, is a reflection of the man's values, decisions, beliefs, thoughts, habits, and motivations.

And he can wear a different suit, if he chooses.

We love you.

WHEN YOU'RE AN emotional eater, food has become your best friend and comfort blanket. You've become a food addict—or a fooddict.

Like the most faithful, loyal and loving friend you can have, the friend that's always there for you and always ready to comfort you. Food can make you feel loved both by triggering the release of loving chemicals, to bringing back memories of wonderful times involving food with loved ones.

This is why it does not work to just tell a person who emotionally binge eats to not do it, to *'just say no'* or—my personal favourite— *'why can't you just have one chocolate and then stop'.*

Ha ha! One chocolate and then stop.

Hilarious.

Telling a binge eater to simply put the packet away after that first cookie is like telling a person who's in chronic, relentless pain to deal with it without medication and suggesting they're weak-willed if they don't. It's like telling someone with chronic diarrhoea to come away from the bathroom because they could stop if they really wanted to, they just need a bit of self-control.

Emotional eaters are self-medicating with food. Whenever you reach for something to eat or drink when you are not hungry or thirsty, there is an emotional component. There's a difference between emotional eating and cravings, though. When you're eating emotionally, you'll inhale everything within reach. When you crave a very specific food, you have an emotional association with that particular food and will get in the car at midnight to drive to the 24-7 store to get it because it has to be that particular flavour and brand of your food drug.

Further down the emotional eating road, you have binge-eating, which is never about hunger. Inhaling a packet of chocolate digestive biscuits dunked in a cup of hot chocolate with cream, followed by half a litre of ice cream eaten straight from the container while standing at the fridge, is not about hunger.

Fooddicts do not think, *'Hmm, I'm feeling a bit peckish, I think I'll eat 17 slices of fluffy, white bread slathered in a layer of chocolate spread, thicker than a shagpile carpet, to keep me going till dinner's ready.'*

For fooddicts, food is emotional. Eating is the symptom—not the problem. The real problem lies buried somewhere in the subconscious and until you dig that evil little root out of your brain soil, you may as well hold onto your 'preferred customer' loyalty card for the local fish and chip joint.

It took me a long time to figure this out. The problem is that knowing it is only half the battle so for a long time I still got sucked in when I heard about a new, *'this time it really will work'* diet. I got lured back into the diet myth time and time again. Like, *'just eat nothing but boiled chicken and egg whites, then your life will totally transform, handsome strangers will give you flowers in the street, and you'll feel happy, fulfilled and worthwhile.'*

They are seductive, these promises of a complete and happy life by just cutting out one or another food type. We are like the puppy that chases every new ball thrown in the park.

SWERVING THE 10 TONNE BINGE TRUCK

When I was in the peak of my binge-eating years from the age of about 14 to 25, I read a lot of advice about how to nip a binge session in the bud. The well-meaning advice included tips like *'go for a walk'*, *'have a big drink of water'*, or *'call your weight-loss buddy for support'*, etc.

These kinds of tips may be helpful to some people (I've never met these people but let's assume they exist somewhere) but they completely missed the point for me.

When you're emotionally triggered and the wheels of an oncoming 10-tonne binge truck start to turn, it's like something or someone else takes over. The clear and rational parts of your brain shut down and a primal lizard brain takes over and all that part of you can do is focus on consuming as much high sugar and high fat foods as possible, as quickly as possible. You become an eating automaton.

Basically for people who choose food to numb their pain and provide a dopamine-induced pleasure fix, the brain has created some unhelpful neural pathways.

How did we get like this? Because no-one is born overeating. While we're floating about in our mother's womb, we have food on tap 24 hours a day so babies are born with the belief that *'food is always available'*. It's after we're born that things go awry.

We're generally okay for the first few years. We've usually had parents who ply us with food every time we cry or ask for it, which is why toddlers will take a bite of something then decide they've had enough (they might throw what's left on the floor for you to clean up, or wipe it artistically over the nearest wall in a life drawing of the dog), they trust there will always be more and they listen to their hunger cues.

Things start to get messed up when we take on social and parental beliefs like *'sweeties and cookies are naughty food that I can only have as a special treat when I'm good'*—talk about mixed messages! No wonder we're all confused. What happens when we're told we can't have something? We want it more. Especially when its subconscious meaning is that we are 'good' and therefore loved. For years and years, we constantly reinforce the belief wired in our brains that food makes everything better, especially junk food.

If, as a very small child, you were rewarded with food such as chocolate, or if you had wonderful times with people who really loved you that involved food, then your brain uses this type of food to flood your system with the same 'feel-good' chemicals that the loving environment triggered. Even if you were too young to actually remember these times now, your brain still retains this information.

Then you've got parents who won't let you leave the table until you've eaten all your dinner. Or maybe you're punished by not being allowed dessert. This turns food and the dinner table into a battleground. Food becomes a war zone; a place for tactics, manipulation and control.

For me, this was definitely a strand of the tangled ball of steel wool that was my weight. Before my parents emigrated from England to

New Zealand when I was three years old, I lived in the north of England amongst grandparents, aunts and uncles, all of whom doted on me. As far as they were concerned, I was the bee's knees.

As the first grandchild, I was enveloped in love and adoration by my grandma Emily, grandad Benny, my Aunty Peg and my Uncle Billy. I don't remember anything about it now but my mum says that I was the apple of my Uncle Billy's eye and, like his little sidekick, I followed him everywhere around the farm.

Emily and Peg were marvellous bakers and, even though I can't remember specific events, I know, because I feel it in my heart and soul, that I spent many happy times with them eating pikelets (like thick, small pancakes) and scones. As well as having my senses overwhelmed with the smell of cakes baking in the oven or the touch of a just-baked warm biscuit.

Back then, part of life on the farm was that every Sunday was baking day. The women, including my mum, would spend all day making piles of cakes, biscuits, slices, scones and more, to feed all the labourers who worked on the farm throughout the week. Those men ploughed through mountains of baked goods during morning and afternoon teas.

My mum was so ingrained with the ritual and tradition of Baking Sunday that she continued it when the three of us moved back to New Zealand. It was quickly apparent though that three-year-old me, my mum, and my dad, just couldn't get through as much cake and baked goods as a team of farm workers (although I gave it my best shot). So the ritual of Baking Sunday fell away. But not before I'd had this association with family, love, laughter and baked goods firmly carved into my neural pathways. So some of the beliefs I needed to shift included *'food is love'*, *'food is family'*, *'food is being accepted'*, *'food is my reward'*, and *'food is how I treat myself'*.

With this kind of powerful wiring going on in my brain, does it seem likely that *'just go for a walk instead'* is really going to work when what my soul is yearning for is to feel unconditionally loved and accepted? Rhetorical question again. Nope, that walk around the block just isn't going to cut it. Even if you do manage to get yourself brisk walking around the local park instead of gorging on warm buttered scones with jam and cream, you're not getting to the root of the problem so another binge attack will soon rear its head.

But wait, that's not even the half of it because we all carry conflicting beliefs in our subconscious. So on the one hand you can be running the programme that *'food is love'* but at the same time you can be running

183

the programme *'food is the enemy'* so you want it but you fear it at the same time. Oh yes, you and me, we're complicated.

Here's the good news though. You can rewire your brain. You can re-organize the files in your brain-computer so that food goes in the food file and loving memories and experiences go into a different file. We then find new ways to feel loved, accepted, rewarded and emotionally nourished without the bar of Cadburys and a hot chocolate.

HEALTHCARE CRISIS

Why then are we still turning to drugs and surgery as solutions for eliminating pain and illness when we are now much more aware that emotions play such a key role in physical diseases and pain?

It's simply because most mainstream medically trained doctors aren't aware of the emotional connection to chronic pain and illness. It's not a part of standard western medical training.

There are other reasons as well. The public health service in many western countries is stretched to the limit. In the UK, many GPs have 10-minute appointment times under the National Health Service (NHS).

Meaningful health care assessment cannot take place in 10 minutes. This is just enough time for the patient to say, *'Doctor, I'm getting headaches every night, please give me more painkillers, I absolutely can't take any time off work or I'll lose my job. Oh, and can I have some antibiotics for my sore throat...'*

Then for the doctor to reply, *'Of course, here's your prescription, come back in a month if there's no improvement... reception, please send in the next patient.'*

NHS doctors in the UK are brilliant and well-intentioned people but they cannot be expected to give a holistic and in-depth service under these conditions. Despite the ongoing budget cuts and ever-stretched services as the NHS is, year-on-year, expected to do more and more with less and less, the people who work within the health system are committed to serving others and doing the best they can. It does feel though, that our public health services are at breaking point thanks to the epidemic of chronic diseases that are sweeping the world.

What's driving the proliferation of these diseases? On the surface, they're a result of the combined effects of our industrialised processed diet, our lack of movement, and our chronic stress levels.

That's just the top layer though, dig deeper and at the root of all of this is our disconnection from Mother Earth and from God, or Spirit, or the Universe, or Divine Source.

The way we're living isn't sustainable and isn't making us happy. This is showing up as disease and disorders and is why we've had an explosion in once rare conditions that are now impacting millions of people. Conditions such as obesity and diabetes, heart disease, dementia, stroke, cancer, high blood pressure, auto-immune diseases, allergic diseases, and various digestion disorders that effect millions of people.

But instead of giving our attention to the real question, which is, what's the cause? We're running around at the bottom of the cliff trying to find many and various different cures. We want one cure for cancer and another cure for dementia and a cure for diabetes... but what if they all root from the same cause and therefore, ultimately, have the same cure? And the same prevention?

EXERCISE:
FAT IS A NOT A FEELING

'FAT' IS NOT a feeling.

So when you say, *'Gah, I feel so fat today!'* this is always code for something else that you're feeling.

Our long-suffering bodies become our scapegoat and whipping boy. When we don't feel good, we blame our bodies. It's easier than exploring, admitting to and expressing our real emotions. Saying, *'I'm feeling hurt, lonely, or depressed today'* is much more vulnerable and painful than, *'Oh my God, I feel so fat and disgusting today."*

When you find yourself saying that kind of thing, or when you find yourself grabbing at handfuls of fat on your belly and calling yourself 'gross' or 'revolting', see if you can rewind a moment and get in touch with what you're really feeling. Ask yourself, *'what am I really feeling when I say 'I feel fat'?'* Or *'what is my weight taking the blame for?'*

What we are doing in this step is unpacking the surface feeling of *'I feel fat'*, getting to the bottom of what you perceive it really means to be fat and what underlying emotions and beliefs are attached to that.

Because physical characteristics are not feelings and yet we assign meaning to them. Humans do this all the time. We take some underlying emotion and transfer it to a body part. That way, this emotion makes more sense; it's something the mind can process. This is why, for example, some men hate being bald or losing their hair. Is being bald so awful? No. But perhaps it's more to do with fear of aging, fear of impotence, losing their testosterone and perceived manliness.

For example, if I said *'I feel tall today'* what I may really be saying is *'I feel proud and confident today'*. Conversely, if I said *'I feel short today'*, what am I really saying about the way I feel? That depends on whether we perceive being short as 'good' or 'bad' but perhaps the real feeling is *'I feel small and insignificant'*. If so, it's not our height that is the issue, it's the sense of insignificance.

The real question then is, what beliefs are underpinning this feeling of insignificance? *'When did I first learn I was insignificant? How did that neural pathway get laid?'*

Using the 'interviewing myself' technique, unpack the idea of *'I feel fat'* by asking yourself some questions, it might go something like this:

Q. 'What is your belly taking the blame for?'
A. 'It's the reason I feel so disgusting and ugly!'

Q. 'Why do you feel disgusting and ugly?'
A. 'Because of all this disgusting fat on my body that I just can't shift!'

Q. 'Why are you so desperate to get rid of your belly fat?'
A. 'Duh! Because it's disgusting, unsightly and unattractive...'

Q. 'Why is it unattractive?'
A. 'It just is! Everyone knows that fat and blubber is ugly.'

Q. 'What's so awful about being ugly? What happens if you're ugly?'
A. 'Oh for goodness sake! Nobody wants to be ugly! If I'm fat and ugly and gross, no one will want me, no one will find me attractive. People will think I'm stupid and lazy.'

Q. 'What's the worst thing about being stupid, lazy and unattractive?'
A. 'Another bloody stupid question! Because no one will want me, of course! No one will love me, no one will like me or accept me or approve of me.'

Q. 'And? So what if they don't...?'
A. 'If no one loves me or likes me I'll be lonely, I won't belong anywhere and I'll feel worthless. I'll feel like a disappointment.'

Q. 'When was the first time you remember feeling worthless and a disappointment? Who made you feel like that?'
A. 'Um I dunno, I guess I felt like a disappointment on my first day at school when my mother told the teacher not to expect me to learn my alphabet as quickly as my older brother did...'

Q. 'Okay and how did that make you feel?'
A. 'Sad and embarrassed and angry and judged.'

Q. 'When you recall that memory and those feelings, where do they live in your body?'

A. 'I feel them in the pit of my stomach, like a ball of fire. And I feel it in my throat as well, like I want to say something but I don't have the words, or they're stuck.'

Q. 'What are the words that are stuck in your throat?'
A. 'I'M JUST AS GOOD AS MY FUCKING BROTHER AND HOW DARE YOU MAKE ME FEEL LIKE I'M NOT! DON'T YOU REALISE THAT I HEARD YOU? THAT I TOOK THOSE WORDS TO MEAN YOU LOVED MY BROTHER MORE THAN ME?'

Q. How do you feel now about what your mother said to your teacher that day?
A. Still fucking angry.

Q. Where do you feel that in your body?
A. Everywhere. It's like my body is burning all over.

Q. Do you think your mother really loved your brother more than she loved you?
A. No, the adult me sees that is not true. My mother loves me.

Q. Do you think there's another way to see the comments that she made?
A. I guess she was probably nervous for me. And she was probably a little emotional, her youngest child's first day at school. I'm not sure, frankly, it was a stupid thing for her to say, she was basically calling me stupid and it really hurt and embarrassed me. I'm not stupid.

Q. What if she didn't mean to say that? What else might have made those clumsy words come out her mouth?
A. Maybe she was feeling emotional, taking me, her youngest child, to my first day of school. Maybe she was afraid for me and wanted the teachers to go easy on me. I think she found school quite tough. Her teachers were strict. Maybe she wanted them to expect less from me so they'd go easier on me? And frankly, maybe I did pick things up a little slower than my brother but so what? Everyone learns at different speeds and has different gifts. My brother is brilliant with words, I'm better with my hands and I'm better with people. My brother's a bit of an introvert at times. I'm the opposite.

Q. Exactly. So, if you could go back now and respond to your mother, what would you say?

A. I'd laugh and say 'oh mum, don't worry about me, I'll be fine! I'm going to love school, I'm going to be really popular and I will discover my talent for art here. I love you!'

And so on. A helpful addition to the exercise above can be EFT Tapping, you can tap on the words, the feelings, the body sensations... to release this trauma that sewed the seeds of not feeling good enough. It is these roots that grow into the experiences we have as adults, including struggles with our weight.

Physical attributes are not feelings but because we assign meaning to them we can unpack and deconstruct these meanings to find the root of what's really going on. When we do that, we're in a position to pull out the roots of the core limiting belief and the negative emotions attached to it.

TAPPING SCRIPT: FREE YOUR FEELINGS FROM FOOD

WE HAVE A lot of really good reasons for binge-eating and turning to food for comfort. The key is not to beat ourselves up for it but rather to understand why we do it.

Do you eat when you're bored? Do you eat to procrastinate? Do you eat to feel better when you're upset? Like on my 40th birthday when I drove home after work via the petrol station, bought three bars of chocolate then ate them while sat in the car and crying about being so old and feeling like I was wasting my life. Maybe you have feelings of being loved or memories of fun times with loved ones that are linked to certain foods—grandma's hot buttered scones straight from the oven or mum's special chocolate cake.

For me, coffee and toast is evocative because that was my mum's daily pleasure when I was young and she made a ritual of it. She would happily butter the toast, fold it in half and dunk it in a big mug of coffee. So yes, I used to go weak in the presence of buttered toast. This tapping script is aimed at reducing your emotional eating habits.

First, using a scale from zero to 10, pick a number that matches how much of an emotional eater you believe you are, or how severe and frequent are your bouts of binge-eating, 10 being the most intense.

Remember that we ideally want to tap on this issue until the number drops to somewhere from zero to three. Even if you don't get it all the way to zero today, keep coming back to this script and theme until it gets closer to zero.

Once you have your number, start by tapping on the karate chop point on the side of your hand and say the following...

Even though I am an emotional eater, I completely love and accept myself.

Even though I've got my emotions stuck in food, and sometimes I eat uncontrollably when these emotions overwhelm me, I profoundly love and accept myself anyway.

Even though I am an emotional eater who uses food like a comfort blanket, I choose to relax and forgive myself.

Pause, take a deep breath and continue tapping around the face and body, starting with the point at the start of one or both eyebrows...

EB: I am an emotional eater
SE: I use food to manage my emotions
UE: I use food to numb my emotions
UN: I use food to evoke loving feelings
CH: I use food to feel better
CB: I use food to stop feeling for a while
UA: I use food to numb the pain
TH: I use food to distract myself from what's really going on
EB: I eat when I'm anxious
SE: It soothes me
UE: It gives my mind and body something else to do
UN: I feel peaceful while I eat
CH: Sure, I feel terrible afterwards
CB: But for a while I am in my happy place
UA: Before the guilt and shame return
TH: These cravings for food are so strong

EB: I can't beat them
SE: These cravings take over

UE: And I become an eating automaton
UN: It's like I'm addicted to these foods [name specific foods here, e.g., chocolate or sugar]
CH: Then when I give in to the addiction
CB: I feel like a failure
UA: Once I start, I just can't stop.
TH: I go on a binge.

EB: My appetite for these foods seems insatiable
SE: And I'm ashamed of eating like this
UE: So I will hide it and do it in secret
UN: Which makes me feel even more shameful
CH: I'm controlled by this food addiction
CB: I can't imagine feeling neutral about these foods
UA: I can't imagine being in control around these foods
TH: It makes me feel helpless

Pause for a moment, close your eyes and take a long deep inhale then exhale through the mouth. Give yourself a couple of seconds to consider anything that came up for you while you were tapping. Any old memories, grudges, emotions, just tap on anything else for as long as you need to and then continue...

EB: I have a lot of really good reasons for eating these foods
SE: In the moment, they make me feel better
UE: Although afterwards, I feel so guilty, regretful and ashamed of myself
UN: I know that there's something else really going on here
CH: I know this emotional eating has underlying issues
CB: What am I really hungry for?
UA: What deeper desires of mine am I suppressing?
TH: What am I waiting for?

EB: What am I weighting for?
SE: I choose to understand...
UE: ... what the emotional eating is masking
UN: And I know that as I get to the real issues
CH: The food addictions and emotional eating...
CB: ...will melt away
UA: I choose to know that these appetites can transform
TH: I choose to face up to what's really going on

EB: *My body has really good reasons for craving these foods*
SE: *My body has really good reasons for storing all the excess body fat*
UE: *In some way, my body is protecting me*
UN: *Keeping me safe*
CH: *But I choose to know that I can be safe...*
CB: *...without the extra weight and food cravings*
UA: *I wonder if my efforts at dieting...*
TH: *... have triggered my body's famine response?*

EB: *Which in turn triggers the cravings*
SE: *Maybe if I focused on nourishing and healing my body*
UE: *Instead of depriving and starving it*
UN: *It would not need to switch on the cravings*
CH: *I choose to know that I can dramatically heal...*
CB: *... my relationship with food*
UA: *I choose to know that it's possible to live without emotional eating*
TH: *I choose new and healthy ways to process my emotions*

Pause for a moment, close your eyes and take a long, slow inhale and exhale. If you feel called to continue tapping positive statements, take some time to do that until you feel finished. A good sign of being finished is when you naturally want to take some extra deep breaths or if you yawn.

When you're bringing the session to an end, cross your hands over your chest, take a deep breath and say 'transform'.

In your mind's eye, imagine this new knowledge of how to live without being an emotional eater pouring into every cell of your physical and energetic bodies until your whole being vibrates with this new frequency.

Take the time to visualise this happening. Watch as every cell of your body absorbs and reflects this new information. Watch your cells release the old patterns and witness the new choices being encoded into your DNA.

Slowly open your eyes onto a world in which you are no longer an emotional eater.

Go back to the number you had at the start of the session and see if it has shifted. If not, keep tapping on whatever came up for you. If you feel called to do so, repeat this script as often as you feel is helpful and tap on anything that comes up as result, especially any memories, emotions or 'aha' moments.

ACTION AND AFFIRMATION

Action: Conscious creators

Instead of being consumers, let's start being creators. How? With this step I invite you to create something. I've put a few ideas below but feel free to come up with your own:

- Draw or paint a picture
- Take photographs of nature. Like a mountain in the distance or a flower in bloom up close. Look for symbols, colours, and shapes that mean something to you. Print the images out, get them framed and hang them in your home
- Make a card for someone—a birthday card, thank you card, get well soon card, etc.
- Build a birdhouse for the garden
- Get some crafting clay and make a pot
- Knit a scarf
- Carve a wooden spoon
- Build a model train set
- Design a teeshirt and sell it on teemill.com
- Write a short story and submit it to a competition

Affirmation

Write the following affirmation on a postcard or post-it note and stick it where you'll see it at least once a day. Repeat as often as possible.

'It's safe to feel and express all my emotions.'

STEP 6
WHAT HAPPENED? HEALING
THE PAST

"Resentment is like drinking poison and hoping it will kill your enemies." — Nelson Mandela, former President of South Africa and anti-apartheid revolutionary (1918-2013)

"We often confuse an emotional wound with the event or experience that caused the wound, but the actual wound is not the situation or circumstance. An emotional wound is the disempowering belief we adopted in response to the experience. Without needing to analyse the details, the core emotional wound is virtually always unworthiness, and, in fact, unworthiness (or conditional worthiness) is the core wound of every other emotional wound." — Nanice Ellis, author of The Infinite Power of You. @Godergy

I HAVE A very good friend called James. Now aged in his 40s, James lives in New Zealand and is an absolutely beautiful, kind and generous soul. He's also very funny, great company, gay and single. Although James has many close friends who love him, he has never had a long-term romantic relationship despite this being something for which he yearns.

James is also extremely overweight at about 265kgs (580lbs). He cannot walk more than a few metres because of his weight and there have been times when he could not leave the house. He wants to have some kind of gastric banding or bariatric surgery but has been told he needs to lose about 100kgs (220lbs) on his own before he can be even considered for this dangerous and expensive surgery.

James' weight has negatively impacted every aspect of his life and every moment of his day. It's stolen away his opportunities, his career potential, his relationships, his health, his finances, and his self-esteem. It is the first thing people see about him and immediately they leap to all sorts of judgments about the kind of person he is. It makes it extremely difficult for him to make new friends. He cannot get into a regular sized car seat and has never been able to ride in an aeroplane.

As far as the physical toll of simply existing, the smallest of tasks, such as standing up to make a cup of tea, or having a shower, or doing the laundry, are difficult.

Even with all these motivations to shed the weight, James has so far found it impossible to shift any weight permanently. He has lost weight in the past but has always gained it back again.

How on earth could James' subconscious mind see this amount of extra weight as a benefit? It's a benefit because as far as the subconscious is concerned, this weight protects him from rape and nothing is more important than that.

As a small boy, James was repeatedly raped by his father. Unsurprisingly, this horrific and shocking violation, done to him by the one person who was supposed to protect and love him, broke his soul and his heart. The experience left him feeling vulnerable, powerless, betrayed, traumatised and unprotected. What subconscious beliefs or decisions might James have formed as a result of this experience? Perhaps at a subconscious level he decided that he would do anything to avoid this kind of betrayal and violation again.

What better way to avoid any kind of physical or sexual intimacy than putting on a massive suit of body fat armour? So the way all that fat is serving James is by protecting him from sexual violation and from sexual interest of any kind, which would trigger those traumatic old memories and have him relive that profound pain.

As a result of his abuse, I would imagine that James formed many other subconscious beliefs, which are contributing to his weight and disordered eating. For example, 'people who love me, abuse me' or 'I can't trust the people who love me' or 'love is violating', 'love is abusive', and so on.

To keep him safe from this kind of attack and also to define his boundaries, his subconscious mind has decided the most effective solution is the body fat suit of armour.

James is an extreme case but it is shocking how many people have experienced some kind of sexual or physical abuse in their lives. It seems to be the silent epidemic. In addition, I've found that the emotional and mental abuse experienced by someone as a child can leave scars just as deep, if not deeper, than physical abuse.

WHAT HAPPENED?

Going back to the BEEBs for a moment—Beliefs, Events, Emotions, and Benefits—the Events part of the BEEB equation refers to anything that occurred in your life, usually up to the age of about eight years old, that led to you forming beliefs about yourself and the world that are served by holding onto excess body fat.

For example, if a young girl is molested by her babysitter, she may gain a lot of weight in order to be less sexually attractive. Over-eating in this scenario has a number of benefits. For a start, the girl may use food as a way to numb the feelings about the abuse. Foods high in sugar will literally alter her brain chemistry and fill her system, temporarily, with feel-good hormones like dopamine, thus providing relief from the memories of the trauma. The extra weight that results from this change in diet may deter her abuser in future, thus validating the belief that *'extra weight keeps me safe'*. The weight may make her feel bigger and stronger, it helps define the boundaries of her body, and it can be the physical symbol of a buffer between her and an unsafe world.

If the abuse does discontinue, the girl's belief that the weight 'helped' keep her safe will root itself even more deeply into the soil of her subconscious mind.

Other Events that can cause the body-mind to see excess weight as beneficial include major life events such as divorce, death, trauma, an accident or natural disaster, moving to a different country or city, abuse, bullying, and so on. However, Events that we may perceive as minor can also form patterns, behaviours and beliefs that cause us to hold onto extra weight.

For example, perhaps you grew up in a tense household with parents who argued a lot before eventually getting divorced. Shouting and slamming doors was the norm in your home and your parents were often upset. Ongoing tense silences was the other side of the coin and both scenarios caused anxiety in the family. You became accustomed to the feeling of walking on eggshells; desperate not to do or say anything that could trigger another shouting match. From an early age, you tried to be the peacekeeper, suppressing your own feelings in the process. The only time you could relax was at your grandmother's house. You were never happier than when you and she were baking in her kitchen before sampling your handiwork. Subconsciously, you

196

came to associate cakes and cookies with love, relaxation and laughter. The body-mind literally holds the manifestation of that love and laughter on your body in the form of the fat that results from eating cakes and biscuits. The fat is like a souvenir of those good times and when you eat cake as an adult, a part of you is back in that safe space of love at Grandma's house.

What do you need to do to start rewiring your brain to start releasing your excess body fat? Figure out the benefits of holding onto it and offer your body-brain alternatives.

ABUSE AND BOUNDARIES

When it comes to avoiding any kind of abuse, your subconscious mind will do whatever it can to protect you. For this reason, your body may use weight to define your boundaries. This is as true of mental, emotional, financial, or spiritual abuse as it is of sexual and physical abuse.

Often the abused becomes the abuser. Their own abuse has left them feeling powerless so in order to try and feel powerful, they abuse others. As the old saying goes, 'hurt people, hurt people'. Schoolyard bullies are never balanced, stable and happy children. Same goes for office bullies and abusive partners.

Much of the time though, all these different forms of abuse tend to come as a package. The mother who hits her child over and over with a belt and locks them in their bedroom without food for a day will also tell this child they are stupid and useless. The father who gets drunk and throws his child down the stairs will also tell the child he wishes they had never been born. The religious leader who sexually violates a member of his ministry will also tell the child that their whole family will be tortured and killed if the child ever tells anyone about the abuse. The husband who beats his wife will also control her spending and isolate her from her family.

While moderate to severe abuse is depressingly and horrifically prolific, the so-called 'smaller' or 'lesser' incidents of abuse, neglect and abandonment can have just as profoundly detrimental effects on a person. Being neglected emotionally can be just as damaging as physical abuse. There is also no hierarchy of trauma in that one person's trauma is 'worse' or 'lesser' than another's. Trauma is trauma. I hear too many people marginalise or deny their pain by suggesting that they shouldn't feel the way they do because something 'worse' happened to someone else. This is another form of subtle self-abuse.

The question for you, though, is what event took place in your life that left the scar of trauma? Chances are you already have some idea of the events from your past that have left you feeling violated or hurt or vulnerable. For this step, we're going to take the ones at the top of the pile, so to speak, the one that brings up the most emotion. Although if it's a series of events involving one particular person, you may be able to address several at once.

Take a few moments to sit quietly and scan back through your life. Let the incident that still stings most when you recall it come to the surface. What happened? Who was involved? Who do you blame? Towards who or what do you hold the most resentment? Take whatever comes to mind first. It doesn't have to be a 'big' thing. You may remember a so-called 'tiny' incident; a throwaway comment said to you by someone. If, though, this comment still brings up a zzzz in your energy field when you remember it, then it's a blockage that needs releasing.

When you have someone or something in mind, go ahead and do the next exercise.

EXERCISE: A LETTER TO MY ENEMY (OR THEIR ANGEL)

FOR THIS EXERCISE, you'll be writing a letter to the person, people, organisation, company, institution or situation who hurt or harmed you. If you cannot bring yourself to address them directly, then write this letter to their guardian angel.

Step one: Dear Enemy

Take a pad of paper and a pen. Find time when you will not be disturbed. Turn your phone off and find a place of privacy, it could be in your own home or in a library or café. Ideally though, you'll be alone at home so, if you choose, you have the space to cry or scream or display any other emotion without inhibition.

Set an alarm for 10 minutes and head up your paper as if you're writing to whoever or whatever it is that has wronged you. You can use their name or just call them Enemy. Begin with 'Dear...' or 'To', whatever you prefer.

Now, start writing and say whatever you need to say to them. Keep writing without lifting your pen from the page. Do not stop to read back what you've written, do not stop to correct punctuation or grammar. Just write whatever is in your heart and head. Don't be concerned about anyone ever reading this, you can destroy it as soon as you've completed the exercise, if you choose.

If you find yourself stuck, write '*I don't know what else to say to you...*' and keep writing that until you do have more to say. Tell them how you feel and how much you hurt and how this has impacted your life and your self-esteem. Howl your rage and sadness and regret. Keep writing till the alarm goes off but if you want to keep writing beyond the alarm, keep going.

When your letter is finished, end it with '*Yours sincerely...*' and your name.

Step two: Breathe and release

Sit back in your chair, close your eyes and place your hands on your knees. Take three long, slow breaths. Visualise all the negative emotions, that are attached to this trauma, floating up out of your body. Visualise the pain releasing from where it's been stored in the cells of your body.

If it's in your belief system, you may like to ask your angels, or spirit friends, or God, for their help with this process. Ponder for a moment, whether this trauma has held any silver linings. Has it benefited you? For example, maybe it taught you to ensure you did not do the same thing to others that was done to you. Maybe it made you stronger, more independent, more discerning over who deserved your trust, etc. Then, when you are ready. Go back to your pad and pen.

Step three: Letter from my enemy (or from my enemy's angel)

This time, you will write a reply letter to yourself from the person, people, or situation to whom or which your first letter was addressed.

Step into the shoes and the perspective of your 'enemy' and write a letter back to yourself as if you are them.

This 'enemy' will respond sincerely and without anger. They will explain the situation from their viewpoint and will respond to any questions you raised in your letter. They will describe how, or if, the situation impacted them in any way—physically, mentally, emotionally or spiritually.

They may apologise and ask for forgiveness but they may not, they may even defend their behaviour.

Again, set an alarm for 15 minutes and continue writing whatever comes to mind. Work intuitively, writing down whatever thoughts come whether or not you know what you're writing is true. For example, a child abuser may disclose their own history of being abused or bullied, don't concern yourself later with discovering whether, or not, this is true.

Step four: Resolution

To finish this exercise, decide what you want to do with the letters. If it feels right, you may want to burn them (safely) or bury them. Alternatively, you may want to hide them away and read them back at a later date.

Finish with some more deep breaths and visualise the burden of this event lifting from your shoulders and then dropping to the floor where it dissolves and melts into the ground.

TAPPING SCRIPT: CLEARING RESENTMENT

RESENTMENT HAPPENS WHEN we create a belief as the result of something that happened to us. That belief may serve us at the time but many years later, this belief may be holding us back in many areas of life.

Close your eyes, bring to mind an event in your life where someone did something to you over which you still feel resentful. Allow all the emotion attached to this to come forward. Let it bubble up. Notice the different emotions that show up. Beneath the resentment and the anger, there is usually fear, pain, shame etc.

Allow yourself to be aware of whatever you believe this event reveals about you. If we understand that what happened is all about the other person, it's easier to let it go. When we take something personally, though, it's harder to let go, so allow yourself to be aware of what meaning you're giving it.

Say the set-up statement three times while tapping on the karate chop point of either hand:

Even though I feel this resentment, I choose to forgive myself and relax now.

Even though I feel this resentment, I choose to love and honour myself.

Even though I feel this resentment, I choose to deeply and completely love and accept myself, and maybe someday I'll forgive this other person. Not because they necessarily deserve that, but because I deserve to be free.

Take a breath then continue tapping around the face and torso:

EB: All this resentment
SE: All this resentment
UE: All this fear of letting go of resentment
UN: I'm afraid that if I let go of resentment
CH: That means that I'm saying what they did was okay
CB: And that it would be okay for them to do it again
UA: And I'm clearing that idea

TH: Clearing resentment

EB: It doesn't mean I'm betraying my values

SE: I know the difference between wrong and right

UE: It means I'm tired of being in prison

UN: Holding resentment is like making poison for someone else and drinking it myself

CH: And I deserve better

CB: They hurt me

UA: But I'm holding onto that pain

TH: They stabbed me but it's me who's twisting the knife

EB: Maybe to teach them a lesson

SE: Maybe just to protect myself

UE: I'm open to the possibility

UN: That there are healthier ways to take care of myself

CH: I am older and wiser now

CB: I have better tools than resentment

UA: And I deserve better

TH: And I can let this go

EB: I'm not bad or stupid for having resentments

SE: I have brilliantly learned these from other people

UE: And as I allow myself to relax while tapping

UN: I choose to think back

CH: And see if that resentment ever helped those people

CB: Probably not

UA: I deserve better

TH: And part of me says

EB: If I let go of this resentment

SE: That means I'm forgiving these people

UE: I'm giving them a pass

UN: That's not what it means

CH: It means I am getting out of the prison I built

CB: Forgiveness isn't something I give other people

UA: It's a gift I give myself

TH: And I choose to love myself so much

EB: That I'm willing to set myself free

SE: And I'm letting go of this belief that what they did meant something bad about me

UE: *That I somehow deserved it*
UN: *That it somehow identified me*
CH: *Letting go of this need to take it personally*
CB: *If they did something harmful*
UA: *It's because there was pain inside of them*
TH: *That's not to excuse their behaviour*

EB: *I'm just letting go of the belief that it was because of me*
SE: *As I set myself free*
UE: *I love and forgive myself for having held onto this resentment*
UN: *Believing that I needed it*
CH: *And maybe I did in the past*
CB: *But I'm setting myself free now*
UA: *To feel peace in body mind and spirit*
TH: *And so it is.*

When you're bringing the session to an end, close your eyes, cross your hands over your chest, take a deep breath and say 'transform'.

In your mind's eye, imagine this new knowledge of how to live your day to day life without shaming yourself for being fat pouring into every cell of your physical and energetic bodies until your whole being vibrates with this new frequency.

Take the time to visualise this happening. Watch as every cell of your body absorbs and reflects this new information. Watch your cells release the old patterns and witness the new choices being encoded into your DNA.

Slowly open your eyes onto a world in which you no longer hold onto old resentments and hurts.

ACTION AND AFFIRMATION

Action: Personal peace process
1. In your Weight-Love journal, write down every person from your past towards whom you still hold some resentment. Even if it's a small incident, such as the classmate in your third year of school who passed you a note with 'I hate you' written on it in her childish script. (Yes, that's mine again. I can't remember her name or what she looked like, but I remember that cruel, little note and how it made me feel.)

2. Put your own name on the list.

3. Sit in a quiet room where you will not be interrupted and read through the whole list. When you're finished, say:

'I forgive you and release you; I hold no forgiveness back. I am free and you are free.'

Next, sit quietly, close your eyes and go within. Imagine all these little resentments living deep inside you as tiny, little bubbles of energy. Using your intention and your imagination, tune in to your Spirit team and ask them to take the negative energy away.

Then, in your mind's eye, visualise this energy looking like the bubbles in a bottle of fizzy drink or champagne. See the bubbles lifting up out of your body through the top of your head and rising higher and higher towards the heavens. See this energy going up, up, up into a bright, white light about 300 feet above your head and then dissolving.

AFFIRMATION

Write the following affirmation on a postcard or post-it note and stick it where you'll see it at least once a day.

'I release everything from the past that no longer serves my highest and best'

STEP 7
UNDO THE DIET DAMAGE

"Diet culture is a really sneaky shape-shifter, and at this point in history it often cloaks itself as 'wellness' when it's really about control and the hope of weight-loss or physical 'perfection.' As an anti-diet professional, I help root out diet culture in all its sneaky forms and help people get to a place where they're truly honouring their bodies' cues and desires—not following external rules, whether those rules come from a formal diet plan, an Instagram 'wellness' influencer, or a 'lifestyle change that's not a diet'." — Christy Harrison, RD, intuitive eating counsellor and the host of Food Psych Podcast. @chr1styharrison

A message from the Spirit Collective: End the war
Dearest One
Stop the battle with the bulge. Simply stop. Decide the battle is done and you are happy with yourself as you are right now. The irony is that you must cease the battle in order to achieve your purpose yet you are locked into the battle. In fact, the battle thrills you in some ways, it is a conundrum that must be solved and you relish the challenge of finding the solution. Stop waiting. Stop weighting. Live now. As you are. As you release this burden of battle energy, your body fat stores will reflect this shift.
How do you do that? Decide that if you stay exactly the same weight as you are today, that is wonderful. You live your life as if you are already at your ideal weight. You wear the styles and lead the life you would lead if you were already at your ideal weight. You tell yourself repeatedly how wonderful you look and feel and you act as if your body already looks exactly how you

would like it to look.

Close your eyes and visualise yourself in a body that delights you. Feel what it is to be lean, healthy and happy with yourself. Feel the joy of this fill your body as a real feeling.

Live, think, behave as if you are a lean, healthy and happy person. The more often you can vibrate at this frequency of health and joy, it is a universal law that this state of being must therefore come into existence.

We love you.

YOU KNOW ALL that dieting and calorie counting you've been doing for years and years?

If you're anything like me, it's triggered, or contributed to, a whole host of real physical, emotional and mental issues that are not only making it nigh on impossible for you to shed weight but are actively pushing you to gain weight.

What kind of physical issues? This could be anything and everything from gut dysbiosis to thyroid function, sugar imbalances, hormonal imbalances, adrenal fatigue, low stomach acid, heavy metal toxicity, candida, parasites, IBS, chronic inflammation, osteoporosis, arthritis, eczema... the list goes on and on.

Unfortunately, years of attempting to follow low fat or low calorie diets has set off a domino-like cascade of ill health symptoms until you're probably at the point where you don't know which condition, or symptom, came first and what is causing what. For example, is your low thyroid function the cause of your thinning hair and brittle nails or are they all the result of unbalanced microbiome?

Are you constipated because of a slow metabolism or because of low stomach acid?

Are you intolerant to gluten and dairy because of your sluggish thyroid or because your low stomach acid has allowed your gut to become overrun with nasty bacteria that have caused leaky gut?

Is systemic candida (aka thrush) causing your low thyroid function, which has given you a slow metabolism? And is the candida itself a result of low stomach acid, triggered by ongoing dieting? Most importantly, how do you heal it all?

THE FIRST DOMINO

Let's follow one of these domino effects from the start; namely, the effects of low stomach acid.

To recap, a lot of the problem comes down to the stress response— 'fight or flight'. The body-brain perceives reduced calories (dieting) as a famine and it activates the famine response to combat this 'threat'.

As an aside, if you're trying to diet while other stressors are playing out in your life—work stress, relationship stress, family stress, money stress, exposure to environmental toxins (a stress to the body)... then it all dumps even more cortisol into your system and triples your trouble.

All these stressors cause the same response in the body and could have just as much to do with your weight struggle as dieting. Stress equals cortisol and cortisol equals weight-gain (especially belly fat).

How does stress give you low stomach acid? The body's stress response diverts resources like blood and oxygen away from the gut and digestive system, instead funneling them to the muscles and organs that enable the body to run away or fight.

As digestion is not an essential function for immediate survival, it is slowed down. The body stops secreting digestive enzymes and juices. Over time, you end up with low stomach acid. As well, you get constipated or have less regular bowel movements. This means the waste products (poop) stays in your colon for longer and the toxins in your poop get recirculated back into your system, putting more pressure on your detoxification organs, namely the skin (adult acne, anyone?), liver, colon, kidneys, and lungs.

As well, suffering from constipation greatly increases your chances of haemorrhoids, anal fissures, diverticulitis, and megacolon (but that's another branch of the diet-damage tree).

Low stomach acid (a sign of this is undigested food in your poop) leads to acid reflux and heartburn. Low stomach acid also affects hormonal balance because if there isn't enough stomach acid to digest fats, this can cause an imbalance in levels of sex hormones such as estrogen, progesterone, DHEA, cortisol and testosterone. Without enough stomach acid, we also get overgrowths in the gut such as candida, harmful bacteria like E. Coli and H. Pylori, fungus and parasites.

These bacterial overgrowths take over your small intestine and cause chronic inflammation, leaky gut, and a bacterial overgrowth condition called SIBO (small intestine bacterial overgrowth). When you get candida running riot, it can turn up as oral and vaginal thrush. All of these conditions lead to yet more weight gain.

Low stomach acid leads us to leaky gut, which is when you have increased intestinal permeability. That means that the tight junctions between the cells that make up the intestinal lining are damaged and become loose, meaning that some microscopic particles, which should remain in the digestive tract, seep into the bloodstream. This activates your immune system and leads to systemic inflammation through the body and the brain. Voila! We have just paved the road to cancers and dementia, amongst other conditions.

In addition, low stomach acid means you're not breaking down and absorbing vital nutrients, you also end up with deficiencies of trace minerals like zinc, iron, magnesium, calcium, selenium, and B vitamins, which sparks a new set of issues.

This is how dieting can lead to conditions like osteoporosis. As well, the body puts bone repair and maintenance on the back burner while it thinks it's fighting for your survival.

When the body-brain notices that you're not absorbing these essential nutrients, it perceives another threat, that is, a nutritional famine, so it sounds a new alarm, which triggers uncontrollable cravings. Your body-brain forces you to become obsessed with food. It's doing this for your own good. It desperately wants nutrients and calories. The foods you crave, though, are often the high sugar and high fat combinations. In other words, ice-cream, chocolate, bread and butter, pastas and pizzas... this is the road to binge-eating disorders and depression.

From there you end up with unstable blood sugar levels, you swing between sugar highs and sugar crashes. Then you develop leptin and insulin resistance and that slows down your thyroid—if adrenal fatigue hadn't already battered your thyroid function.

You end up with Hashimoto's Thyroiditis, your hair thins, your brain fogs, your memory deteriorates, etc.

Another weight-loss red herring is then born.

You realise you have a slow thyroid and a slow metabolism and you think, 'Aha! That's why I'm fat. It's my thyroid!' Your doctor puts you on synthetic thyroid medication for the rest of your life, which brings a host of other side effects, when in fact your thyroid is not the root cause of the problem; it's the symptom of a different issue and of a system out of balance—all of which can perhaps be traced back to low calorie dieting or other chronic stresses on your system.

If you're like me, you may have spent years, decades, slowly creating the perfect conditions for all sorts of other physical ailments. And you'll have gone down many false trails, thinking you've found the answer ('*it's my thyroid!*' '*it's leptin resistance*', '*it's dairy intolerance!*', '*it's gluten intolerance*') but nothing really gives you the results you're looking for. There are two reasons for this.

First, it's none of these false trails but it's all of them. They are all branches on the tree; they are not the roots.

Second, you're still living in the diet mindset. Congratulating yourself for 'being good'. Restricting yourself just enough to keep your highly trained sniffer dog Brain on high alert for an oncoming famine. Your focus is still on your weight as opposed to your body's nourishment, health and healing.

If you haven't yet done so, now is the moment to really start shifting your focus. It's about setting aside the desire to be thinner and understanding that something much bigger and more important is at stake. Your overall health and wellbeing. It's time to turn your back on quick-fixes and empty 'lose weight now' promises and get on a deep, cellular healing journey.

You are the ultimate authority on your body, mind and spirit. We disempower ourselves when we think that the answer to our issues lies outside of ourselves. I don't care if you've read an article by someone calling themselves a 'holistic life coach and intuitive yoga teacher' (I've used that title myself) who says that eating her dinner off a child's plate helped her lose 10lbs (5kg).

That's not to say that we can't learn from others—both from their knowledge and the example they set—but how you translate that information into your own life and situation is something only you can do. And if what helped them does not help you then you have not failed in some way.

Finding our way back to our natural equilibrium is a journey and, at this stage, all I ask is that you be open to the possibility that all hell will not break loose if you get off the dieting misery-go-round.

Ask yourself this, how did the human species survive for about 200,000 years before we came up with the concept of dieting?

How did Neanderthal woman and man maintain an ideal weight without vanilla flavoured diet shake powder and microwaveable lite meals? How did Neanderthal woman and man maintain their muscle mass without calculating how many grams of protein and carbs they were consuming each day? How did they stay fit without wearing a gadget that told them how many steps they'd taken in a day?

Could it be that the human body comes with its own inbuilt intelligence? Could this reliance on external information about what is right and wrong for your body be part of the much wider and deeper human disconnection with nature and our innate natural rhythms?

GETTING OFF THE HAMSTER WHEEL

I'm not suggesting you jump off the diet hamster wheel while it's spinning at its fastest though. Let's just slow it down first. If you've been keeping your weight in control artificially with dieting then, if you stop dieting now, you will gain weight. It's like stretching a rubber band and then suddenly letting go.

As well, if you're like me, I know what you're scared of. You're scared that if you take off the limits and restrictions of dieting and give yourself free rein to eat whatever you want, then you'll eat nothing but cookie batter and donuts washed down with chocolate milkshakes all day.

This is why the self-love part of healing your weight comes before we start looking at what you put in your mouth. The reason being that binge-eating is a form of abuse. The question changes from, *'How much do I need to starve myself to get rid of this disgusting fat...'* to *'How would I eat if I really loved and valued my body?'*

For now, let's consider the possibility that the restrictive diet mentality is not the only way to live or eat. And let's plant the seed in our subconscious mind that giving up the rigid adherence to dieting rules, set by someone we've never even met, will not result in an avalanche of body fat coming our way.

Because what are you telling your body and brain when you defer to some bestselling diet book author, who's never met you, over the messages of your own body-brain? You're essentially saying, *'I don't trust myself to make my own decisions. I give my power to others and let them decide because others know what is best for me.'*

What does this do? It disempowers you and when you feel powerless, this leeches into every area of life and gets reflected as weight on your body.

BODY WISDOM

What if the best person to decide what's best for you, is you? And what if, intuitively, your body-brain knows how to heal itself back to optimum health and is constantly providing you with the information and feedback about where imbalances lay? For example, do you get indigestion? This is your body-brain providing feedback. It's telling you that your digestive system is struggling with whatever you've consumed. What do you do with that feedback? Do you offer your system different foods or do you swig on a bottle of neon-pink anti-acid liquid to silence your body's messages to you? (Which is, in essence, telling yourself to shut up. As an aside, who from your past does that remind you of? Who silenced you, or wouldn't listen to you, or stopped you expressing your feelings?)

For this step, I invite you to be open to the possibility that if you love, honour, respect and nourish your body, your body will transform to reflect this new mindset by releasing excess weight as a result of being allowed to get on with the work of healing and repairing itself.

Getting closer to a place of inner peace and harmony will reflect in the physical by way of a healthier body. So, if you're ready, let's start loosening the shackles of the dieting mentality wrapped around your mind and soul.

EXERCISE: FILL YOUR LIFE WITH PLEASURES

YOUR MISSION FOR this exercise is to go on a search for all the things that add pleasure and sweetness to your life and doing more of them. You basically need to bring as much sweetness into your life as possible (the non-edible kind) in order to reduce your food cravings.

This is an essential part of the process of erasing that *'must deprive myself for my own good'* mentality of the diet industry... the very mentality that has you rushing off to stuff your face with sugars in a desperate search for the pleasure and enjoyment in life you've been denying yourself.

When I say 'pleasure', I'm not talking only about sex, although if you want more of that, great. Self-pleasuring is one of the loveliest pastimes so, whether you have a partner or not, I encourage you to make love to yourself. And approach it like a considerate lover would, ensure you're comfortable, put some music on, dim the lights, kick things off with an erotic novel.

However! The word 'pleasure' is so much broader than this. Pleasure, sweetness and enjoyment is always uplifting; it nourishes the soul and it never causes harm to any other sentient being.

So, what brings you pleasure?

If you're thinking, *'umm... gee... well, I dunno... I guess I like chocolate and peanut butter cups...'* then, my darling and gorgeous friend, you have some wonderful self-exploration to do. Your purpose here on Earth in this life is to experience joy and pleasure. Your soul is nourished by pleasure. You were not put on this planet to be miserable nor to deprive and whip yourself for your so-called 'failings'.

You are part of the divine, you are here to experience wonder, joy and pleasure on behalf of God. Because God exists within you. You are a part of God and your life is enabling God to experience God.

Your job, therefore, is to uncover new ways to bring yourself pleasure. Now, work out a plan for the next seven days where you will do at least one of your fun things. Diary them, set a time for them, put them in your calendar. Then, of course, do each of them when the time comes. To get you thinking, here are some of the things that bring me pleasure;

1. Sitting on the sofa of an evening, stroking my cat Jake while he dozes on my lap and purrs loudly
2. Listening to whatever piece of music I'm loving right now (favourites include Jai Jagdeesh, Christine and the Queens, Beth Ditto...)
3. In winter, snuggled up by a crackling fire with a good book
4. Putting rose, or lavender, or jasmine essential oil into the palm of one hand, rubbing my palms together, cupping them over my nose and mouth, and deeply inhaling several times
5. Smelling my husband's neck when I kiss him there
6. On a sunny day, sitting on the grass with our chickens
7. Getting a full body aromatherapy massage
8. Watching stand-up comedy (Sarah Millican, Sara Pascoe, Jo Brand, Michelle Wolf...)
9. Painting
10. Guided visualisation meditation (the kind where you lie on your back and listen to a voice that transports you off to a beautiful world filled with unicorns and angels...)
11. Slipping between clean sheets after having a shower
12. Dancing around the living room to 'In and Out' by Beth Ditto and 'Shape of You' by Ed Sheeran
13. Relaxing in a hot tub
14. A yoga class

When you fill your life to the brim with a huge variety of pleasures, you will be less inclined to search for a pleasure substitute in the arms of food. And as you continue to explore what brings you pleasure and fulfillment and joy, you may surprise yourself as you realise your pleasures are evolving and shifting. You may realise the things that you thought brought you pleasure, no longer do in the same way. Or you may realise that things you did not think of as pleasurable may start to offer you a new sense of fulfillment.

You will never, however, begin the unfolding of this process while you're stuck in the denial, deprival and struggle mentality of the diet culture.

Before you start though, let's address the issue of selfishness versus self-love. A lot of people feel like there's something selfish or shameful about putting their needs and desires first.

Selfishness and self-love are polar opposites. Selfishness is when someone does not know how to love themselves so looks externally for that hole inside to be filled. They come from a space of internal starvation so they grab at every scrap of anything that poses as love within reach.

Self-love is an extension of Divine Love. It is a reflection of God's Love. When you love, care for and nurture yourself and your body temple, you are honouring God.

TAPPING SCRIPT: LOVE LETTER TO MY BODY

YOUR BODY LOVES you.

Your body is performing many millions of functions right at this very moment in order to keep you alive and thriving. It's so important to repay some of that love. Even simply putting your hands on your tummy or heart and saying, '*I love you, body, thank you,*' can be so powerful. Loving your body doesn't mean that you think you have the best-looking body in the whole world, it simply means that you love it because it's yours and it's the one thing keeping you alive on this earth at all times, no matter how you feel about it. That's some real unconditional love your body is giving you.

Body image is a tricky thing to deal with. It's tempting to think that we can 'solve' our body image problems with the latest crash diet or workout plan, but feeling good about your body is never dependent on outside circumstances—it's all a matter of choice and perspective. We all have the ability to feel better about our bodies at any given moment. So if those negative body beliefs come sneaking in, always remember that your body loves you and that you have the choice to feel however you want.

As you start to lift the mental needle in your brain that's been stuck in a groove of self-judgment for goodness knows how long, you pave the way for changing the record and playing a new, more uplifting song.

Beating yourself up for being overweight is never, ever going to get you thinner. You cannot shame yourself slim and happy. You cannot hate yourself slim and happy. You cannot bully, criticize, judge or berate yourself thin. On the contrary, this relentless, internal dialogue of self-abuse is the perfect way to make sure the excess weight never goes away.

Bullying yourself is as mean and cruel as bullying anyone else. It's time to change your relationship with your body to one of love and appreciation.

So to kick off this whole new road you're now walking down, begin with the following script to start changing your internal conversation.

This tapping meditation script is worth doing as often as you can, try doing it every day for 21 days and see how your life starts to shift.

Say the set-up statement three times while tapping on the karate chop point of either hand:

Even though my body carries more fat on it than I think is desirable or acceptable, I still choose to completely love and accept myself.

Even though I'm carrying more fat on my body than I believe is desirable and I would like to release some of this excess fat, I know that my body has valid reasons for keeping this weight and I deeply love and accept myself regardless.

Even though my body is holding more fat than I would like and I feel bad about feeling bad about myself, I accept my feelings about this.

EB: My dearest body
SE: I've directed a lot of hate at you over the years
UE: I've criticized you
UN: I've judged you
CH: I've deprived you
CB: I've been ashamed of you
UA: I've punished you
TH: I've abused you

214

EB: I've rejected you
SE: I've hated you
UE: I've told you that there was something wrong with you
UN: I've compared you unfavourably with other bodies
CH: Telling you you're not as good as them
CB: I haven't appreciated you
UA: I've taken you for granted
TH: I haven't looked after you properly

EB: I've filled you with toxins and pollutants and chemicals
SE: I've over stuffed you with unnatural foods
UE: I've overloaded you, tripling your workload in order to keep me healthy
UN: And then I've still found fault with you
CH: I've forgotten what an incredible gift you are
CB: I've forgotten that you are a walking miracle
UA: I've forgotten that just one cell of you is more intelligent than the best computers on earth
TH: I've neglected to nurture you properly

EB: I've neglected to take proper care of you
SE: I've neglected to give you enough quality food, water, air and sleep
UE: And yet still you work for me tirelessly, relentlessly and thanklessly
UN: Dearest body, please forgive me
CH: Forgive me for the love I've denied you
CB: Forgive me for the acceptance I've denied you
UA: Forgive me for insulting and rejecting you
TH: I'm ready to change my ways

Pause. Take some deep breaths and continue tapping...

EB: Dearest body, I offer you my apologies
SE: I know that every single thing you do is for my benefit
UE: I know you have really good reasons for holding onto this excess body fat
UN: I know that you believe I need this extra fat
CH: And as long as you believe I need this fat
CB: You will fight to keep it where it is
UA: And you're doing this because you love me
TH: Maybe this fat makes us feel safer against the threat of famine

215

EB: Maybe this fat makes us feel stronger when facing the world
SE: Maybe this fat is our emotional armour
UE: Maybe this fat is a substitute for love and affection
UN: Maybe this fat keeps unwanted sexual attention at bay
CH: Maybe this fat is holding all the emotions and feelings that I dare not express
CB: Maybe this fat is quarantining heavy metals where they can't hurt my organs and brain
UA: Maybe this fat is filling an emotional hole within me
TH: Maybe this fat gives me a great excuse for not living life fully

EB: Maybe this fat is about rebelling against a world that refuses to approve of me
SE: Maybe this fat is about something else completely
UE: Dearest body, I know you have good reasons for keeping this fat
UN: And if you want to keep all this fat, I will no longer fight you
CH: I will attempt to understand your good reasons
CB: And maybe we can change some of the reasons
UA: So maybe you won't see benefits to keeping the fat anymore
TH: But there is no hurry

EB: I'm going to start loving you exactly as you are
SE: Please be patient with me though
UE: I need to change some life-long and deeply ingrained patterns
UN: Patterns of self-criticism and self-judgment
CH: So I may not always be consistent
CB: But I will now be aware of when I am not being kind to you
UA: And I will change that
TH: Dearest body, thank you so much for everything you do to keep me safe and well in this world

EB: Thank you for my heart that has pumped every second or so from the day I was born
SE: Thank you for the lungs that keep oxygen and prana flowing through my body
UE: Thank you for my liver, kidneys, and pancreas
UN: Thank you for my skin
CH: Thank you for the feet and legs that attach me to this earth and move me wherever I want to go
UA: Thank you for my incredible hands that never stop working, creating, expressing

TH: Thank you for my bones that give me support and structure
EB: Thank you for my eyes, my ears, my nose
SE: Thank you for my throat and neck
UE: Thank you for my reproductive organs and genitals
UN: Thank you for my stomach and intestines and digestive system
CH: Thank you for my amazing brain
CB: This brain that filters two billion units of information per second...
UA: ... deciding what I need to notice and what I don't
TH: I know there is so much more to my beautiful body than all this...

EB: Thank you for every molecule of this incredible vessel
SE: This incredible vessel for my soul
UE: This miraculous body that enables my soul to experience this 3D world
UN: I know I am blessed to have this body
CH: Body, I love you
CB: Body, thank you, I love you
UA: Body, I love you, thank you
TH: I love you my beautiful, incredible body

Continue tapping positive statements around the body until you feel finished. A good sign is when you naturally want to take some big deep breaths or you feel like yawning.

When you're bringing the session to an end, close your eyes, cross your hands over your chest, take a deep breath and say 'transform'.

In your mind's eye, imagine this new knowledge of how to honour, nourish and listen to your body is pouring into every cell of your physical and energetic bodies until your whole being vibrates with this new frequency of unconditional love.

Take the time to visualise this happening. Watch as every cell of your body absorbs and reflects this new information. Watch your cells release the old patterns and witness the new choices being encoded into your DNA.

Mindfully open your eyes onto a whole new world in which you no longer neglect to honour and appreciate your body. A world in which you recognise that your body is a miracle.

ACTION AND AFFIRMATION

Action: Sun power
Absorb the sunlight. Go outside and either stand or sit facing the sun. Close your eyes and feel the light on your eyelids. Let this light absorb into your skin for at least five minutes. Aim to do this daily. If you can do it in bare feet, even better.

Affirmation
Write the following affirmation on a postcard or post-it note and stick it where you'll see it at least once a day. On the bathroom mirror is great, look into your eyes and, using your name, say this to yourself as many times as you can (aim for 100 times a day and every time you see your reflection).

'I am willing to see the very best of myself. I am willing to learn to love myself.'

STEP 8
YOUR HORMONES ARE MAKING YOU FAT

"Obesity is a disease caused by excessive insulin, not excessive calories. It is a hormonal imbalance, not a caloric one." Jason Fung, author of The Obesity Code. @DrJasonFung

AS WE'VE EXPLORED, when it comes to the hormonal dance that causes fat storage, the four biggest hitters are Insulin, Leptin, Cortisol, and Ghrelin. I like to think of them as the four horsemen of the fatpocolypse—the fab four of fatness.

This four-piece band of blubber play a huge part in why you're losing the obesity battle, here's a quick look at each of them before we got deeper into your hormones:

Ghrelin - the hunger hormone

Ghrelin stimulates appetite. In other words, this is the guy that makes you feel hungry. Ghrelin is produced in the stomach and small intestine and one of its roles is promoting digestion and fat storage. In fact, when ghrelin is given artificially to humans, studies have found that food intake increases by 30 per cent[25].

Ironically, for would-be dieters, ghrelin levels go through the roof when calories are restricted as this is one of the methods the body-brain has to get you eating more. In other words, dieting makes you

---

[25] [https://www.hormone.org/hormones-and-health/hormones/ghrelin]

hungrier. The same effect is triggered by a lack of sleep. If you don't get enough sleep, your ghrelin levels soar and you eat more.

Cortisol - the stress hormone

When you're stressed, the brain instructs the adrenal glands to release cortisol to deal with whatever is perceived as a threat. This is the 'fight or flight' state. So cortisol adjusts all your bodily functions to prepare to fight or run. Ongoing low-grade stress means an ongoing supply of cortisol, which means high blood sugar and ultimately ongoing fat storage. In today's world, the stresses that trigger this knock-on effect include:

- Physical stress (too much high intensity exercise, demanding job),
- Social stress (peer pressure, relationship tension);
- Emotional stress (abusive relationship, past emotional trauma, emotional event such as divorce or job loss);
- Environmental stress (exposure to chemicals or toxins, poor air quality, too much time indoors, a stressful workplace with lots of noise, artificial lighting, etc.);
- Health related stress (depression, chronic illness, nutrient deficiencies, hormone imbalances).

Insulin - the sugar police hormone

When too much sugars, or glucose, is present in the blood stream, the brain instructs the pancreas to release insulin and it is insulin's job to get it out of the blood stream and into the muscles so it can be used for running or fighting. Insulin is basically like a key that unlocks the cells of your muscles and liver so they can take in the sugars for fuel. Once the sugar moves into the cells, it's no longer circulating in the blood stream, which makes the brain happy and pancreas is told to 'relax, take a break, we don't need any more insulin for now.' Any excess sugars or glucose that can't be stored in the liver or muscles are shunted into fat cells, usually around the belly. The problems arise when there's too much glucose in the blood (from sugar or stress) and your system becomes insulin resistant, which makes weight-loss nigh on impossible.

Leptin - the fat messenger hormone

The hormone leptin is produced within your fat cells and its job is to let the brain know how much fat is on the body. This is how the brain 'sees' the amount of fat you're carrying. The brain then either instructs the body to store more fat, or to shed fat, depending on whether the brain perceives too much, or not enough fat, is on the body for your survival. The problems come when your system becomes leptin resistant and, even if you're carrying a significant amount of excess weight, your brain can't 'see' the weight because it can't 'hear' leptin's messages. The brain believes you're starving and resets the body to store as much fat as possible.

Bottom line, being leptin-resistant means you'll be carrying excess body fat and if you're carrying excess weight, particularly around the belly, I'd bet good money that you are leptin resistant to some degree — and you may very well have got that way through low calorie and low fat dieting.

KEEP THE FAITH

One last point to make here is to be patient and give your system the time it needs to heal.

You may have been eating and living in a perfect 'hormone balancing and leptin re-sensitising' way for weeks and yet not be seeing much, if any, change in your body. At some point, the doubts will creep in. You'll think, *'Darn this isn't working! I'm not losing any weight... maybe this isn't the answer and I should go back to calorie counting...'* Take a deep breath and stay the course.

It's probably taken you many years to damage your system to the extent it is today. If, like me, you'd persevered with the reduced calorie and excessive exercise regime for decades then you've done a really great job of turning your body-brain into a sugar-burning, fat-storing machine. Chances are the leptin receptors on your cells' membrane need to completely grow back once you've removed the inflammatory triggers that blunted them, like stress, sugar and gluten. You need to give your body-brain time to adjust to a different fuel source—namely, fat stores instead of sugar. This can take months, depending on how much damage has been done to your system.

Know that you're not just focusing on your weight, you're focusing on your total mental, physical and emotional health. You've spent years (well, I did) training your body to operate under the blood sugar swings brought on by yo-yo dieting and carb cravings yet turning all that around will take just a few months.

It won't, though, happen overnight so relax, love your amazing body as it is right now, and keep going while noting all the other subtle improvements such as energy levels, clearer skin, clearer mental focus, better bowel movements, stronger fingernails, better sleep, and so on.

Ultimately though, to state the blindingly obvious, I'm not a nutritionist or a functional medicine doctor, I'm just a journalist and anti-dieting obsessive who's done a massive amount of research and I'm sharing the information that made sense to me and also what worked for me.

When it comes to a holistic view of nutrition, there are some real, actual, qualified, smart people doing some ground-breaking work so for a more in-depth look at the nutritional side of hormonal balance and food check out people like:

Mark Hyman at www.drhyman.com,
Magdalena Wszlaki at www.hormonesbalance.com,
Christiane Northrup at www.drnorthrup.com,
Andrew Weil at www.drweil.com,
Anthony Williams at www.themedicalmedium.com,
Jonathon Bailor at www.thesanesolution.com,
Tim Noakes at www.thenoakesfoundation.org,
Jason Fung at www.idmprogram.com,
Christy Harrison at www.christyharrison.com.

EXERCISE: HORMONAL REBALANCE

WHAT TO DO if your hormonal dynamics are wildly out of whack? Here's how to bring everything back into balance:

1. Stop dieting and start nourishing your body

Pack your day with a rainbow of fresh colourful, wholefoods and lots of vegetables and fruit. What are whole foods? They're foods that don't come wrapped in tinfoil or polystyrene; they're foods that have one ingredient, e.g., 'eggs' or 'broccoli' or 'almonds'. Ask yourself the following: Does it still look somewhat like it did when Mother Earth made it? Is what you're about to eat full of life force energy? Are there five or fewer steps in the process from taking that food from planet to plate?

2. Protein, fat and fibre for breakfast

Eat a filling amount of protein, plant fibre and healthy fats in the morning. This gives your body the building blocks to make hormones and fuels you easily through till lunchtime.

3. Stop the snacks between meals

You need to give your liver a chance to recuperate and it can't do that if you're making it work constantly by eating little and often. The key is to eat enough at breakfast to easily get you through till lunchtime. Leave four to six hours between meals and ideally stop eating four hours before you go to bed. You know the old saying, *'Breakfast like a king, lunch like a lord and dine like a pauper'*. There's a similar old Chinese proverb as well, it goes something like *'Breakfast like it's your friend, lunch like it's an acquaintance and dinner like it's your enemy'*.

4. Eat low to no simple starches.

Cut out refined foods, sugars and fructose. This includes everything from white table sugar to high fructose corn syrup, bread, pasta and pastries, etc. Avoid anything that has more than 10gms of sugars per 100 grams.

5. Sleep early

Sleep! Get as much sleep as you can. Sleep like it's your job. Sleep rebalances your hormones and that will both stop you gaining more weight as well as help it melt away. Be in bed by 10pm at the latest (unless you work night-shifts or similar obviously). A lack of sleep can cause leptin resistance and see your hunger cravings skyrocket so getting plenty of sleep is literally good for your waistline. Ideally you want to have at least 12 hours of fasting between dinner and breakfast. Aim for 12 to 16 hours to allow cellular clean-up to take place.

6. Drink green tea. A lot of it.

A study on mice[26] showed that green tea decreases leptin resistance.

7. Get in touch with nature

Humans love to pretend that we're somehow 'above' the natural rhythms of the Earth when in fact we are intrinsically connected to the

---

[26] https://www.ncbi.nlm.nih.gov/pmc/articles/PMC3371013/

movement and cycles of this planet. We are part of Mother Earth but we've become disconnected from her and isolated ourselves in air-conditioned, concrete boxes in the sky. At least once a day, let your bare feet feel the earth beneath them. Let the energy of the planet come up through the soles of your feet, waking up every cell in your body and reconnecting you to the energetic ebb and flow of this planet and this universe. When we're not in balance with the world, it shows in a lack of internal balance in our bodily systems such as our hormones.

8. Move your body

To support your hormone levels, take a walk outdoors, especially in the evening, or do some restorative yoga or yin yoga. If you feel like it, weights and strength-training is good but keep it moderate. For now, lay off the intense anaerobic exercise. Frankly, if you've been dieting for years, or if you're constantly stressed and your whole system is exhausted and depleted, for goodness sake just let yourself rest and recuperate for a while without the added stress of a punishing exercise regime. If you're a chronic dieter who's been eating reduced calories on an ongoing basis and, as a result, your body-brain has assumed you're in a famine situation, it's triggered all the various methods it has to keep you alive and keep fat on your body. Therefore, as far as your body-brain is concerned, doing a lot of exercise makes as much sense as telling a starving person to go for a long run. In an effort to mitigate the effects of what it views as downright insane behaviour, the body-brain will up the ante on its fat preservation efforts and really bring out the big guns. For example, your cravings for a quick carb hit will skyrocket and the urge to reach for that sandwich, croissant, muffin, chocolate bar or biscuit will become monumental. Just walk, every day if you can, for 30 minutes.

9. Up your omega-3s

Increase your omega-3 essential fatty acids intake to bring down inflammation in the body. A lot of people take fish oil supplements and if you think they're helpful for you, fine, but I've found that my body doesn't like anything in supplement form that much. My body wants its nutrients from whole, real food sources and for omega-3s this means wild-caught, sustainably sourced seafood, in particular oily fish like sardines, mackerel, kippers and herring. Yes, salmon and tuna can be great but the world is over-consuming these bigger oily fish and for the sake of the oceans we need to spread the load a little more, so to speak. As well, salmon and tuna, particularly from the Atlantic Ocean, now contain toxic levels of mercury and that's one heavy metal you do not want in your system.

In addition to sustainably sourced seafood, you can get omega-3s from grass-fed, free-range meat, sea vegetables, seeds such as pumpkin, flax and chia, walnuts, eggs, and more.

10. Drop the fake and inflammatory fats
Slash your omega-6 intake, which includes avoiding so-called 'vegetable' oils like canola, sunflower and safflower.

11. Go gluten-free
Yes, I know that 'going gluten-free' has become a global movement but we have still managed to mess this up by replacing foods containing gluten with some really unhealthy but gluten-free junk food. The basic premise is that, in many people (some experts argue it's *all* people), gluten causes intestinal permeability, which causes inflammation in the hypothalamus and results in reducing leptin sensitivity. How do you know if you're gluten sensitive? Do you get any kind of reaction to breads or baked products like acid reflux, indigestion or bloating? Although you may not always have an obvious physical reaction.

My view is that if you think you're leptin-resistant (and if you have a load of excess belly fat that won't shift, I'd bet my last donut that you are) then for a couple of months just lay off all gluten, which is in foods and food additives containing wheat, rye, and barley. Don't replace these foods with the highly processed 'gluten-free' alternatives, just eat whole foods. Removing gluten from your diet can help heal leaky gut, improve gut health and gut barrier function, and incite less inflammation throughout the body, especially in the brain.

12. Turn on to turmeric
Get turmeric into your diet. It's a powerful anti-inflammatory. For optimum results though, it needs to be taken with fat and black pepper. Here's a recipe for a daily turmeric tonic: Combine a heaped teaspoon of coconut oil with a heaped teaspoon of turmeric powder, cover with boiled water to mix, add a dash of black pepper then cool with some cold milk (dairy or non-dairy as desired). To make this more palatable, try making it with coconut milk and a dash of cinnamon and ground ginger, or with half a teaspoon of cacao.

13. Rock your probiotics

Probiotics are live, friendly bacteria and micro-organisms that live in our gut (microbiome) and keep us healthy. This community of microbes do a lot of work for us. From metabolising hormones, and stress hormones, and digesting the foods we eat, these friendly gut bacteria control our bio rhythms ad our sleep cycles, they metabolise all the drugs we take in so a drug can be effective or not, based on our unique microbiome. Upping your probiotic intake can make all the difference in the world to rebalancing gut flora and bringing your hormonal dynamics back to normal. As well as taking probiotic supplements, add natural sources of these living organisms by eating foods such as yogurt, kimchi, sauerkraut, miso and kefir.

TAPPING SCRIPT: 'I'M DESPERATE TO LOSE WEIGHT NOW'

I KNOW HOW you feel! You're just so desperate to lose weight, you feel like you'd do anything. You've tried everything! Nothing works! You're so frustrated and disappointed. You're at your wit's end and this battle colours your whole life. You don't understand it, you've followed all the rules and done all the right things. Why won't the weight budge?!

Take a big deep breath.
Pause and take another.

Because this feeling you have now, this desperate, anxious, panic type emotion... it's flicking your 'fat storage' switches. This constant pressure you're putting on yourself, this constant subtext that you're telling yourself about not being okay as you are, that you have got to change before you're 'acceptable' and allowed to just enjoy life, it's a major stress. That stress switches on all your body's inbuilt store-fat programmes.

Ironically, one of the first things you need to do to lose weight is take off all the pressure you've been putting on yourself to lose weight. Like

I've said though, this is probably the hardest part of this process.

So, take another deep breath and let's go...

First, using a scale from zero to 10, decide how strong is your desperation to lose weight, 10 being the strongest. Ideally you want to tap on this until the number drops to somewhere from zero to three. Even if you don't get it all the way to zero today, you may find that the remaining energetic residue works its way out after a sleep cycle. Repeat this script every day, even several times a day, until this energy starts shifting and you get a glimpse of what's driving it... so you can tap on that.

Once you have your number, start by tapping on the karate chop point on the side of either hand and say the following:

Even though I feel so desperate to lose weight, I completely love and accept myself.

Even though, I'm so desperate to lose weight that it's all I can think about, I accept that these are my feelings and I completely own these feelings.

Even though this desperation to lose weight colours my whole life and I just can't stop trying to lose weight because I think that it's the answer to my ultimate happiness, I choose to relax and forgive myself now.
Pause, take a deep breath and continue tapping around the face and body, starting with the point at the start of one or both eyebrows...

EB: I am so desperate to lose weight
SE: I'd give anything to lose weight
UE: It's the one obstacle to my happiness
UN: I feel like I've tried everything to lose weight
CH: But nothing works
CB: So I keep searching for the answer
UA: Keeping my life and happiness on hold until I'm thinner
TH: I feel this desperation to lose weight like a physical ache

EB: I've spent so much time and money on trying to lose weight
SE: My whole life would be on track if I could just lose weight
UE: My life is on hold until I figure it out and lose the weight

UN: Losing weight is on my mind all the time
CH: I'm sure I would be so much happier and more successful without this excess weight
CB: But I can't get rid of it!
UA: And I am so desperate to get rid of it!
TH: It's so unfair

EB: I'm so angry and frustrated that nothing has worked
SE: I've been battling this weight for so long
UE: But I'm still overweight
UN: And I hate it
CH: I'm so desperate to lose weight
CB: So so desperate to lose weight
UA: What will it take to lose this weight?!
TH: I'm so tired of thinking about this all the time

EB: I'm so tired of being so obsessed with my weight
SE: I feel so trapped
UE: How do I free myself from this miserable place?
UN: What is all this extra weight doing on my body?
CH: I don't understand it and I don't want it!
CB: This desperation consumes me
UA: I don't want to feel this desperate any more
TH: Even if my weight never changes, I wish I could stop caring about it

EB: Is that possible?
SE: Could I just stop caring so much about what I weigh?
UE: Maybe I could
UN: I'm willing to give it a try
CH: Because I don't want all this stuff in my head anymore
CB: I don't want to think about this all the time anymore
UA: It's draining away my life and my joy
TH: I choose to let this desperation go now

Pause for a moment, close your eyes and take a long deep inhale then exhale through the mouth. Give yourself a couple of seconds to consider anything that came up for you while we were tapping. Any old memories, grudges, emotions, etc. Just tap on anything else for as long as you need to and then continue...

EB: Maybe I can live my life without this desperate feeling

SE: Maybe it's possible for me to give up the fight
UE: But if I give up the fight, won't I get fatter?
UN: What if that's not true?
CH: What if all this desperation is keeping the excess weight in place?
CH: Maybe I believe that this desperation motivates me to do something about my weight
UA: But maybe that's not true
TH: Maybe if I stopped resisting, everything would change

EB: Even if I stayed overweight, at least I'd have my sanity back!
SE: Fat and miserable or fat and joyful?
UE: I know which sounds better
UN: And I've been desperate about this for years
CH: Where has it got me?
CB: Fat and desperate
UA: I am ready to call time on that
TH: I'm ready to find a new relationship with my body and weight

EB: I'm ready to accept myself
SE: I'm ready to love myself
UE: I'm ready to release all this desperation
UN: I'm ready to live my life to the full regardless of my size
CH: I'm ready to buy myself beautiful clothes regardless of my size
CB: I'm ready to do lovely things for myself regardless of my size
UA: I'm ready to take my foot off the brake of my life
TH: Because maybe all this desperation and resistance has contributed to the excess weight

EB: This fat has good reasons for being on my body
SE: Instead of fighting my body, I shall work on understanding what's really going on
UE: I will be kind to myself
UN: I will show myself compassion
CH: I choose to accept myself and my body
CB: I choose to focus on the wonderful things that my body is capable of doing
UA: I am so grateful for the joy that my body brings
TH: I release all desperation to lose weight now

Pause for a moment, close your eyes and take a long, slow inhale and exhale. If you feel called to continue tapping positive statements, take some time to do that until you feel finished.

When you're bringing the session to an end, imagine that this new knowing of how to live without harsh self-judgment is pouring into every cell of your physical and energetic bodies until your whole being vibrates with this new frequency.

Take the time to visualise this happening. Watch as every cell of your body absorbs and reflects this new information. Watch your cells release the old patterns and witness the new choices being encoded into your DNA. Slowly open your eyes onto a world in which you are no longer desperate to lose weight.

Go back to the number you had at the start of the session and see if it has shifted. If not, keep tapping on whatever came up for you. If you feel called to do so, repeat this script as often as you feel is helpful and tap on anything that comes up as result, especially any memories, emotions or 'aha' moments.

ACTION AND AFFIRMATION

Action: Start a new habit
Choose at least one health-affirming behaviour that you can add into your daily routine, here are some examples but you can also come up with your own:

1. Start the day by drinking a large glass of warm water with the juice of a lemon.

2. Find a way to add at least one cup of organic dark green leafy vegetables into your day—kale, spinach, chard, silverbeet, rocket, arugula, microgreens, mustard greens, bok choi, lettuce, collard greens, etc. You can whizz them in a smoothie (e.g., spinach with banana and avocado), steam them with butter or coconut oil, eat them raw in a salad with grated beetroot and carrot dressed in cold pressed virgin olive oil and organic apple cider vinegar, add them into scrambled eggs or an omelette, add them into your vegetable juice, cook them in your soup, stir fry with a selection of vegetables like onion, mushrooms, tomatoes, etc.

3. Responsibly dispose of any fake, processed, industrial oils like

margarine and so-called vegetable oils like canola, safflower or sunflower, that you have in your kitchen cupboards. Replace them with organic fats such as lard, butter, and coconut oil for cooking and cold-pressed virgin oils for dressings, always organic when possible. When it comes to oils a good tip is the packaging. If it's quality, it will be in glass. Don't buy the rubbish that comes in plastic. Avoid plastic whenever you can in every part of life.

4. We've talked about it before but I'm going to say it again. Drink at least one cup of green tea a day (but five or six is better).

5. If you normally eat commercial breakfast cereal, swap that out for one week with whole foods such as eggs, meat, fish, oats, or beans with avocado and vegetables.

6. On an evening, make a pot or plunger of nettle tea (great for the adrenals and liver). Leave it overnight to steep and drink in the morning. I put a tablespoon or two of loose nettle tea into a plunger and half fill it with boiling water. The next morning, I pour some of the steeped tea into a cup then top it up with boiling water to warm it up again.

7. For one week, be in bed by 9pm. Every day for that week, write in your Weight-Love journal how you feel when you first wake up and rate your mood on a scale from zero to 10—zero being 'awful' and 10 being 'fabulous'. The following week, go back to your normal routine but keep up the morning mood assessments.

Affirmation
Write the following affirmation on a postcard or post-it note and stick it where you'll see it at least once a day. As often as you can, say it out loud while looking at yourself in a mirror.

'Every area of my life is coming back into balance and harmony for my highest and best.'

STEP 9
SUGARHOLICS ANONYMOUS

"Want to solve the obesity epidemic in one stroke? Eliminate sugar from the world." — *Dr Zoe Harcombe, obesity researcher and author of The Obesity Epidemic and The Diet Fix. @zoeharcombe*

Hi, my name's Tamara and I am a sugarholic.
I've been sugar-sober for 18 months now but I take it day by day.
I know that in every moment I'm just one sugar-dusted donut bite away from losing control. Sugar has robbed me of my dignity, my health and my self-respect. But every day is still a struggle. Sugar calls to me from every corner... cafes, restaurants, supermarkets, TV screens, magazines, outdoor advertising, movies... it's everywhere I turn and sometimes, when I'm feeling low, the urge to taste its silky sweetness and slip into that other world where everything is ok, is almost overwhelming.

AH YES, SUGAR. That deadly but irresistibly, sweet killer. I know that you know that virtually the whole world is addicted to refined sugar. We're all using this drug to get ourselves through the day, to feel good, to feel calm, to feel loved, treated, and rewarded.

We're wrapping ourselves in the cotton wool of sugar to float through life buffered by a gentle sugar buzz because the harshness of reality without our sugar-coated glasses on often seems too painful, too stressful, too dull.

What would celebrations and good times be without sugar in one of its many forms? What would birthdays or weddings be without cake?

What would movies be without popcorn? What would achievement or success be without a toast with sparkling wine? What would a reunion of friends be without alcohol? What would Easter be without chocolate eggs and hot cross buns? We consume sugars as a sign of celebration, happiness, good times, reward, relaxation... so of course we are going to want it, crave it, look forward to it.

SUGAR BUZZ

What do we do when all this sugar is making us sick and killing us?

We find ways to ramp up the love we have for ourselves more so that we fill our lives with so much enjoyment and satisfaction, as well as rest and sleep, that we simply won't need to use sugar to get us through another day in a job we hate, or to cope with an unfulfilling relationship, or to numb our feelings of hopelessness, despair, and disempowerment.

When you love yourself enough, you engage with life. You press 'eject' on any person or situation that is not making you happy. You make love to life and life makes love to you. When that happens, a short-lived sugar buzz seems a poor substitute.

I know what you're thinking though.

'That's all lovely hippie talk, Tamara, but I still have a really sweet tooth and there's a tub of salted caramel ice-cream calling me, what can I do?'

I hear you Sister.

We're going to work through a few things with regards to sugar but the first thing I want you to do is drop the sugar guilt.

That's right, quit feeling guilty about eating sugar. Shut down the sugar shame! I know, I know, this seems to go against everything I've been saying but hear me out.

While you're working through the steps of this book and going through the process of uprooting your limiting beliefs and un-installing your diet mentality mindset, you're still going to reach for the odd chocolate bar or whatever sugary treat floats your boat. When you do this, don't guilt yourself about it and don't be sneaky about it. Eat the treat fully conscious and mindfully, choose to eat it, take your time over it, breathe slowly while you're eating and enjoy every mouthful. If you can though, choose quality treats. If you're going to eat chocolate, eat the best chocolate you can find. Not some cheap nasty thing full of 'vegetable' oil. Get the real thing! Proper organic dark chocolate made with cacao beans and cocoa butter by people who care about their product and its carbon footprint.

THE DEMON BEHIND DEMON SUGAR

And I know that my 'eat sugar mindfully' suggestion may seem to contradict all the 'sugar is the most terrible thing ever' implications in this book—so yes, just to reiterate, as a species we ARE eating WAY too much refined sugars and processed foods (which the body treats as sugars) and we have to stop—but the only way we will ultimately and profoundly change our relationship to food, to sugar, to our bodies and ourselves, is by changing our minds.

Demonising sugar also deflects our attention from the real issue. Because sugar is ultimately not the real problem—the real problem is WHY do we need so much sugar? What is the pay-off? Who's getting the pay out? Because there must be a pay-off and it must be a pretty huge one if it's worth the misery of hauling around mounds of excess fat, type 2 diabetes, the risk of limb amputation and cancerous growths, to name just a few of the side effects.

Of course awareness is the first and crucial step in the process of changing our minds. Just like with the cigarette industry, we needed to be consciously aware that cigarette smoking caused lung cancer, as well as a host of other horrific diseases, to begin changing attitudes.

But we all know that now, yet it still hasn't stopped us all from smoking so there must be another, bigger, pay-off. There is. Just like food, alcohol, recreational drugs, shopping, gambling, etc., cigarettes change our brain chemistry. We feel better, empowered, included, defiant, more popular, calmer, less stressed... there are huge pay-offs in these addictions. That's why they're addictions.

There is no point attaching a load more guilt and shame to sugar consumption. That will simply tighten the hold it has on us. Waging war on anything has only ever made that thing stronger—whether you're talking about the War On Drugs, the War On Terror, or the war on anything else, when you give these things this type of resistance energy, you're essentially giving them more power than ever. More importantly you're ignoring the underlying drivers of these phenomenon, behaviours or conditions.

Okay, so, here are the four points to work on in this step.

First, drop the sugar guilt: It is counterproductive.

Second, delve into your unconscious mind: Continue working on the unconscious emotional issues and beliefs that are at the root of your excess weight and/or abusive relationship with food. This is the work that will reap massive transformation in the long term. Even if you see no effect on your weight for months, just keep chipping away at these issues and know that a whole lot is going on in the background metabolically. So, by the time you do start losing weight, you've already achieved a huge amount. In your Weight-Love book, write down these questions:

'What problem does food solve for me?'
'What emptiness does food fill for me?'
'What need does food meet for me?'
'What pain does food numb for me?'
'What boredom or irritation does food distract me from?'

Using stream-of-consciousness writing, set an alarm for 10 minutes and let your subconscious mind give you the answers.

Third, ramp up your life non-food pleasures and enjoyments: We turn to food for pleasure when our life is devoid of other pleasures. The answer? Fill your life with all sorts of pleasures and joys. From cuddling your cat, to getting a massage, sitting for hours reading a novel, painting, singing, or just sleeping more. Find out what brings you real, heart-lifting pleasure and do more of it. The action coming up will help with this.

Fourth, nourish yourself properly: Instead of focusing on depriving yourself of sweet treats, focus instead on significantly ramping up your nourishment and your non-sugar pleasures. This is vital for switching off the cravings that are triggered by dieting and nutrient deficiencies.

Start the day with a nourishing, filling breakfast of whole foods that Mother Nature made—free range eggs, avocado, spinach, nuts, mushrooms, tomatoes, free range chicken, oily fish such as mackerel, pickled vegetables, sauerkraut, and so on.

'Real whole foods' do not include commercial cereals that you can eat straight from the box. Any cereal that can be eaten with your fingers straight from the box is actually dessert. Nor does it include white bread, especially any that's packaged in plastic and claims to be 'enriched with vitamins and minerals'. This means the ingredients they've used are so cheap, processed, and devoid of nutrients, that they needed to add nutrients back in to avoid their product having about as much benefit as eating polystyrene. Your body and brain have a huge amount of work to do every day, nourish them so they can serve you to their best ability.

EXERCISE: CAKE DATE

WHAT I'M ABOUT to say next is a little controversial and not the kind of suggestion you'd normally find in a book about weight-loss. Nor is it probably what you'd expect me to say after having ranted like a banshee about how sugar is basically Satan.

I'm suggesting you try taking yourself out on a cake date.

If cake is not your 'poison' then replace it with whatever food is your weakness, pizza, ice-cream, chips, etc.

You might even decide to make this a regular thing. For example, on the last Friday of every month, take yourself to that fabulous cafe you know with all the colourful cakes displayed in the window, and order a slice of the most gorgeous-looking one. Ideally, choose a cafe that has beautiful handmade cakes baked with quality ingredients. Don't go for some mass produced, highly processed thing full of chemicals, food colourings and preservatives. Nothing that is wrapped in plastic is good enough.

Find a table and make yourself comfortable. While away some time with your cake and hot beverage, and maybe a thick novel (that's my perfect afternoon fantasy popping in—cake and crime fiction) and slowly eat that cake fully present and mindful of every mouthful.

Take your time over your cake; appreciate it. Think about what it means to invite this substance into your body. Say a silent prayer of thanks for this food and its nourishment.

Like a wine connoisseur, lift the plate to bring it to your nose and inhale its fragrance. What can you smell? Cinnamon? Walnut? Vanilla?

Take a photo of the cakey gorgeousness and put it on social media #cakelove.

Put your fork down between mouthfuls and take a few slow breaths. This is important because it keeps your stress response turned off, which means that sugar you're eating doesn't so immediately get pushed straight into your fat cells.

Close your eyes and imagine for a moment the person who might have baked this cake. Visualise your fantasy baker, imagine them doing their work with pride, care and love. Know that they baked this cake in the hope that someone would enjoy it. Imagine the energy of their love and pride being absorbed into the cake.

Think about the ingredients and how many people and animals have contributed to bringing this food to you. If the cake has eggs in it, imagine the hens that laid them. Imagine the people who care for the hens and who collected these eggs. If there's flour in the cake, imagine the wheat growing in the field, absorbing the sunshine.

Imagine the baker carefully piping and spreading the icing on and considering what they can do to make the cake look as good as it can. Imagine the pride taken in placing this beautiful piece of baking in the shop window.

Look closely at the texture of the cake, notice the different tastes of the cream, the filling, the icing. Do they complement each other? Notice the sweetness. Take a bite and hold it on your tongue for a moment with your eyes closed. Feel the sweetness and imagine you can see your brain lighting up like a Christmas tree as the sugar triggers the release of dopamine. Sit with that feeling, let this dopamine high course through your blood stream.

Also, stop eating when you've had enough. You might finish the whole slice, you might eat just a quarter of it but listen to your body and let it tell you when it's had enough. Only stop eating when you really want to stop—not because you think you should stop.

Now, chances are you will find this exercise really challenging. I did. It'll trigger all that guilt, panic and fear that the diet industry has instilled in you.

It's okay though, just slow down and breathe and, if you can, do the tapping meditation that comes up next.

It's ironic that we can easily eat a family-sized cake by ourselves when we do it in secret and mindlessly, shoving the cake in without thinking or even chewing properly, but when we choose to eat just a slice in a mindful way, out in the open, allowing ourselves to enjoy it, our demons start thrashing.

TAPPING SCRIPT: DROP THE SUGAR GUILT

THIS TAPPING SCRIPT is for those times when you eat something that you then feel guilty about.

You can do this tapping meditation here and now, whether you have eaten any foods you feel guilty about or not. If not, just bring up a memory of a time when you did feel like this. The key is in giving the shame a voice because you had good reasons for eating the way you did. Then, using a scale from zero to 10, pick a number that matches how guilty you feel, or felt, about eating all that unhealthy food.

Once you have your number, start by tapping on the karate chop point on the side of your hand and say the following out loud...

Even though, I just ate all that sugar [insert your food shame here] and I'm so angry and ashamed of myself for doing that, I choose to relax and forgive myself.

Even though I ate all that rubbish food and I wish I could somehow get it back out of my body, I'm so ashamed of eating all that! But I choose to love and accept myself anyway.

Even though I am so ashamed of eating all that sugar... again! I've done this before, why do I keep doing this to myself when I know I'll hate myself for it? But still, I choose to accept myself anyway.

Pause, take a deep breath and continue tapping around the face and torso, starting with the point at the start of one or both eyebrows...

EB: All this shame about what I've eaten
SE: I feel so ashamed
UE: All this shame in my body
UN: The way I eat is shameful
CH: I'm ashamed of myself
CB: Ashamed and angry with myself
UA: Why do I keep doing this?
TH: I'm ashamed of my weakness

EB: I feel so ashamed

SE: *All this sugar shame* [replace 'sugar' with your food shame]
UE: *This sugar shame*
UN: *Ashamed of myself*
CH: *I'm ashamed of myself*
CB: *All this sugar shame I'm feeling*
UA: *I ought to be ashamed of myself!*
TH: *Sugar shame*

EB: *I wish I hadn't eaten that*
SE: *I wish I could turn the clock back*
UE: *And not eat that*
UN: *Why do I keep doing this?*
CH: *Why am I so weak and pathetic?*
CB: *I want to punish myself for eating that*
UA: *Punish myself with more dieting!*
TH: *I'm so upset with myself*

Pause for a moment, close your eyes and take a long deep inhale then exhale. Give yourself a couple of seconds to consider anything that came up for you while we were tapping. Any old memories, grudges, emotions... tap on anything else for as long as you need to and then continue...

EB: *Okay so I ate a load of sugary junk*
SE: *And, sure, I wish I hadn't!*
UE: *But is it really the end of the world?*
UN: *Eating some sugar?*
CH: *Maybe it's not the shameful heinous crime I'm making out*
CB: *I ate that sugary stuff because part of me wanted it*
UA: *It made me feel better for a moment*
TH: *Who can blame me for wanting to feel better?*

EB: *Maybe I don't need to beat myself up about it*
SE: *Maybe shaming myself is more harmful than the sugar*
UE: *And shaming myself doesn't stop me eating badly*
UN: *I've been sugar shaming myself for years*
CH: *I'm still eating the sugar!*
CB: *So maybe sugar shame is a waste of time*
UA: *Maybe sugar shame stops me from seeing the real issue*
TH: *Maybe sugar shame gets in the way...*

EB: ... of understanding why I crave sugary foods
SE: What if this shame isn't really about sugar?
UE: Maybe my real shame runs deeper than this
UN: By shaming myself about sugar and weight...
CH:... maybe I'm avoiding addressing the real issues
CB: What if this sugar and body shame is a convenient distraction?
UA: A masking agent
TH: A disguise to hide behind

EB: Does body shaming myself mean avoiding the real issues?
SE: Which means never healing
UE: Stuck going round and round in circles
UN: What if I need less self-shame and more self-compassion?
CH: Maybe I can release all the shame now
CB: I now release all the sugar shame
UA: I let go of all the shame
TH: I am ready to have a new relationship with my body

Pause for a moment, close your eyes and take a long, slow inhale and exhale. If you feel called to continue tapping positive statements, do that until you feel finished.

When you're bringing the session to an end, with your eyes closed, cross your hands over your chest, take a deep breath and say 'transform'.

In your mind's eye, imagine this new knowledge, of how to live without sugar shame, pouring every cell of your physical and energetic bodies until your whole being vibrates with this new frequency.

Take the time to visualise this happening. Watch as every cell of your body absorbs and reflects this new information. Watch your cells release the old patterns and witness the new choices being encoded into your DNA.

Slowly open your eyes onto a world in which you no longer an emotional eater.

Go back to the number you had at the start of the session and see if it has shifted. If not, keep tapping on whatever came up for you.

If you feel called to do so, repeat this script as often as you feel is helpful and tap on anything that comes up as result, especially any memories, emotions or 'aha' moments.

ACTION AND AFFIRMATION

Action: Sweet surrender

Find a refined sugars-free recipe of your favourite treat, make a batch to share with family, friends or colleagues, or neighbours. There are thousands of sugar-free recipes online, try https://recipes.28bysamwood.com/

Affirmation:

Write the following affirmation on a postcard or post-it note and stick it where you'll see it at least once a day. Say it as many times as you can in the day. When you can, gaze into your own eyes and say it to your soul.

'I embrace and explore all the sweetness life has to offer.'

STEP 10
STRESS IS A WEIGHT-GAIN
SHAKE

"Weight-loss is not about willpower and discipline. It's about certain chemical and hormonal things that can be triggered by stress and emotion that are causing your body to hold on to weight. If your body wants you to hold onto weight for protection it's going to force you to eat. Then you get this shame and we think we're sabotaging ourselves, and we think our bodies are out to get us when in reality that's not at all the case, our bodies are trying to preserve us and we have to deal with the real issues."

— Jon Gabriel, weight-loss coach, author, and founder of The Gabriel Method @GabrielMethod

IF I HAD TO boil the biggest physical drivers of excess weight down to two factors, they would be these two bad boys: Sugars and stresses.

Why? Because of their devastating impact on your hormonal dynamics and your microbiome.

The problem is that 21st Century human is getting more of both refined sugars and stresses than ever before in our history. This dastardly duo are fat-makers and ongoing, low-grade stress is one of the most overlooked components of excess body fat. Feeling stressed is like drinking a weight-gain shake. It's like having a bartender inside of you who just won't stop mixing weight-gain cocktails. Even mild stress, tension or anxiety, can cause your body to maintain a low-level stress response. Researchers have found that just thinking about a stressful incident increases the levels of C-reactive protein, a marker of inflammation, in your body.

Let's briefly revisit what we know about the stress response—aka the 'fight or flight' response. Feeling stressed means your adrenals are spurting out cortisol and that puts your body into fat storage mode. When you've got cortisol, you've got insulin. They work together as a pair and it is insulin's job to push sugars out of your bloodstream and into your ever-obliging adipose tissue, aka fat cells, once there's no more room in your liver or muscles. Insulin particularly likes storing sugars as fat around the belly because this area is viewed as a relatively safe holding space.

Having high blood sugar levels leads to strong food cravings, over-eating, and weight gain.

Ongoing high levels of cortisol also compromise the immune system and reduce the effectiveness of the digestive system, which leads to low stomach acid, pathogen overgrowth in the gut, nutrient deficiency, and more.

The problem is, we're all living such busy 24-7 lives, that our bodies are in that fight or flight state more frequently and for longer than ever before in our history. 'Work-related death' is now actually a thing in the 21st century. Japan and China even have a special word for death from overwork – *karoshi* and *guolaosi* respectively.[27]

The emotions associated with living on 'high alert' all the time—which is what happens when you're chronically stressed—include anger, guilt, aggression, hatred, fear, prejudice, anxiety, insecurity, hopelessness, and other negative states that feed the energetic chaos that manifests as physical pain and disease. All of these emotions are derived or produced by stress chemicals.

Our stresses can be emotional, physical, mental, as well as subconscious but your brain reacts the exact same way to all of them. That is, it releases cortisol into your bloodstream and kicks over the first domino in the get-fat-quick chain.

That domino can be kicked over by anything from putting on jeans that are too tight; to getting stuck in traffic; a snarky comment on your Facebook post; receiving an overdue notice on a bill; being put on hold for 45 minutes when you call your gas supplier; having to stay late at work to meet a big deadline; worrying about plastics in the ocean; a

---

[27] https://www.ncbi.nlm.nih.gov/pmc/articles/PMC3341916/

pending exam that your life seems to depend on; reading another ignorant, racist, misogynist, raving tweet by someone's who running an entire country; a child who just won't stop crying... basically, life in the modern world is just one stress after another.

Or, to put it another way, one spurt of cortisol after another.

The result? We're all getting fatter.

MANAGING YOUR STRESS

The different stressors that lead to the metabolic syndrome that's keeping you fat, can be broken down to the following categories: refined sugars and processed foods; unprocessed emotional trauma from the past; sleep deprivation; famine or calorie restriction; over exercising; exposure to toxins such as heavy metals or pesticides; medication; digestive issues, artificial flavourings, and food sensitivities; financial stresses; relationship conflict; isolation and loneliness; limiting beliefs and negative thinking; hectic lifestyle; juggling work and home commitments; unresolved trauma from your past... and more. All these things can cause chronic low-grade stresses that tell the cells to stop listening to leptin and insulin, causing you to be leptin and insulin resistant. Reverse these stresses and your body will no longer perceive a need to hold onto the weight.

It's key, though, to address stress at every level. You've got to heal your mind and your emotions by doing emotional work, especially if you've experienced any emotional traumas. You must also address physical stresses, like food intolerances or the stress of leaky gut, which is when your intestinal wall has become permeable and toxins are leeching into the bloodstream. This toxic matter cannot go into your cells, it stays in the bloodstream where it gets picked up by your immune system up as a foreign invader. This triggers an inflammatory response. Your immune system gets constantly activated and the inflammatory hormones, called pro-inflammatory cytokines, tell the cells in your body to stop listening to leptin and insulin.

LOW STRESS LIVING

By switching to low stress living, you reverse the hormonal dynamics that are making you fat. To start the process of reducing your daily stresses, here are some ideas.

1. Calm the mind

Activities like meditation and visualisation help by putting your brain in the alpha or theta brainwave state, which means you're no longer pumping out stress hormones and your brain gets better and better at being calm. This is why people can lose weight from doing regular meditation. It's not about burning calories, it's about switching off the stress response, metabolising stress hormones, and getting the body back to a state of fat burning instead of sugar burning and fat storing. Download the free meditation app called Insight Timer.

2. Tap daily

EFT tapping is one of the most effective ways of managing stress so developing a daily tapping practise is a habit that will transform your life. One landmark, randomised controlled trial compared an hour-long EFT tapping session with an hour of talk therapy. It found that anxiety and depression dropped twice as much with tapping and that cortisol declined by 24 per cent in just a single hour. (Church, Yount & Brooks, 2012)[28] Whenever you're feeling stressed or anxious about anything, take yourself off for a few minutes of tapping about it.

3. Heal your digestive system

Proper nutrition on a regular basis can help to combat your stress levels. Take the time and effort to heal your digestive system and be aware that this can take months. Use probiotics, fermented foods, bone broths, collagen, and plenty of foods rich in vitamins and minerals—real wholefoods made by Mother Earth. Eliminate all fake, refined and processed foods as they're inflammatory.

4. Gently move your body

Interestingly, studies show that slobbing on the sofa all evening in front of television does not reduce stress hormones in the body. What does metabolise stress hormones is gently moving your body with activities like yoga, walking in nature, dancing, cycling, swimming.

5. Au naturel

Get out in nature every day and live as if you don't have access to a pharmacy of chemical drugs, which is how we did it for thousands of years.

6. Detox your body and life

Excess toxins and heavy metals could be part of the reason that your

---

[28] https://www.ncbi.nlm.nih.gov/pubmed/22986277

body-brain is stubbornly holding onto excess fat.

Heavy metals like mercury, cadmium, nickel, fluoride, aluminium, arsenic and lead, can be extremely harmful so your body-brain quarantines these dangerous toxins into your fat cells to stop them harming the delicate tissue of your organs.

Reduce your exposure, as much as possible, to environmental toxins such as pesticides, herbicides, industrial chemicals, plastics and cleaners, etc. These toxic substances and more are, unfortunately, used with abandon in the modern world in everything from our carpets and paint to plastics, dental amalgam, household cleaners, in personal products like shampoo and anti-perspirant.

Toxic metals also block the absorption and utilisation of essential minerals, this can bring on an avalanche of symptoms that get gradually worse and worse. This includes chronic fatigue, chronic pain, nervous system disorders, digestive issues, migraines and headaches, visual disturbances, infertility and miscarriage... to name just a few.

What to do? Support your body in safely removing the heavy metals. Detox with natural foods, herbs and spices. Eat whole, real foods, especially cruciferous veggies like broccoli, bok choy, kale and Brussels sprouts to maximize your dietary phytonutrients and increase your body's ability to detoxify. Choose foods high in antioxidants like dark, green leafy veggies and berries. Garlic and onions can also help you detoxify. For more, see Dr Mark Hyman's excellent documentary series, Broken Brain[29].

7. Sleep away the fat

A lack of sleep can make you fat. Why? Because the body-brain views this as a stressor and so reacts in the same way as it does to any stress, that is, your cortisol, insulin and blood glucose levels rise. Sleep is restorative. Not getting enough sleep is a chronic stress on the body, and anytime you have added stress, you also have higher blood sugar levels, which leads to laying down belly fat and cravings for comfort foods. This is why the winner of a UK reality TV show, where a big cash prize went to the person who stayed awake the longest, gained 6lbs in one week, simply from not sleeping and having her hormone balance thrown out of whack. Sleep is restorative and rebalances your hormones. Make sure you get plenty.

If you're getting plenty of sleep but still feeling tired on waking. Your

---

[29] https://brokenbrain.com/01-epidemic/

hormones may be out of balance or you may have sleep apnea, which is when the weight of the neck and chest compresses the windpipe. It basically means you're choking a little as you sleep.

If you're a big snorer then you probably have some degree of sleep apnea. This is more than just heavy snoring though. Sleep apnea is a serious medical condition that many people don't even realise they have—although they can't understand why they often feel tired even though they get eight or so hours in bed. You think you're sleeping but if you measured your brain waves during the night, you'd see that you're never getting into the deeper sleep states of alpha, delta and theta that we need to get into in order to repair and regenerate. An hour before you go to bed, drink a cup of tea prepared from fresh ginger, cinnamon, and hot water.

8. Avoid caffeine, alcohol, and nicotine

These substances interfere with your sleeping cycles and so contribute to excess weight. As well they can contribute to inflammation of the airways, which causes sleep apnea.

9. Talk to someone

Possibly the most important action. Keeping everything all bottled up inside you gives these stressors an ideal environment for growing deeper roots and spreading. If you don't want to confide in friends or family then go and see a healer or counsellor.

10. Keep a stress diary

Writing about your daily stresses in your Weight-Love journal will highlight any recurring themes as well as help you shift the way you see things. Writing it all out can defuse the stress and open up creative areas of your brain that can offer solutions to challenges you're facing. When you're stressed, you're unable to access those creative, problem-solving areas of the brain.

Now, let's go a bit deeper into uncovering what's really eating you...

EXERCISE:
WHAT'S EATING YOU?

LOSE THE STRESS to lose the weight.

How? It's key to address stress at every level. You've got to heal your mind and your emotions by doing emotional work, especially if you've experienced any emotional traumas. You must also address physical, mental and spiritual stresses.

The first step here is to identify your different stresses. In simpler terms, what's distressing you? What's eating away at you? What do you lie in bed worrying about at 3am?

The following list is not exhaustive, you'll probably think of your own but they are intended to get you thinking about the kinds of things that can be adding stress to your life:

Physical stresses
- Low calorie dieting
- Sleep deprivation
- Refined sugars and processed foods
- Exposure to environmental toxins
- Heavy metal accumulation in the body
- Leaky gut and inflammation
- Food sensitivities and allergens
- Nutritional deficiencies
- Sedentary lifestyle
- Medication

Mental stresses
- Bullying or intimidation at home, work or school
- Work pressures such as exams, sales targets, and deadlines
- Work overload and time pressures
- Financial difficulties
- Limiting beliefs with regard to self-worth or capability (all disempowering beliefs, such as unworthiness, powerlessness, and victimhood, put us into survival mode)
- Performance anxiety and the demanding expectations of others
- Negative criticism or judgment (from yourself or others)

- Major life event such as divorce, death, redundancy, job change, relocation, baby, etc.

Emotional
- Unresolved past traumas or childhood abuse
- Conflict
- Unmet emotional needs
- Negative emotions such as anger, resentment, rejection, guilt, shame, betrayal, etc
- Fears such as fear of the future, or the fear of old age
- Isolation and loneliness
- Abusive relationships

Spiritual
- Lacking a sense of life meaning or purpose
- Life devoid of passions or satisfaction
- Disconnection from the natural world
- Sense of unrealised potential or life regrets

In your Weight-Love journal, turn to a new page and write: *'The stressors in my life are...'* and write about everything that comes to mind. This might be as a list or you might want to free write about the things that are worrying or upsetting in your life.

When you've finished writing about all your stressors, go back and choose one that, at the moment, feels stronger than all the others. Sum this stress up in a single sentence. For example, 'I'm just so exhausted from a lack of sleep', or 'I'm so upset about this family conflict', 'I'm worn out from struggling with money', 'My boss is bullying me', 'My son isn't speaking to me', 'I'm going crazy from trying to meet everyone's needs', 'I hate my boring job but I can't afford to quit' and so on.

Take note of your summed-up stress sentence, and use this sentence in the tapping script up next.

TAPPING SCRIPT: STRESS RELEASE

FOR THIS TAPPING script we're going to focus on the stressor you identified in the What's Eating You? exercise.

Say your sentence out loud to yourself and pick a number that about matches how strong, or true or upsetting that statement feels on a scale from one to 10, with 10 being the most upsetting. Once you have your number, start tapping on the karate chop point on the side of your hand and say the following out loud...

Even though I have all this stress in my life and [insert your sentence here], I choose to relax now.

Even though I have all these stresses in my life and [insert your sentence here] and I'm not sure how to release all this tension, I accept that I have every right to feel like this.

Even though, I have this stress in my life and I can feel this stress in my body, I choose to love and accept myself.

Take a breath and start tapping around the face and torso, beginning at the eyebrow point...

EB: [insert your sentence here]
SE: [insert your sentence here]
UE: [insert your sentence here]
UN: [insert your sentence here]
CH: [insert your sentence here]
CB: [insert your sentence here]
UA: So much stress around this
TH: [insert your sentence here]

EB: All this stress in my body
SE: I feel all this stress in my body
UE: It makes me feel panicky
UN: And out of control
CH: My breath gets shallow
CB: My heart races

UA: My palms sweat
TH: I feel afraid

EB: All this stress in my body
SE: So many stresses in my life
UE: It seems overwhelming
UN: I can't see a solution
CH: Life always brings challenges
CB: That's not going to change
UA: But what if I handled them differently?
TH: Maybe I could be less effected

Pause and take a big deep breath before continuing...

EB: All this stress in my body
SE: Maybe I can start to release it now
UE: Because this stress isn't helping!
UN: It's making things much worse
CH: What if I could deal with this calmly?
CB: Without getting stressed?
UA: What if these things just didn't stress me anymore
TH: Maybe it's all not as bad as it seems

EB: What if there was a solution?
SE: A solution I can't see when I'm stressed
UE: I can't think clearly when I'm so stressed
UN: Maybe I can see this in a completely different way
CH: What if I could release all this stress in my body now?
CB: I choose to release all the stress...
UA: ...in my body now
TH: I inhale calm

EB: And I exhale stress
SE: I inhale calm
UE: I exhale all the stress in my body now
UN: Right now, I am safe
CH: Right now, I am calm
CB: Right now, I am blessed
UA: Right now, I am loved
TH: Right now, my world is wonderful

Pause for a moment, close your eyes and take a long, slow inhale and exhale. If you feel called to continue tapping positive statements, take some time to do that until you feel finished, remembering that natural urges to yawn or sigh or take really deep breaths are a sign of shift and release.

When you're bringing the session to an end, imagine this new knowledge of how to live your life without unhealthy levels of stress is pouring into every cell of your physical and energetic bodies until your whole being vibrates with this new frequency.

Take the time to visualise this happening. Watch as every cell of your body absorbs and reflects this new information. Watch your cells release the old patterns and witness the new choices being encoded into your DNA.

Mindfully open your eyes onto a whole new world in which you feel calm and safe.

Check in with the number you had at the start of the session. Has it shifted downwards? If your number is still high, do this script again and change the words to be more relevant to your situation.

ACTION AND AFFIRMATION

Action: Stress killers

Managing your stress levels is one of the most crucial components in managing your weight. If your stress levels are out of control, then so is your weight. Regulating the breath is a powerful way to quickly change your brain wave state and dissolve stress. The breath is one of the ways that the body communicates with the brain. When we consciously regulate our breath, making our exhales longer than our inhales, the message to the brain is *'Relax! Everything's fine, turn off the panic alarm.'* Just making our exhales longer than our inhales switches our brains from the sympathetic to the parasympathetic nervous system. In other words, from stress to peace. Breathing like this metabolises the stress hormones in our system and brings us back in to balance.

One particular breathing exercise that is highly effective for relieving stress is Alternate Nostril Breathing, also called Nadi Shodhana, if you're using its Sanskrit name.

Every morning for at least five mornings, set your alarm 15 minutes earlier than usual and do 10 minutes of Alternate Nostril Breathing. Set a timer for 10 minutes so you don't need to clock-watch.

Alternate Nostril Breathing

- First, seat yourself comfortably, this could be in a chair or seated on the floor. Keep the spine comfortably straight, shoulders relaxed, tongue gently touching the roof of the mouth.
- Close, or lower, your eyes and place your right thumb on the side of your right nostril, inhale deeply through your left nostril and count to four.
- Close your left nostril with the ring finger of your right hand and hold your breath, with both nostrils closed, for a count of four.
- Release your right thumb from your right nostril and exhale slowly through your right nostril.
- At the end of the exhale, take an inhale through your right nostril for a count of four.
- Close your right nostril with your right thumb and hold your breath for a count of four.
- Release your ring finger from your left nostril and exhale. At the end of the exhale, inhale through your left nostril for a count of four.
- Close the left nostril and hold the breath for a count of four.
- Continue with the alternating inhales and exhales on each side until the timer goes off. Finish your rounds with an exhale through your left nostril.
- Sit quietly while breathing normally before opening your eyes.

Affirmation

Write the following affirmation on a postcard or post-it note and stick it where you'll see it at least once a day. Say it as often as possible.

'It gets easier every day to release tension and stress from my body and mind.'

STEP 11
MICROBIOME MYSTERIES

"Are we humans hosting a whole lot of bacteria, or are we bacteria having a human experience?" We appreciate that we are living with a parallel civilization inside of us, each assisting the other." Dr. Tom O'Bryan, author of The Autoimmune Fix @theDr_com

BELIEVE IT OR not, toxic bacteria that live in your gut may be keeping you fat.

In a nutshell, scientific studies show that an imbalance of the 'good' and 'bad' bacteria in your gut, along with low gut flora diversity, is a recipe for obesity. As well, it's a recipe for depression, auto-immune conditions, and a host of other chronic diseases but for now we'll keep the focus to weight.

They've done the studies on poor, long-suffering lab mice. The researchers discovered that obese mice had different gut flora to thin mice. Amazingly, when they transplanted the gut flora from the thin mice into the fat mice, the fat mice lost weight. And vice versa.[30] Thin mice that were given fat mice gut flora, gained weight.

The gut health step was a total game changer for me. It was the final key that unlocked the last barrier to fat freedom. In fact, I suspect it was the biggest key and, had I dealt with it many years earlier, my battle with weight may have been over years ago. But I didn't know. I was stuck in dieting world. I'd never imagined that vast communities of different life forms, which lived in my belly and intestines, profoundly affected how my body dealt with what I ate.

---

[30] https://www.ncbi.nlm.nih.gov/pmc/articles/PMC4695328/

The reality was that, my years of dieting, restrictive eating rules, binge-purge swings, and high intensity exercise, had destroyed the health of my gut flora. Also called microbiome, this is the community of friendly bacteria that lives mostly in the gut.

By the time I turned my attention to my gut flora health, I had only about 35 per cent of the diversity I needed for optimal health, thanks to all the dieting rules that had seen me eat basically the same foods every day for years. A lack of food diversity means a lack of microbiome diversity. Plus I was riddled with an overgrowth of candida albicans, and had been for decades. These factors alone make it pretty much impossible to shed excess body fat permanently.

How can an unbalanced gut microbiome make you fat? One way is that the bad bacteria cause leaky gut, which causes the systemic inflammation that triggers fat storage. As well, the bad bacteria influence you to choose the sugars they need to survive. Happily though, when you change your gut bacteria, you change how your body produces and metabolises energy and you release weight. Before we go further into that, let's take a closer look at what's going on in your digestive system.

YOU ARE NOT ALONE

Here's what you probably believe. You believe that your body is yours and you live it in alone. You don't, though. You share your body with a host of other microbial life forms. We humans are a collection of about 100 billion cells but we have more bacterial, fungal, and viral cells in our body that we have human cells.

These life forms, or bacteria, are essential to the health and vitality of your body. These microbes need you and you need these microbes because the body is a complex microbial eco system. Without these friendly little bugs, your body would die. All these little life forms have their own consciousness, their own needs and desires. Sometimes, the thoughts you have aren't actually your thoughts, they're messages to your brain from your microbiome. Like when you've eaten your dinner and suddenly find yourself in the kitchen hunting out 'something sweet'. That may be your not-so-friendly gut bacteria sending a message to your brain via the vagus nerve that triggers your hunt for the food that this bacteria needs to live. This is also why, when someone does a detox and these bacteria start dying off, the person may feel depressed themselves. They're feeling the bacteria's feelings about dying.

So you think you're running the show but you're not. For every message from the brain to the gut, telling it what to do, there are nine messages going from the gut to the brain telling it what to do.

It's your microbiome, or gut flora, that gets the last say on everything. From how you're feeling, to how you digest and absorb nutrients, to whether you metabolise hormones. Your microbiome changes the foods you eat, controls your bio rhythms and your sleep cycles. That's not all though, our gut flora is also our biggest detox organ and our biggest nutrient generator. As well, our gut flora metabolises any drugs we take so certain bacteria can block the effects of your medication. This has been proven in cancer and diabetes therapy. A drug that's not working can then start working when the gut microbiome is altered.[31]

Without the right gut bacteria, our bodies can't produce serotonin. Without the right gut bacteria, our bodies can't regulate our thyroid hormones or convert T4 (thyroxine) to T3 (triiodothyronine). So you think your problem is depression, or hypothyroidism, when in fact your problem is low gut flora diversity.

Your microbiome conducts the orchestra that is you, your body. You are the puppet and the bacteria is the puppet master pulling your strings. So make sure it's the friendly bacteria that's holding the reins.

What do these friendly bacteria get in return for doing all this work for us? We give them a home, a place to live, and we eat to feed them. We have a beautiful and synergistic relationship with these organisms and it is in our best interests to look after these friendly microbes. Our happiness and health depends on their happiness and health.

YOUR INNER GARDEN

Bottom line, if your gut microbiome is out of balance and you don't have the 'thin mouse' bacteria, the extra weight will stay and probably increase.

How does your microbiome get out of balance? The usual suspects. Stress, sugars, restrictive eating rules and dieting, toxic exposure, unprocessed emotional trauma, alcohol, anti-inflammatory drugs, aspirin and antibiotics, anti-acid formulas, and even high intensity exercise. These factors destroy your friendly bacteria and pave the way for the toxic bacteria to run riot. Bacteria like E. Coli, H. Pylori, candida, salmonella, campylobacter, ... to name just a few.

Candida, for example, is a fungal bacteria. It overgrows when there's

---

[31] www.interconnectedseries.com

not enough stomach acid, or friendly bacteria, to keep it in check and when its host (you) offers it a constant supply of the sugars it thrives on. If you get a white coating everyday on the back of your tongue, or if you're regularly getting oral or vaginal/genital thrush, then you've got a problem with candida and you have a microbiome that's out of balance. Other symptoms of candida include fungal infections like athlete's foot, acne and bad body odour.

When candida spreads out of control, it pushes bigger holes in your intestinal gut lining. That's when you get pathogenic intestinal permeability, aka leaky gut. As well, though, it starts secreting toxins that impact brain function.

Leaky gut is the gateway to autoimmune diseases—everything from hashimoto's thyroiditis to Parkinson's, lupus, muscular sclerosis, and more. It allows all sorts of toxic bacteria to leech into the blood stream. One of these toxic bacteria is called LPS (lipopolysaccharides) and it wreaks havoc. Once LPS gets in the bloodstream, it triggers the immune system, which leads to systemic inflammation and the body flicks its 'store fat' switch. This is a slippery slope to all sorts of problems—weight gain being just one of them.[32]

When LPS runs amok in the body, it's called metabolic endotoxemia. This condition triggers obesity, leptin and insulin resistance, depression, and diabetes.[33]

If you can heal the gut and get rid of the endotoxemia, you lower the fat signals, turn off the fat cells, and lower the inflammatory signals.

HOW TO HEAL YOUR GUT GARDEN

Promoting a healthy microbiome is key to getting well and losing weight. You might find it helpful to get comprehensive microbiome testing from a functional or integrative medicine practitioner to uncover any specific issues unique to you but in general, these guidelines to support your gut flora could make a massive difference.

Here are the DOs

1. Pack in the probiotics: To help your gut bacteria work better, take quality probiotic supplements, digestive enzymes, and fermented

---

[32] https://chriskresser.com/how-inflammation-makes-you-fat-and-diabetic-and-vice-versa/

[33] https://www.ncbi.nlm.nih.gov/pubmed/17456850/

foods—which are natural probiotics—to reset your gut. Eat as wide a diversity of plant foods as possible.

2. Don't forget your prebiotics: Prebiotics are the food for your probiotics. These are starches that you can't digest but that your good bacteria thrive on. If you don't feed your good bacteria, they die. Good prebiotic foods include plant fibre like banana, plaintain, konjac. Eat a lot of plant-rich foods, vegetables, fruit, nuts and seeds, wholegrains and beans. These provide the nutrients for the friendly bacteria to grow and flourish. Eat two prebiotic foods every day.

3. Resistant starch: This is a top tip. Your friendly bacteria really love resistant starch and a great way to get that is from potato or rice that's been cooked and then cooled before you eat it.

4. Rock your fermented foods: Eat a tablespoon of fermented food every day and alternate varieties. Go for different colours. Choose from pickled onions, pickled beetroot, kombucha, kefir, sauerkraut, miso... as many different varieties of fermented foods as possible to increase diversity. (If you have an intolerance to dairy, don't consume the cow milk kefir products.)

5. Boost your gut healing nutrients: This includes glutathione and glutamic acid. Cabbage and cabbage juice is a great source of glutamic acid. Cabbage juice is given to people to heal stomach ulcers.[34] To boost your glutathione, eat plenty of sulfur-rich foods like garlic, onions and the cruciferous vegetables (broccoli, kale, collards, cabbage, cauliflower, watercress, etc).

6. Eat a root vegetable every day: Carrots, beetroot, parsnip, turnip, sweet potato, etc. I like to grate a carrot on a morning, add a tablespoon of apple cider vinegar, a tablespoon of olive oil and a pinch of sea salt. I eat this first thing in the morning, after my warm water with the juice of a lemon.

7. Eat your good fats: Good fats help reduce inflammation. This is mainly your omega 3s—oily fish, olive oil, avocado, nuts and seeds.

---

[34] https://www.ncbi.nlm.nih.gov/pmc/articles/PMC1643665/pdf/califmed00295-0012.pdf

8. Sort out the stress: Your microbiome listens to your thoughts and changes the flora in your gut as a result so deal with your stress. Meditation is very powerful for switching the body over from the sympathetic to the parasympathetic nervous system—sympathetic is 'fight or flight' and parasympathetic is 'rest and digest'. It makes a world of difference to the hormones your body-brain is pumping out, as well as the impact of these hormones on your system. And don't forget to sleep! Studies[35] show that sleep deprivation causes weight gain because it significantly changes your gut flora.

Here are the DON'Ts

1. Ban the big three: Say no to sugar, dairy and wheat. If your gut flora bacteria is struggling, give them a break with a complete ban of this terrible trio for a month at least. Ideally permanently but at least for a few weeks.

2. Don't feed the trolls: Similar to above, to get rid of the toxic bacteria, stop feeding them refined sugars, processed foods and refined oils. Sugar, in particular, destroys microbiome diversity and healthy gut flora. If there's just one thing you do, get rid of the sugars and the white flour. Remember, if you find yourself craving sugars, it might be the dying toxic bacteria urging you to seek out these sugars for them.

3. Eliminate the chemical gut busters: Avoid when possible the antibiotics, acid blockers, anti-inflammatories, and aspirin. These are all damaging your gut. If you do have to take a course of antibiotics, follow it up with a concerted effort of gut flora rebuilding.

4. Dump the 'no pain no gain' mentality: While regular, moderate exercise is awesome for your body and mind, high intensity anaerobic exercise is not so great for people with digestive issues. Hard core exercise, outside of your aerobic range, releases stress hormones, which tear your gut lining, leading to pathogenic intestinal permeability (leaky gut).

---

[35] https://www.sciencedirect.com/science/article/pii/S2212877816301934

EXERCISE:
BACTERIA AND EMOTIONS

FROM AN ENERGETIC healing point of view, all imbalance in the body stems from an imbalance in the emotions. When these emotions are not processed or resolved, they manifest as physical issues.

These physical ailments are like a message from the universe. They're telling you that something in your life is out of alignment and is showing up because it's ready to be healed.

Toxic bacteria, for example, is given an opportunity to take hold when the immune system isn't strong enough to fend off these 'enemies'. A weakened immune system can be the result of ongoing suppression of emotions like anger, resentment, fear, guilt, and regret.

As a ThetaHealing practitioner, I believe that toxic bacterial conditions are linked to suppressed guilt; that fungal overgrowths are linked to suppressed resentment, and that viruses indicate self-esteem and worthiness issues. Until these emotions and feelings are processed and released, the physical condition will continue to return.

If your digestive tract has become overrun with nasty bacteria, think back to the time in your life when it first began and ask yourself:

'What in my life was so hard to stomach?'
'What in my life did I have no choice but to stomach?'
'What in my life was difficult to digest?'
'What gut intuition have I been suppressing?'

Open a new page in your Weight-Love journal and answer one of these questions using stream-of-consciousness writing for at least 10 minutes.

When you are finished, read through what you wrote and take the insights, memories and feelings that the writing evoked as targets for the tapping script up next.

TAPPING SCRIPT: CLEANSING THE SOLAR PLEXUS

FOR THIS TAPPING script we're going to focus on any stuck resentment, guilt, old childhood victimisation, inability to accept affection, feelings of being shouted down, railroaded, over powered... or whatever else came up when you did the previous exercise. These emotions can get stuck in our solar plexus and sacral chakra. You may feel them as an ever-present subtle anxiety. They leave us feeling weak and powerless, which can show up in our physical bodies as the overgrowth of harmful microbes in our gut. As your feelings and experiences are unique to you, please alter the script to use whatever language makes it more relevant to you and your situation.

To pick your number, think about what it is from your past that you simply couldn't or wouldn't stomach or absorb. How strong or upsetting does it feel on a scale from one to 10, with 10 being the most upsetting? Once you have your number, start tapping on the karate chop point on the side of your hand and say the following out loud...

Even though I couldn't stomach these things, I choose to forgive myself.

Even though I can't digest these things, I accept my feelings.

Even though, it's hard to stomach, and part of me refuses to stomach it, I accept my feelings and the right to feel this way.

Pause for a breath and continue tapping around the points on your face and torso:

EB: I can't stomach it
SE: I won't stomach it
UE: It's too painful to digest this stuff
UN: Too much to absorb
CH: So I'd rather not
CB: Part of me refuses to fully digest these things from my past
UA: So many old emotions
TH: Old resentment

EB: Old guilt
SE: Old bitterness
UE: Some old stuff that I still can't stomach
UN: Energy I'm holding onto
CH: Suppressed feelings
CB: Unresolved upsets
UA: Simmering resentment
TH: Feeling aggrieved

EB: I hold onto these old emotions in my solar plexus
SE: I hold these old emotions in my sacral chakra
UE: It's like an enemy is inside me
UN: I hold my fear in my solar plexus
CH: Alongside my sense of self
CB: This ever-present subtle anxiety
UA: Lives in my solar plexus
TH: Lives in my sacral chakra

EB: This energy from my past is stuck there
SE: This energy from when I felt taken over...
UE: ... bullied
UN: ... colonised
CH: ... over powered
CB: ... shouted down
UA: ... out numbered
TH: ... victimized

Pause and take a big deep breath before continuing...

EB: These old emotions
SE: These old internal battles
UE: I've held onto them for long enough
UN: They're showing up as digestive issues
CH: Energies I can't stomach
CB: Energies I won't stomach
UA: Maybe I've held onto them for long enough
TH: I'd really like to let them go now

EB: Maybe it's time to shift these old energies
SE: Move them along
UE: Pass them through my system

UN: These feelings may have helped me once
CH: But they are no longer helpful
CB: They're harming me
UA: That time is past now
TH: I no longer need these energies to stay safe

EB: I'm done with feeling victimised
SE: I'm done with feeling shouted down
UE: I now set myself free from the past
UN: I release all my attachments to people...
CH: ...who have hurt me in the past
CB: I release all my attachments to situations...
UA: ...that have hurt me in the past
TH: I am free and they are free

Pause for a moment, close your eyes and take a long, slow inhale and exhale. If you feel called to continue tapping positive statements, do that until you feel finished.

When you're bringing the session to an end, imagine these old emotions and beliefs lifting up out of your cellular memory. Imagine this old energy being released from your stomach and colon. See this part of you being flooded in healing white light. Imagine the new knowing of how to live without these old feelings and beliefs pouring into every cell of your physical and energetic bodies until your whole being vibrates with this new frequency of empowerment.

Take the time to visualise this happening. Watch as every cell of your body absorbs and reflects this new information. Watch your cells release the old patterns and witness the new choices being encoded into your DNA.

Slowly open your eyes onto a world in which you are no longer anxious and victimised or over powered or shouted down.

Go back to the number you had at the start of the session and see if it has shifted. If not, keep tapping on whatever came up for you. If you feel called to do so, repeat this script as often as you feel is helpful and tap on anything that comes up as result, especially any memories, emotions or 'aha' moments.

ACTION AND AFFIRMATION

Action: An apple a day

Homemade stewed apples, or apple sauce, can help you lose weight. How? Because the pectin in the apples rebalances and rebuilds a healthy microbiome[36].

According to Dr Tom O'Bryan,[37] author of *The Autoimmune Fix*, pectin increases a substance in our gut called Intestinal Alkaline Phosphatase (IAP) and stimulates the production of more probiotics. IAP prevents the toxic bacteria LPS from getting into the blood stream, when this happens it's known as metabolic endotoxemia. IAP grabs LPS and escorts it out with the bowel movement. As well, IAP stimulates the genes to heal intestinal impermeability and stimulates the good bacteria to colonise and rebuild. It enhances the binding of the good bacteria to the gut wall so they're stronger to protect you from the bad bacteria. This is the real reason why an apple a day keeps the doctor away.

So, make your own batch of the miraculous apple sauce and eat a couple of tablespoons per day.

To make the sauce, take four organic apples, wash and slice them, put them in a pot of water that covers about one third of the sliced apples. If you want, add raisins or cinnamon. Bring to a boil and boil for about five to 10 minutes. When you see the shine on the skin, you're done, you've released the pectin from the apples. Mash them up and store the sauce in a glass container in the fridge.

I got this tip from the wonderful Dr Tom O'Bryan, when he was a guest expert on the excellent documentary series *Interconnected - The Power To Heal From Within*, see www.interconnectedseries.com.

Affirmation

Write the following affirmation on a postcard or post-it note and stick it where you'll see it at least once a day.

'I love and appreciate how my body expresses my truth for me.'

---

[36] https://www.ncbi.nlm.nih.gov/pubmed/26938554

[37] https://thedr.com/

STEP 12
FAT SELF INTEGRATION

"Food is a substitute for the symbolic reflection that you feel you are starving spiritually, not physically. Do what excites you." — *Bashar, a multi-dimensional being channeled by Darryl Anka @Bashar_ET*

I HAD AN unsettling blast back to the past recently. My mum (who lives on the other side of the world) went through that huge bag of photos that's been sitting in the back of a closet for the last few decades. This huge back is stuffed full of old-style envelopes full of photos. My grandparents are in there, preserved forever in black and white on little squares of cardboard, as well as my parents as young people, and me and my little brother at every stage of our lives.

Pictures of me from birth. You can watch me grow up in an afternoon by sifting through this enormous bag of photos.

Since social media kicked in, this bag has stopped expanding. Now, all our memories are on our computers and phones but when I was growing up, memories were imprinted on glossy squares of cardboard held in envelopes with a little inside pocket for keeping the negative film, in case we wanted more copies of any photos made.

On one of our Skype chats, I'd asked Mum to sift through this bag and find a few examples of what I call my 'fat photos' and what Mum more kindly calls my 'chubby photos'. I needed them for a weight-loss workshop I was running. I wanted some credibility in the eyes of the workshop participants. Proof that I've gone through this battle and that I know what I'm talking about when it comes to what works and what doesn't in the minefield of weight-loss. I weigh about 15kgs less now than I was at my heaviest. I wanted to hold these photos up and boast, *'Look at me now! Haven't I done well!'* But I got more than I bargained for.

These images of younger me that I haven't looked at in decades dragged up some old feelings and memories that I hadn't counted on. I'd forgotten how overweight I'd been. My initial reaction, though, was to laugh at that fat girl in the photos who was me. I was laughing at myself like one of those mean girls at school. Who needs enemies? I had split off the 'fat me' and cast her adrift. She was other, separate, unacceptable. She was not, I told myself, the 'real me'. But I was lying to myself about that.

That girl in the photos had battled through life. She got out of bed every morning and put a smile on her face when inside she felt lost. She was following the rules of life to the letter but not getting the promised results. She played the game of 'everything's alright' because part of her didn't know it wasn't. She didn't know life could be different. Better.

Low level anxiety was the default state that had become so normal that she didn't realise she was anxious all the time. Like background noise you stop noticing. That girl looked outside of herself for approval and love. Ironically, she thought the answer to a happier life was more self-punishment and self-criticism. That if she just punished herself enough, she'd lose the weight and finally be happy. Ironically, it wasn't until she stopped punishing herself—I stopped punishing myself—that the weight would slowly, slowly reflect this new attitude by vanishing.

RESISTANCE IS FUTILE

Why has your excess weight persisted for all this time despite all your desperate, frantic, relentless, and determined efforts to shift it?

It persists precisely because you have resisted and rejected it with such force.

By doing so, you have been pushing part of yourself away. Essentially, you split yourself in two as you try to distance yourself from her; this unacceptable, fat you. You are ashamed and embarrassed by this version of yourself so you reject and disown your fat self in disgust.

By doing so, you are offering yourself conditional love. You are telling yourself that you must meet certain expectations, certain conditions, before you can be loved and accepted. This is abusive, corrupted love and it is learned behaviour. You are playing out a pattern that was taught to you. By splitting off your supposedly 'unacceptable and unlovable' parts into a 'fat self', you contain them in a form that feels understandable and separate from the 'real you'. This means the part of you that rejects your fat self is able to blame her for this feeling of shame. Your fat self takes the blame for everything that's wrong in your life; for all your so-called failings. It means that you feel the rest of you is worthy of being loved and accepted.

Your fat self, therefore, is doing you a service. She plays this role out of love for you, taking on the part of outcast so the rest of you doesn't have to. The trouble is, it doesn't ultimately work. That's because there is not a fat you and a thinner you. There is only you.

Until you integrate all the parts of yourself that you have been taught are shameful and unlovable; until you accept and love these parts, and release the idea that any part of you has ever been, or could ever be, unacceptable or unlovable, you will never feel completely whole, accepted and loved.

What do you need to do? Stop pushing your fat self away and instead welcome her, own her validate her and reintegrate her into your whole self.

To do this integration exercise, find some time when you can be alone. Cross your hands over your heart and repeat the following out loud.

"Fat self, you are welcome here. I see you, I accept you and I love you.
"Fat self, please forgive me for pushing you away.
"Fat self, please forgive me for shaming you. Forgive me for denying and disowning you.
"Fat self, I acknowledge you. I see your hurt and I see your pain. I see your shame. I see your embarrassment. I see your despair and your sense of worthlessness.
"Fat self, please forgive me for contributing to your pain and hurt. Please forgive me for rejecting you. Please forgive me for being yet another person in your life who offers you only conditional and grudging acceptance. I know how much this hurts. Forgive me for telling you to get lost; that I don't want you here.
"Fat self, I now offer you my wholehearted and unconditional love. I see your courage and your bravery. I see and feel your love for me.
"Thank you for bearing the brunt of all the criticism. Thank you for bearing the brunt of the judgment and negativity.
"Fat self, I love you."

Now, close your eyes and see your fat self standing in front of you. In your mind's eye, imagine walking over and hugging her. Take as long as you want over this hug and if you feel like saying anything else to her, do so. If she has anything she needs to say to you, give her the opportunity.

Next, imagine her shrinking in size so you can hold her in the palm of your hand. Now place her into your heart and breathe her in.

EXERCISE: REWIRE YOUR BRAIN

I LOVE THIS exercise. You can really play with it and make it fun. It's the power pose exercise, aka postural feedback. What it basically involves is you standing tall with your hands in fists on your hips, legs apart, as per Wonder Woman or Superman. You stand like a superhero for a minute at least, ideally two minutes, and you say '*I am enough! I am enough! I am enough!*' for the whole time.

You can switch it up, though, if '*I am enough*' gets too repetitive. You can add in whatever makes you feel uplifted. I did this exercise myself a couple of hours ago and found myself up saying things like, '*I am brilliant! I am unstoppable! I am gorgeous! I am stylish! I am vibrant, healthy, and slim! I am toned and strong and youthful! I attract amazing opportunities...*' that kind of thing.

Even though it will feel like you're just playing around and being a bit silly, what you're doing is actually fundamentally rewiring your brain and therefore transforming your life.

Here's why. We know that our emotions effect our physical bodies but it works the other way as well. It's that bi-directional relationship we've touched on before. This means that, if you assume a depressed stance, with sloped shoulders, crossed arms and a frown, it will cause your brain to produce the chemicals in the brain that support a depressed mood. By the same token, if you adopt a strong, powerful, confident pose, your brain will pump out the chemicals that support you feeling this way, so you will feel this way.

But here's the really important part. Your brain will actually grow new branches, or neural pathways, that support the feelings engendered by the way you use your body. This is neuroplasticity.

So when you consistently hold and move your body in a new way, it actually wires the brain to maintain those feelings. In other words, 'fake it till you make it' is actually a thing. This has been proven in proper studies by intellectual, sciencey types. The most well-known one is Harvard psychologist Amy Cuddy, who first introduced power posing to the world in 2012 through her very popular TED talk called 'Your body language may shape who you are'.[38] The talk went viral and everyone was power posing but then there was a backlash. Cuddy received some severe criticism from some of her peers. Undeterred, she did all the studies again, even more thoroughly than the first time.

Then, in 2018, she published even more research[39] that proves the power of postural feedback. Cuddy took saliva samples of volunteers to measure levels of hormones like cortisol and testosterone before and after 'power posing' and 'weak posing'. Just two minutes of power posing made significant changes to confidence levels, with cortisol falling and testosterone rising (women have testosterone as well).

STRIKE A POSE

Let's do it then. Take yourself somewhere you can be alone and adopt your Wonder Woman or Superman pose. Stand tall, lengthen the spine, shoulders down and back, legs apart, chest proud. Repeat 'I am enough', or a similar uplifting phrase, over and over again for two minutes. Vary your tone of voice but keep it confident, assured and comfortable.

Make this practise a habit to really root in the new wiring. Maybe do it after you brush your teeth on a morning, or in the shower. Do it at least once a day for a month and notice how these new neural pathways of self-love bring positive changes into your life.

38

https://www.ted.com/talks/amy_cuddy_your_body_language_shapes_who_you_are?

39 https://journals.sagepub.com/eprint/CzbNAn7Ch6ZZirK9yMGH/full

TAPPING SCRIPT: DROPKICK YOUR INNER CRITIC

DO YOU HAVE an inner critic squatter living in your head? Let's serve that miserable git an eviction notice with this tapping script.

Sometimes our inner critic is so entrenched in our internal dialogue, we don't even realise it's the critic speaking to us. The inner critic also disguises itself as our friend—the kind of friend who says, 'Now, I'm telling you this because I care so much about your happiness... you really need to get back to the gym and do something about your arse.'

How can you tell when your inner critic is having a go at you, yet again? They're usually around if you're feeling guilty. Like when you sleep through the alarm and miss an early gym class, it's your inner critic who makes you feel bad about it. By contrast, your inner cheerleader would tell you that you were right to sleep in because your body obviously needed the extra rest. (I've given my inner cheerleader a name, she's Oprah.)

When you look in the mirror and your hair and make-up looks fantastic, it's your inner critic who dismisses that and whispers, *'ah yes but your thighs are still fat'*. Your inner cheerleader will say *'wow, you look fabulous, your eyes are so beautiful and I love your hair like that...'*

When you get top marks in an exam or win praise at work, your inner critic whispers *'yeah great but I bet you'd still swap it all to be thinner...'* Your inner cheerleader would say, *'you are so brilliant, I am so proud of you, you can achieve anything you want'*. Who would you rather hang out with?

Let's start dialing down the volume on your inner critic. Using a scale from zero to 10, pick a number that matches how strong your inner critic feels, 10 being the strongest.

Once you have your number, start by tapping on the karate chop point on the side of your hand and say the following out loud...

Even though I have this loud and annoying inner critic in my head, I love and accept myself completely.

Even though I have this horrible inner critic stuck in my head, constantly making me feel anxious and guilty and not good enough, I profoundly love and accept myself anyway.

Even though I have this inner critic relentlessly judging everything I do and say, I choose to relax and forgive myself.

Pause, take a deep breath and continue tapping around the face and body, starting with the eyebrow point...

EB: *This inner critic is stuck in my head*
SE: *This voice in my head telling me I'm fat, lazy, not good enough...*
UE: *Like a record player in my brain that's stuck in a nasty groove*
UN: *Relentlessly banging on about how I'm not quite enough*
CH: *Not thin enough*
CB: *Not pretty enough*
UA: *Not sexy enough*
TH: *Not clever enough*

EB: *Not funny enough*
SE: *Not smart enough*
UE: *Not ambitious enough*
UN: *Not thoughtful enough*
CH: *The list goes on and on...*
CB: *According to this voice in my head*
UA: *I'm just not good enough*
TH: *This voice suggests I would be good enough...*

EB: *...if I were thinner*
SE: *But then it tells me I'll never manage to get thinner*
UE: *I'll fail at that*
UN: *Just like I've always failed at it*
CH: *What a failure I am*
CB: *Says this internal voice*
UA: *'You shouldn't eat that!' says the voice*
TH: *'You haven't been exercising enough this week' says the voice*

EB: *'Get up off your fat backside and clean the house / get to the gym / call your parents... do more, be more, achieve more...*
SE: *Then this voice tells me...*
UE: *... it's saying all this for my own good*
UN: *'If I can't tell you the painful truth, who can?' whines the voice*
CH: *'I just want you to be the best you can be...' says the voice*
CB: *'So I have to push you to work at it', says the voice*

271

UA: But what if this voice is making everything worse
TH: Maybe I can tell this voice to shut the fork up

Pause for a moment, close your eyes and take a long deep inhale then exhale through the mouth. Give yourself a couple of seconds to consider anything that came up for you while we were tapping. Any old memories, grudges, emotions. Tap on anything else for as long as you need to and then continue:

EB: I am fed up with listening to that stupid inner critic
SE: I am fed up with it droning on and on
UE: Droning on about what's wrong with me
UN: God that inner critic is boring!
CH: It's time to turn the volume down on the critic
CB: I'm giving my inner critic a name – his name is now Homer [or any other name you want to use]
UA: Homer, you need to shut up for a while
TH: It's time to turn the volume up on my inner cheerleader

EB: My inner cheerleader is so much more fun
SE: Her name is Oprah [or any other name you want to use]
UE: I feel better when she's around
UN: She's so uplifting
CH: She always sees the bright side
CB: She always notices how well I've been doing
UA: And how good I look
TH: She says, 'girl, you are rocking that look today!'

EB: Why on earth have I been listening to Homer?
SE: When I could have been listening to Oprah?
UE: Homer has nothing helpful to say
UN: He is always so negative
CH: I'm so done with that
CB: Homer can pack his bags and move on
UA: It's time for Oprah to be heard
TH: Listening to Homer has left me fat and feeling like a failure

EB: Time's up on that shit
SE: Oprah and I will have a much better time together
UE: Oprah is my fabulous inner cheerleader
UN: She's so much fun

CH: If Homer tries to pop up again
CB: I'll just tell him to shut up
UA: I'll tell him to go away
TH: I'm so bored with him

EB: He's a bit too stupid to be of use to me
SE: Oprah is brilliant, clever and funny
UE: And she says I am as well
UN: Oprah says I'm beautiful and sexy and smart
CH: Oprah says I can be anything I want to be
CB: Oprah says the world is my oyster
UA: And she is absolutely right
TH: I now listen only to my inner cheerleader, Oprah

Pause for a moment, close your eyes and take a long, slow inhale and exhale. If you feel called to continue tapping positive statements, do that until you feel finished. A good sign of being finished is when you naturally want to take some extra deep breaths or if you yawn. When you're bringing the session to an end, close your eyes, cross your hands over your chest, take a deep breath and say "transform".

In your mind's eye, imagine this new knowledge of how to live with an inner cheerleader is pouring into every cell of your physical and energetic bodies until your whole being vibrates with this frequency.

Take the time to visualise this happening. Watch as every cell of your body absorbs and reflects this new information. Watch your cells release the old patterns and witness the new choices being encoded into your DNA.

Slowly open your eyes onto a world in which you no longer listen to your stupid and boring inner critic.

Go back to the number you had at the start of the session and feel if it has shifted. If not, keep tapping on whatever came up for you. If you feel called to do so, repeat this script as often as you feel is helpful and tap on anything that comes up as result, any memories, emotions or 'aha' moments.

ACTION AND AFFIRMATION

Action: Create your new life

The way to profoundly and powerfully change your life and reality is to choose different thoughts. Our brain is just a neural network, trillions of neural connections and patterns that have coalesced in these associative patterns, so when we want to achieve a new goal, vision, pattern of behavior thought or emotion, we need to visualise ourselves at that new level of success. The brain cells (neurons) grow new branches, make new connections, and the seeds of your new life are sewn. In your Weight-Love journal, create a picture of your new desired life and body. You may write a description, you may draw a picture, or paste a photo into your journal.

Affirmation

Write the following affirmation on a postcard or post-it note and stick it where you'll see it at least once a day. Repeat as often as possible.

'I notice more of the things that bring me pleasure and I welcome them into my life at every opportunity.'

STEP 13
FAT AND FORGIVENESS

"The quality of mercy is not strain'd, it droppeth as the gentle rain from heaven upon the place beneath. It is twice bless'd: it blesseth him that gives and him that takes."—William Shakespeare, English poet, playwright and actor (1564-1616)

YOU'VE PROBABLY ALREADY heard that forgiveness is the path to your own freedom and liberation. Part of you probably would love to be able to forgive, the only problem is that you just can't quite get there.

Here's the thing. If forgiveness were easy, we'd all be doing it. We'd offer our forgiveness without any hesitation and take our place amongst the ascended masters and angels.

But we are human and it's not always so easy. What's easy—or what seems easier—is clinging onto our resentment, anger and bitterness. Even when research has shown over and over again that forgiveness makes us happier and healthier.

All the studies show that without any doubt, forgiveness sets us free. People who forgive enjoy lower blood pressure, lower stress, and a stronger immune system making them less susceptible to anything from a cold to cancer. Health issues such as back pain, stomach problems, and headaches can disappear and depression is lifted. Still, we stubbornly cling to our seething resentments, bitterness and grudges.

According to Duke University, the University of Tennessee, and Stanford University, holding onto hurts, grudges, annoyances, pet peeves or old wounds hurts the body, especially when the memories are triggered by current life events. As well, in accordance with the

Universal law of attraction, we unconsciously attract people into our lives who trigger our emotional wounds. Did you feel rejected or conditionally loved as a child? If that wound is unhealed, it's why you attract rejection and conditional love as an adult. This is not some kind of punishment or karmic slap in the face. It's your external world reflecting your inner world to you. In other words, it's your inner self being projected onto the external screen of your life. It is also your Higher Self showing you what needs healing by bringing your wounds to the forefront.

You'd think, then, that we'd all be queuing up to heal our inner children and forgive everyone and everything in our lives, wouldn't you. Yet we don't. Instead, we spend decades clinging to old hurts like a beloved security blanket that we cannot be without.

Why? Because we have a lot of really good reasons to hold a grudge. We wrap ourselves in resentment armour, that often looks like body fat, to keep that dangerous person away; or maybe we wear our resentment like a badge of honour to garner sympathy or to manipulate others; or maybe we use this resentment to blame others for our failures in life, or we may hold onto this resentment as a reason for excluding someone dangerous from our lives in which case it genuinely helps us to do so. Or maybe when we're constantly pointing the finger of blame at others, it deflects attention from our own misdeeds. Or maybe by finding fault with others we feel more virtuous, more blameless.

There are loads of 'good' reasons for withholding forgiveness. There are limitless situations where it seems justified to hold a grudge and keep our defensive walls up.

From the personal to the political, the world is over-flowing with egregious and indefensible acts of horrific abuse and corruption on a macro and micro level.

How do you forgive the woman who killed your child while riding their bike because she was sending a text message while driving? How to you forgive the man who raped you when you were six years old? How do you forgive the corporation who polluted the river that was the lifeblood of an Amazonian tribe? How do you forgive the person who shot the last animal of an endangered species? How do you forgive the people who turned the gas on in the holocaust chambers? How do you forgive the sex slave trafficker who abducted your child? How do you forgive the President who rained missiles on children in a foreign city in the name of national security? How do you forgive the school bullies who drove your gay son to suicide? How do you forgive your best friend for having an affair with your spouse? How do you forgive your mother for telling you you'd never make it? Or forgive your father for walking out on your family?

FORGIVENESS AS A SPIRITUAL PATH

'They don't deserve my forgiveness!' our egos howl.

And you're probably right so why should you forgive? The simplest reason is because not doing so means walking through life beneath an ever-present black cloud whilst having a ball and chain attached to your ankles.

The question is not whether they deserve your forgiveness; it's about whether you deserve to be free of this trauma.

Here's another thing though. Holding onto our resentment can be a way of protecting ourselves by keeping distance between us and our abuser. If you are still in a position where you could be hurt, forgiveness could take away the only defence you have. That's something that your protective ego will never allow to happen. Other times, the act of withholding forgiveness feels empowering when it's the only thing you have to throw back at someone who's hurt you. It is, therefore, necessary to develop new ways to empower and protect ourselves before we feel safe to forgive. No one said this forgiveness stuff was straightforward.

The catch-22, however, is that our own healing cannot be completed until we're ready to forgive. That doesn't mean though, that you can bully yourself into forgiving before you're ready. Like grief, it is a process.

The process of forgiveness can take much more time, courage, and commitment when the transgression is larger, or when it happens repeatedly, or to whole groups of people, or to nature. It can take months, years, and decades to forgive, and when we are locked in the righteousness of our pain and hurt, there is an insidious illusion that these pains and hurts are our identity. In that space, it may even seem impossible to forgive what appears to be unforgivable: abuse, atrocities, and large-scale and intergenerational trauma.

True and heart-felt forgiveness is a critical part of the healing process but forcing yourself, through gritted teeth, to forgive prematurely can feel like another form of abuse for someone who already feels they've been robbed of choices and power. Nor will that result in true forgiveness.

So what do you do?

Simply decide to entertain the idea of beginning the process. This can start with just exploring the possibility and concept of forgiveness with no pressure on yourself to do it.

Also exploring how withholding forgiveness may be harming you.

The comedian, actor and author Russell Brand gives a wonderful summation of this in an interview that's been doing the rounds on Facebook. The interviewer asks Brand how he got past judgment and blame of his own parents.

Brand replied: "Of course people make mistakes but the older I get, the easier my childhood was. The more I recognise that my parents were just ordinary people, like me, making their way through life. By justifying your pain and by blaming, we recommit to the pain. 'Well of course I feel like this, this happened to me, that happened to me...' you're signing another contract to continue with the pain.

"If you say, 'okay those things happened but I want to let go of them now and move forward,' you have an opportunity to re-imagine your world and re-imagine your place within it.

"I'm sure terrible things have happened to people. People are abused, people are let down, people don't do what they should do as parents. People make all sorts of mistakes but by holding onto that pain you recommit to re-living it. Of course it's wrong that you were abused, if you were abused but what's even more wrong than that is that you continue to allow it to effect your consciousness now, in this moment, when you could be free."

WHAT IS FORGIVENESS?

How do we start the process of forgiving? First, let's establish what forgiveness is not.

As Anita Sanchez writes in her book, *The Four Sacred Gifts: Indigenous Wisdom for Modern Times* (Simon and Schuster), forgiveness is not forgetting.

> "Forgiveness is not condoning vile, ignorant or atrocious acts. Nor does it mean the perpetrator skips having to atone for any wrongdoing.
>
> "Contrary to what many people believe, to forgive does not mean you give up your power. To forgive does not negate the wrong that was done to you or the feelings you are experiencing.
>
> "The power to forgive the unforgivable does not mean that you are lacking confidence in yourself, or in your values and principles, or in your strengths. The power to forgive the unforgivable does not indicate weakness nor does it mean giving up on creating

justice for yourself or others who have been wronged on a small scale or on an unthinkably huge one.

"The power to forgive the unforgivable does not mean pardoning or helplessly accepting an act that is horrific against human beings, other species, or nature. It does not mean no longer requiring an apology, an assurance that mistreatment will not happen again, and even some kind of reparation for the mistreatment.

"Forgiving the unforgivable does not mean the avoidance of justice. It does not mean the mistreatment or the harm is forgotten. In fact, most of the acts that people think are unforgivable cannot be forgotten; they are remembered for us to learn from. Forgiveness is not about forgetting.

So, why should you forgive? Because it sets you free— emotionally, mentally, physically and spiritually.

"You can at last lay down the anger, hate, resentment, revenge, and distrust that is poisoning your body and your life.

"As you learn forgiveness, you learn compassion and empathy, creating the possibility to live as a whole human being, experiencing the joys of being alive and the joys of being in connection to people, earth, and spirit."

As both Brand and Sanchez so beautifully put it, forgiveness sets you free.

So are you ready to begin? First though, let me assure you I'm not going to make you forgive someone you don't want to.

Chances are that some, if not all, of the issues you are dealing with, involve someone else. Someone who, you perceive, did something or said something that has hurt or harmed you in some way. This could have been deliberate or it could have been inadvertent.

This person could be a parent, a teacher, a mentor, an abuser, a stranger, a friend, a loved one, a family member, a politician, a priest, a peer, a colleague, an employer, an authority figure... it could be a group of people, a community, a church group, a family. There are so many people involved in our lives.

You may have nursed your grudge or resentment for years. You may be certain to your core that this person is evil, wicked, despicable and unforgivable. And you may be right. It may be that this person does not deserve your forgiveness. Maybe what they did was truly egregious and unspeakable. Lord knows, we live in a world where people carry out unspeakable acts of atrocity and horror every day.

You may have very good reasons for holding tightly onto that resentment or grudge. It may be keeping you safe by putting distance between you and this person. It may help you feel empowered when this person took away your power in some way.

The anger and rage that still burns hot in your belly, when you remember, may be easier to feel than the raw and unbearably painful emotions and vulnerability that lay beneath these ones.

I invite you to hold onto that resentment, that hatred, for as long as you need it. I hope though, that in time you do get to a place where you feel safe to relax your grip on the resentment to which you're determinedly clinging.

THE RAGE BASEBALL BAT

Believe me, I get it. As much work as I've done on myself, as much as I talk about everyone being a divine spark of God, as much as I believe in love and light, as much as I believe in compassion as being the only approach we should take to anything... still, there are moments when I find my mental fingers curling once again around the resentment baseball bat that I would still like to swing at the skull of someone from my past. These moments are now fewer and farther between but I remember it was not that long ago that I would imagine, with graphic detail, smashing this person's skull in with my imaginary baseball bat as the rage and hurt bubbled up again from the pit of my stomach.

I know though, that the effort of holding this harsh resentment energy in my system is blocking me in so many other ways. It takes huge energy to hold onto heavy emotions like resentment, bitterness, rejection, revenge... it leaves us depleted in other ways. I know that while this energy still lives in my cells, in my heart, in my throat, in my belly, I am not free. This energy blocks my spiritual evolution. It keeps me stuck and stagnant. So you'd think I'd want to get rid of it, wouldn't you?

Yet it's still there. Much less than it used to be but some debris, some last little splinter, is still there, which means it is still serving a purpose.

I also know that, until I can completely forgive this person, it's me who remains trapped.

We do not forgive for the sake of the other person, we forgive for the sake of ourselves.

We forgive because by not forgiving, we are drip-feeding ourselves poison.

So, I'll be doing the following exercises again as well, in my continued efforts to loosen my grip even more on that resentment baseball bat.

My hope is that I can one day drop this bat completely.

I hope that I can one day see this situation and my life from a completely different, higher, perspective. That I can understand more clearly my own role in this drama. That I can see this person as a spark of God who is simply doing the best they can in this life, based on their own learnings, resources, experiences, and suffering.

I hope that one day, I not only forgive this person (and all those people against whom I harbour resentment) but find it in my heart to love them. To see them from the perspective of God. That's probably the day a few more grams of excess body fat will melt from my body.

I'm not quite there yet though, so shall we get on with these exercises?

EXERCISE: THE ENERGY OF FORGIVENESS

THIS IS AN exercise designed to release negativity from your energetic body. If we cling on to the emotions of grudge, resentment, hatred, bitterness, anger, and so on, this can over time manifest in the physical body as disease and ill health.

The energy of forgiveness is the most powerful energy of transmutation and liberation. You may find it helpful to do this exercise a few times before you feel fully cleared.

1. Be clear on who you are holding resentment towards. On a piece of paper that you can later burn if you wish, write down the main players against whom you're holding a grudge for having hurt, harmed or disappointed you.

2. Write down why you are angry with them, what they did to hurt you, how they hurt you, how you feel about it... write down everything that's in your heart about this person, or people, and the situation. Get it all down on paper and out of your system.

3. Feel the feelings about this rise up in your body. Let all these feelings bubble to the surface and let them come. Acknowledge these feelings and know that you have every right to feel the way you do.

Know that these stuck emotions are the very things keeping your vibration low and if you keep them held in your energy field, they will attract more situations and circumstances that trigger these same emotions. If nothing is changed or healed, you will always get more of what you've already got.

4. Say to the Universe: *'I now decide and declare that I am no longer holding onto any negativity in my energy body that is related to this issue. I choose to see that this person (or people) was just doing their best with the resources and experience that they had up to that point.*

'I am open to the idea that I played a part in creating and attracting this, even if I'm not sure how. I humbly accept the learning that this opportunity has given me and I forgive all aspects of it. This learning is now complete. I command that all vows, oaths and obligations related to this learning, across all lifetimes, are now completed and finished. I release all aspects of this issue and I am free.' Go outside and safely burn the piece of paper.

6. If you're suffering from guilt about something you did then the person you resentful towards is you. Do this exercise again but direct it to yourself as a journey towards self-forgiveness.

TAPPING SCRIPT: FORGIVING SOMEONE WHO DOESN'T DESERVE IT

TO TAP ON this issue, pick a person, group, or situation that has part of you crying, 'They don't deserve my love!' or 'They don't deserve my forgiveness!'

As you think of this, rate your resistance to forgiving on a scale from zero to 10, with 10 being the highest intensity. What's the emotion around this situation? Feel it in your body, and let's tap! Saying the set-up statement three times on the karate chop point of either hand:

Even though they don't deserve my love, and I just can't forgive them, I choose to relax and feel safe now.

Even though I just can't let this go, I can't condone this behaviour, they don't deserve my love, I choose to relax and feel safe now.

Even though part of me refuses to forgive them, I can't open my heart, it's just too hard, I love, accept and forgive myself.

Pause, take a breath and continue tapping:

EB: I can't let this go
SE: They don't deserve my love
UE: So I'm going to withhold it
UN: Since they don't deserve it
CH: They're not going to get it
CH: All this anger in my body
CB: All this bitterness towards them
UA: I just can't let it go
TH: I still feel so much emotion about this

EB: What they did was unforgivable
SE: Why should I be the one who has to forgive?
UN: Wouldn't that let them off the hook?
CH: They can't be allowed to get away with this
CB: They have to be held accountable
UA: So I will not forgive them!
TH: But holding onto this resentment is hurting me

Pause to take a couple of deep breaths. Tap on any other words or phrases that you feel you need to say and then continue...

EB: What if I could start to forgive them?
SE: For my sake if not for theirs
UE: What if I could release some of this resentment and anger?
UN: Wouldn't that be a relief!
CH: It's hard to keep this resentment fire burning inside me
CB: I'm so tired of being this angry and bitter
UA: It's me who would be freed by forgiving them
TH: And it's time for me to be free

EB: So maybe part of me could forgive them a little
SE: Even though they don't deserve it
UE: I can start to consider

UN: *Opening my heart*
CH: *Even though it feels so difficult*
CB: *This bitterness runs so deep*
UA: *I'm not sure I can let it go*
TH: *But what if I could?*

EB: *What would it take to move on from this?*
SE: *What would it take to finally let go of this hurt?*
UE: *Could I love them when they least deserve it*
UN: *Because that's when they need it most*
CH: *Feeling safe to let go of this now*
CB: *Feeling safe sharing my love*
UA: *Feeling safe opening my heart*
TH: *Choosing to be free*

Take a few deep breaths and check back in with the intensity of your bitterness and anger.

Look at your original number again, where is it now? Up, down or the same? If anything else came up for you while doing this script, tap on those new things now, be they memories, emotions, thoughts... keep tapping till you feel a shift and your emotional intensity comes down. We want to get your number to zero. If that doesn't happen today, come back to this issue daily until it shifts.

When you're bringing the session to an end, close your eyes, cross your hands over your chest, take a deep breath and say 'transform'.

In your mind's eye, imagine this new knowledge of how to live your day to day life without holding onto resentment pouring into every cell of your physical and energetic bodies until your whole being vibrates with this new frequency.

Take the time to visualise this happening. Watch as every cell of your body absorbs and reflects this new information. Watch your cells release the old patterns and witness the new choices being encoded into your DNA.

Slowly open your eyes onto a world in which you know what it feels like and how to forgive old hurts.

ACTION AND AFFIRMATION

Action: Forgiveness ritual

For this step, the action is a ritual so you're going to need a sacred space or altar. This can be just a small corner of a table, on a mantelpiece or window ledge if you're short of space.

Your altar is simply a collection of things that feel nourishing to your soul, this could include poems, candles, incense, feathers, crystals, stones, photographs, books, your Weight-Love journal, etc.

Light a candle and place it on your altar.

Write a list of all the people or situations you find it difficult to forgive. This can include individual people, groups of people or organisations, e.g., Monsanto, oil companies, paedophiles, Nazis, right wing extremists... You may even put your own name on this list if there are regrets from your own life.

At the bottom of the list, write:

'Just for today, I am open to the possibility that I can live without the weight of this anger and hurt.'

'Just for today, I am open to the possibility that I can forgive the unforgivable. Even though I'm not sure how.'

Roll this list up and place it on your altar. Spend a few minutes in quiet meditation.

Affirmation

Write the following affirmation on a postcard or post-it note and stick it where you'll see it at least once a day.

'I choose to see the love and light in every person and situation.'

STEP 14
DNA AND ANCESTRAL
TRAUMA

"The reason you feel lost? Because of lack of purpose. The way to discover purpose? To look at yourself and ask the higher aspect of yourself to reveal to you, through synchronicity, the nature of your purpose. And know that it will feel beautiful. And know that it will involve helping others." — Russell Brand, actor, author and comedian.[40] @rustyrockets

A message from the Spirit Collective:
Seeing your light
Dearest One,
Reconnection. Living light. Channelling light into this world.
This is ultimately expressing God in the physical world.
Live light.
How?
Intend it and ask. Slough off the vanity, fear, greed, darkness, sadness... all the emotional layers that block out your light like blankets draped over a glowing bulb.
Imagine a lightbulb secured at the top of a lampstand, shining brightly. Then a lamp shade is placed over the bulb to dim the light a little and make it softer. Next, a blanket is draped over the lampshade. The bulb still shines as brightly beneath these layers but it is less noticeable from the outside. Then another blanket is layered over the lampshade, and another and another. Until all

---

[40] https://www.facebook.com/21641548176/videos/257311258532639/

an external observer can see is what appears to be a large pile of blankets. Yet beneath these layers, the light bulb continues to shine brightly.

These blankets are the layers of your karma, which includes residue of other lives and the inherited experiences of your ancestors, ancient vows and oaths you or your ancestors took in many lives past, commitments, traumas, obligations, beliefs, decisions... all written on your soul and encoded into your DNA and therefore recreated, like an echo, in your experience in this life. Echoes from your past lives and echoes from your inherited genetic material.

Added to which are your own learnings from this life, the misinformed beliefs that you are not worthy, not enough, not deserving. The beliefs that life must be hard, that you must struggle... is it any wonder that you groan and stumble beneath the weight of these blankets?

How to remove these layers? How to shed the weight of the blankets and reveal your light? How to shine the Divine light of Source into this physical world of the Earth plane? Tools are available to you. The Divine always has a solution. The violet flame of Saint Germain is one such gift. We would urge you to make use of these tools, these gifts.

We would urge you to explore why you may be choosing to hold onto these blankets, what purpose are they serving you? What misinformed beliefs do they align with?

We would ask you to ask us to help you.

Just like the bulb fastened at the top of the lampstand, there are two options for the bulb. It can pull more power through from Source and set fire to these blankets to burn them away or it can have these blankets pulled off by a friend.

We can help remove these layers but you must ask for it and you must allow it. It is you who cling to your security blankets, believing they keep you warm and protected. In reality, you yourself are the Source of heat and light so you can never be cold and you do not need the blankets.

We love you.

FAT IS AN emotional issue. Excess fat on the body is the emotional made manifest in the physical.

It might get there via a circuitous route that detours through food intolerances and auto-immune disorders but if you follow that string down the rabbit hole all the way back to the root, there is ultimately an emotional layer of causality.

However, this idea that all physical symptoms, including excess weight, root from beliefs and emotional issues is a tough one for many people to grasp and accept. Especially when we take it one step further and even include events such as accidents or unprovoked attacks as being in some way the result of a belief or programme vibrating in our energetic body that attracts these things into our reality.

The next step from there is understanding that illness can also be the result of limiting beliefs we carry in our DNA that have been passed down to us from ancestors. Intuitive channel Wendy Kennedy touches on this in the documentary movie *Tuning in: Spirit Channelers in America.*

"The emotional body creates the physical template. All illness starts in the emotional field—without exception. If it's a genetic mutation, that starts in the emotional field and it is something that has been so generously left behind by one of your ancestors. They had a big emotional issue, a block, and it altered their genetic material and got passed down through the genetic line," says Kennedy, acting as a channel for information from higher dimensional beings.

"Many people carry with them, even throughout their life to their deathbed, resentments, guilt and worry, and that is where all physical illness comes from. From negative emotions that people even nurture.

"It all goes back to the emotions. The emotional body creates the physical reality so if you're talking about weight and health, how you are feeling about yourself is determining your physical body more so than what you're consuming and how you're exercising. Which is a very different way of thinking for many. Because you're conditioned to think it's all physical. But it's not. It's all emotional," says Kennedy.

FAT AND BROKE

Do you have too much fat on your body and not enough money in your life? It's a common partnership although, of course, it's not true for every person who struggles with their weight because you also get obese people who are very rich. That's why there is no cookie cutter solution to weight issues because nothing is true for everyone. As I've said before, my reasons for holding onto body fat are unique to me and to my experiences in this life, in my past lives, as well as to the experiences of my ancestors that I have inherited in my genetic coding.

288

You have experienced and inherited a whole load of different stuff however there are still common themes because the human condition dictates that we all face many of the same challenges. That's why psychics and clairvoyants generally get asked the same big four questions – love, money, career, and health.

However, weight issues and money issues often go hand in hand. People with weight issues often also have abundance issues. It makes sense when you consider the theme of 'lack'.

If someone feels like there just isn't enough for them, not enough food, money, love, support, attention, etc. then it may follow that they desperately hold onto whatever they do have; so they pack on weight from a perspective of survival. This behaviour can also be the result of ancestral coding or past life experiences.

For example, although I was born in New Zealand, most of my ancestors were Irish (thus the red hair, freckles and white skin) and they experienced life during the devastating famine caused by failed potato crops, also called the Great Famine or the Great Hunger. It was a time of mass starvation, disease, and emigration from Ireland between 1845 and 1852. About one million people died of starvation during this time and another million or so emigrated to countries like America to find work.

During my own weight healing journey (which I'm still on, by the way), I discovered that somewhere in my genetic coding, I was carrying the memories, emotions and beliefs of my ancestors around famine that were formed as a result of them living through this traumatic experience. This experience altered their genetic coding and this was passed on to me, written into my DNA. These subconscious fears of famine became part of my (many, many) reasons for clinging onto extra body fat because you never know when there'll be another potato famine!

If you're having doubts about how it could be possible that you're carrying memories and trauma from experiences of your ancestors, consider for a minute that there is so much more to these incredible physical and energetic vessels, that we call our bodies, than meets the eye.

We can all accept that it's possible to inherit physical characteristics like our great grandfather's hair colour or the shape of his nose. We can also stretch that to accept that people can inherit personality qualities and talents of their ancestors, our grandmother's artistic flair for example, or our great grandfather's sense of humour. However, we also inherit their emotional baggage and beliefs, as well as the emotional response to a trauma that they experienced. It gets passed down in our DNA.

This can explain why someone can have an inexplicable fear of water, perhaps an ancestor almost drowned (it has to be 'almost' because if they actually died from drowning then they would not pass on the subsequent genetic mutation as a result of the trauma).

It can also explain why people who are not of a religious persuasion themselves, still have deep-seated fears of purgatory and beliefs about sin. Ancestral inheritance is not the only reason for behaviours and phobias but it can be a contributor.

GENETIC PREDISPOSITION

Someone who has written a great deal about genetic predispositions that we inherit from our ancestors is Yvette Rose, author of *Metaphysical Anatomy*.

In an online interview with Wisdom of the North in 2016, Rose explains: "I realised in my work that... you are an expression of your ancestry."

"No one really realises that medical conditions and emotional patterns have a very big tendency of repeating every three generations from the mother's side," Rose said.

"So if you want to look at what's happening in your life and you're thinking, 'why am I feeling like this when nothing has really happened to me that justifies that?' Yes there are predispositions but the question would really be, 'what happened to grandma?' Because you already existed in your mother, when your mother was in the womb in your grandmother, so the stress that she was experiencing was already being programmed.

"There's all this juicy information being captured and plugged in so mum goes through her stress and you go through your stress and you have this big mess of 'okay, I'm having my experience but where do I stop and start and where does my mum's stuff stop and start?'

"You're having this collective experience and you accept these feelings as yours because you're feeling it so you think, 'it has to be mine', but it's not," Rose said.

When it comes to weight, an ancestral experience of famine, or other trauma involving a lack of food or starvation (war rationing, for example), can trigger this sense of feeling deprived but many other factors can also lead to this feeling or belief of deprivation.

When it comes to abundance—or a perceived lack of it—one of the most important themes is feeling deprived and this often has a direct relationship with weight issues.

When a person feels that there is not enough; when they feel deprived in some way, be this feeling deprived of money, food, services, love, attention, time, care, or something else, then they have a scarcity or poverty consciousness. As a result they vibrate at this frequency of 'not enough' and of 'lack'. They send this vibration out into the world and because the Law of Attraction is irrefutable, then this is the vibration that the universe mirror reflects back.

Conversely, if you really feel that you are prosperous, that you always have plenty, and that you are wealthy and abundant, then you're sending that vibration out into the world and so you attract even more prosperity. This goes in part to explain that old saying 'the rich get richer and the poor get poorer'.

How does a feeling of deprivation keep us fat? If you're vibrating at this frequency of lack and scarcity then you may turn to food for a whole host of possible reasons. For example, if someone is financially destitute and they don't know where their next meal is coming from, they will eat everything available at the time in case it's a long wait before the next opportunity to eat.

This is why some people will hoard food and over-eat to prevent feeling any deprivation. Also, people can use food to fill an emotional hole or emptiness that's caused by feeling deprived or neglected. When a person feels deprived, they may have a tendency to cling on to things, these things can be as varied as the fat on their stomachs or their dysfunctional relationships. It all stems from a place of insecurity.

How to tackle this? Ironically, you need to feel abundant in order to attract abundance. This can be monumentally hard to do though if you've just lost your job, if the rent or mortgage payment is due, and your credit cards are maxed out. In cases like this, it's about nudging the needle the other way, even just a small shift. This happens when you take time to notice the abundance and richness in your life. You may have to widen your definition of abundance as well, it's not just about money.

Abundance is every part of life where your needs are met—this includes friendship, health, laughter, sunshine or rain (rain nourishes the Earth and its vegetation), love that's offered to you from any source—pets, partners, peers... so it's about really starting to notice where abundance flows to you. And being thankful for that.

If you can get up out of bed by yourself and walk up a few stairs then you are already wealthier in health than millions of people on the planet who cannot do these things.

If you had breakfast this morning, then you are doing better than a lot of people. If you have access to a tap from which clean water flows then you have more than millions of people on this planet. If that water is hot, then you're ahead of many more millions.

If you are able to read the words on this page then you have something that 760 million adults on the planet do not have.

Even if you can't read the words on a page but you have the eyesight to see those words, then again you have a blessing. The blessing of vision. A blessing that millions of visually impaired people on this planet do not.

The key is not to feel bad about your blessings. The key is to feel thankful, grateful and appreciative of the many and varied ways the universe showers you with love.

TAPPING SCRIPT: CLEARING ANCESTRAL FAMINE

SIT QUIETLY, CLOSE your eyes and say to yourself: *'I'm terrified of starving,'* and *'I'm terrified of poverty'* and *'I'm terrified of not having enough'.*

Roll these phrases around and see how they feel in your body. How true or intense does this feel? Give this a number from zero to 10.

When you have your number, begin tapping. Start by saying the set-up statement three times while tapping on the karate chop point of either hand, taking a deep breath after each one.

Even though, part of me is clinging onto extra body fat for fear of famine and starvation, I still completely love and accept myself.

Even though, part of me is scared that there's not going to be enough so I need to save for a rainy day, I accept my feelings and love myself anyway.

Even though, part of me doesn't believe that I'll always have enough, I still profoundly love and accept myself.

Pause to take a deep breath and then continue tapping around the face and torso:

EB: Somewhere inside me there is a deep fear of famine and lack
SE: This deep terror of starving
UE: Somewhere in my DNA, I'm terrified of famine and starvation
UN: Poverty
CH: I'm terrified of starving
CB: Because it's happened before
UA: It's happened to me in past lives
TH: And it's happened to my ancestors

EB: The horror of famine can happen
SE: So part of me wants to be prepared for that
UE: I need to stockpile
UN: I need to make sure I've got reserves in
CH: I need to be ready for an emergency
CB: This extra weight will keep me alive in a famine
UA: This extra weight will protect me from starvation
TH: I feel safer when I have this extra weight with me

EB: I might die without this extra weight
SE: I know that can happen, it happens all the time
UE: People starve to death all over the world
UN: You never know what the future holds
CH: So it's safer if I store away as much as I can in case of disaster
CB: I feel protected and safer when I'm carrying extra weight
UA: Although, there are many downsides to holding onto this extra weight as well
TH: Carrying all this extra fat is tough on my body

EB: This extra weight hurts my joints and my organs
SE: My body has to work a lot harder with all this extra weight
UE: It might even cause me to die a lot sooner than I would without it
UN: That's probably more likely to happen than famine
CH: So it would be great if I didn't need to burden my body...
UA: ...with extra fat in case of an emergency
TH: Is there another way to survive famine?

EB: What if I didn't need to stockpile this extra weight?
SE: What if I had other options for surviving famine without carrying extra weight?
UE: Maybe my body already has built-in tools for tackling famine?

UN: Maybe all this extra weight just makes my body's job harder
CH: My body already knows how to survive famine...
CB: ... without me holding so much extra fat
UA: It has a built-in famine response that adjusts my body's chemistry
TH: It has already allowed for extra energy in emergency situations

EB: It doesn't need or want the many extra weight I've packed on
SE: That's like jumping into a lifeboat with so many suitcases that the lifeboat sinks
UE: So maybe this is the wrong way to prepare for famine
UN: Maybe some past experience of famine is written on my DNA
CH: That doesn't mean it will happen again in this life
CB: That time is in the past and over now
UA: I now live in an abundant universe
TH: I trust my body's wisdom in caring for me

EB: I trust that my body knows best how to look after itself
SE: I trust that my body has a vast array of tools for surviving
UE: So maybe I can let this extra body fat go now
UN: Maybe I don't need to be locked into the fear of famine
CH: It's like living life through the cross hairs of a loaded gun
CB: It's time to stop living from a place of fear
UA: It's time to start living from a place of love and safety
TH: I know what it feels like to always have plenty

EB: I know what it feels like to be abundant
SE: I know what it feels like to be prosperous
UE: I let go of the fear now
UN: I let go of the fat now
CH: I receive and accept the energy of abundance
CB: I receive and accept the energy of plenty
UA: I receive and accept the energy of prosperity
TH: I release the fear and the fat now

EB: I now cancel and delete any ancestral famine trauma in my DNA
SE: I release all fear of famine from every cell of my body now
UE: Part of me already knows how to live without fear of famine
UN: That part of me is informing the rest of me now
CH: This new information is pouring like white light into every cell of my physical and etheric bodies now
CB: My mind, body and spirit are now sparkling with this light

UA: I release all fear of famine from every cell of my body now
TH: And so it is

Check back in with your original number to see if it has shifted. Tap on anything that came up for you while doing this script. When you're bringing the session to an end, close your eyes, cross your hands over your chest, take a deep breath and say 'transform'.

In your mind's eye, imagine the inherited DNA code that carries the trauma of your ancestor's famine being switched off.

Take the time to visualise this happening. Watch as every cell of your body absorbs and reflects this new information. Watch your cells release the old patterns and witness the new choices being encoded into your DNA.

Slowly open your eyes onto a world in which you no longer hold an inherited fear of famine in your cells.

EXERCISE:
VIOLET FLAME

FOR THIS EXERCISE, we will invoke the power of the violet flame to transmute all our inherited ancestral baggage—not just for ourselves but also for our ancestors. An invocation is a call to Light that is transmitted from your heart to the heart of God instantaneously.

The violet flame is the key to individual and world transmutation. It works in microcosmic and macrocosmic worlds, from the smallest particle of matter to molecule, to mind, to materialisation.

The violet flame, or violet fire, is a gift from God and a tool of self-transformation. Its guardian for use on the Earth plane is Ascended Master Saint Germain. A powerful spiritual energy, this fire burns up karmic debt and negative energy. It helps us in all areas of life and yet too few people ever call on the power of this violet fire simply because they don't realise it's available to them or they do not believe in such things thanks to the five-sensory-blinkered mainstream culture of the developed world. If we regularly visualise ourselves standing in this ball, or flame, or bonfire, of violet light and feel the violet fire passing through all of our consciousness—our mind, our feelings, our emotions—we can undo psychological problems, hang-ups, depressions, records of the past.

The Spirit world wish more people would call on this energy to transmute their karma and transform their energy and their lives. In fact, I get the feeling that they are a little exasperated that such a powerful tool is so rarely utilised on the Earth plane when it is there for using at any moment. Spirit see and hear us struggling with our lives yet not realising that we have this powerful tool at our fingertips that could change everything. It's like watching a blind person starving while they sit near a table groaning with a smorgasbord of food.

How to use the violet flame

Find a place and time that you won't be disturbed, sit comfortably with your spine straight, your legs and arms uncrossed and feet flat on the floor. Although sitting cross-legged is fine as well if you'd rather. Rest your hands on your upper legs, with palms facing upwards. You may like to slightly tilt your head forward with your tongue on the roof of your mouth. Say out loud, or in your head:

'I call on the power of the violet flame to transmute the energies contributing to the excess weight on my body now. I call on the power of the violet flame to transmute the trauma of my ancestors' famine experience.'

Then, take a deep breath and repeat:

'I RAISE the power of the violet flame, I RAISE the power of the violet flame, I RAISE the power of the violet flame...'

Keep repeating this phrase like a mantra but stop when you've had enough. Meanwhile, focus on visualising the violet flame in your mind's eye. As you do so, bring your awareness to your third eye, the area between your eyebrows.

See yourself in front of a large violet bonfire. Visualise the soft, dancing flames flickering and undulating. Notice the many shades of violet that appear and fade, dark violet, light violet, shimmering violet, silky violet. Shot with pinks and purples.

Next, see yourself stepping into these flames and imagine they feel soft and caressing and warm. See your body as transparent and see the flames working into the most microscopic cells of your being. See the flames flowing under your feet, curling around your legs and arms, passing through your body and over your head. Imagine breathing the flames into the deepest part of you. Watch as this fire instantly transmutes all the energy within you that is not for your highest and best. Witness yourself being purified at the deepest level. See the flames permeate every cell and atom of your body, mind, emotions, subconscious, and memory.

Do this every day for a week for five to fifteen minutes and take note of any shifts in your life and experiences.

Using the violet flame for others

This flame can be used for cleansing others as well as cleansing situations, animals, places and things. I often cleanse my home with the violet flame, taking my time to see our whole house engulfed in this flickering violet light. I watch in my mind's eye as this energetic fire cleans the walls, ceilings, carpets of our home. I send the flame into every corner, under every bed, up into the attic and under the floorboards to the very foundations of the house. I watch in my mind's eye as the flames burn away all the negative, stale, old, stagnant energy that gets stuck in corners and seeps into the walls and furnishings. There are no limits to how you can use the violet flame. Use it to cleanse a room where people have argued, use it to cleanse your workspace, see the whole Earth being cleansed in this fire, send it to loved ones, or use it on pets. Most of all though, use it on yourself.

ACTION AND AFFIRMATION

Action: Paying respects

If you know where any of your ancestors are buried, visit their grave or memorial and thank them for all the talents and wisdom you've inherited from them. If it's possible, offer them a gift such as flowers (but don't leave plastic!). Ask Spirit to bless their souls.

If you're unable to visit their resting place, light a candle on your altar in their memory and offer them a prayer of thanks and blessing.

Affirmation

Write the following affirmation on a postcard or post-it note and stick it where you'll see it at least once a day.

'I know how to honour my ancestors without recreating their burdens and struggles.'

STEP 15
FOOD, LOVE AND VIBRATION

"You are a light being and your body is a portal to bring Heaven to Earth." — Vanya Silverten, intuitive healer; *www.vanyasilverten.com*

"Emotions are feeling states that well up from inside of us spontaneously. Wanting to 'control' one's emotions is a desire, luckily often frustrated, to repress and deny a part of ourselves that is simply expressing itself."
— Javier Regueiro, author of *San Pedro Huachuma: Opening the Pathways of the Heart; www.javierregueiro.com*

A message from the Spirit Collective: Food is Love
Dearest One,
Food is Mother Nature's love offering to you. It is God's love offering to you.
The planet supports you. She grows foods and herbals that can heal all your ailments. This wisdom has been lost or ignored in favour of drugs that mask instead of heal. Cover-ups. Masking agents. Denial and secrecy.
It reflects a culture of secrecy and hiding.
Shrouding in darkness when what is needed is light. In all senses. Look to the light. Be light. Eat light.
Blessings, gratitude, appreciation. These are lighter energies.
Food is connection. When you continue to over fill your bodies with processed foods, you are searching for spiritual nourishment that these foods cannot provide.

They instead offer numbness, disconnection, illness.

Everything is energy. Food is energy. In all senses of the word.

Food provides energy and food comprises energy. On a physical level, your body converts food through complex biological and energetic processes into fuel. These processes are not fully understood by your scientists however the energy of food is also transmuted by you; by your energy and intention. This energy is then sent back into the world as your love or your hate, your passion or your lethargy, your joy or your resentment.

When your vibration is raised, you choose high vibration foods; foods of light. As well, you can transmute low vibration foods.

Saying a prayer, even over what you would call junk food, enlivens it somewhat. We say that your attitude to the food is more important that the molecular make-up of the food. Food has energy. You are able to convert this energy. Whether or not this energy is used for your benefit or your detriment is up to you.

You can eat the most organic, lovingly prepared dish of vegetables and wholefoods but if you do so with bitterness in your heart, with anger, with frustration pouring out of you and into the world, this beautiful dish cannot lighten you in the way it could if you approached it with gratitude and appreciation.

However it is more likely that a bitter and angry person would not be drawn to eat this light, high vibration food as it clashes too much with their own energetic vibration. They will instead gravitate towards low vibration, mass produced, factory processed food-like products that do not contain the love and energy of human hands and care. This food matches their view of the world as a harsh, uncaring and scary place.

It is no coincidence that people feeling emotions such as hopelessness, despair, frustration, guilt, shame, and anxiety, are drawn to foods and substances that match this vibration. Alcohol, drugs, cigarettes, and processed foods made with factory-farmed animals.

Choosing to care what you put in your body is choosing to care about yourself. You only do this when you love yourself enough. When you do not love yourself enough, it is only because you do not see who you really are. You do not comprehend your Divinity. Because if you could see yourselves as we see you, your magnificence, your power, your limitless capacity for Love, you

would no more feed yourself toxins than you would feed petrol to your baby instead of breast milk.
We love you.

AS THE AUTHOR and angel expert, Kyle Gray, said in an interview, high vibration is happy, loving, kind and generous. Low vibration is feeling angry, irritated, intolerant etc. When you raise your vibration, you consciously choose to move into these higher vibrational states. There are various ways to raise your vibration, including through the body.

"How you treat your body has everything to do with your spiritual practice," Gray says, "simply because it's the home of your soul."

Honour your body as befits the temple of your soul. And the soul, of course, is of God/Creator/Universal Energy, etc. Honour your body temple with appreciation, love, tender care, and nourishment. Let your foods be the best quality available and may you be appreciative of them. Choose clothes, creams, lotions and cleansers that are supportive and non-toxic to your body.

As mentioned by The Spirit Collective in the channelled information for this step, choosing to care what you put in and on your body is choosing to care about yourself; is choosing to value yourself. You only do this when you love yourself enough.

When you do not love yourself enough, it is only because you do not see who you really are, which is a Divine spark of God. As a result, we feel unworthy of nourishment and nurture—which are expressions of Love. When we do not believe we are worthy of nourishment (worthy of Love), we may starve ourselves, we ration ourselves, we feed ourselves nutritionally empty substances, or we develop digestive issues. When this happens, we are, at some level, refusing even to accept the love of the Earth through the nourishment She provides. So food passes through our systems undigested. There are other reasons why we may be resistant to loving ourselves and these include having a corrupted view of love.

THE CORRUPTION OF LOVE

Ah yes, love. That many splendored thing that has been so distorted and corrupted through human abuse of the concept. Love has been manipulated into something that can be traded, earned, leveraged, and used as a bargaining tool—*'if you really loved me you would...'*

But true, divine and unconditional Love does not come with ties and conditions or limits. Nor is it given with ties, conditions or limits. Which is why so many of us are confused about Love. We've been mostly exposed to the conditional type. We've been taught that to receive love, we have to behave in a certain way. Most of us, then, grow up believing that we're not worthy of love, having judged ourselves as failing to meet the conditions. Or we've subconsciously decided not to accept love because the price is too high.

This translates into a screwed-up relationship with both food and our bodies because we redirect this lack of love onto ourselves. We over-eat to feel better—temporarily—and we over-eat to create excess weight on our bodies. We can then turn the blame on our bodies for why we feel unloved and unworthy. By doing so, we bring an emotional problem into the physical. Our lack of love worthiness becomes quantifiable in grams of body fat. *'Well, of course no one loves me, look at how fat and unattractive I am. If only I could lose this weight, then I'd be loved and happy.'*

In fact, the unworthiness came first. We've simply tried to make sense of our painful feelings by turning them into fat on our bodies. The twist in this tale comes when we are subconsciously holding onto the excess weight as an excuse for rejecting the love we see as conditional.

So this becomes: *'Well, of course no one loves me, look at how fat and unattractive I am (and, phew, thank goodness for all this fat because it's protecting me from conditional love that demands so much of me in return).*

We're so distrustful of love we don't even offer it to ourselves without conditions attached. *'I will love myself when I'm thinner but until then, the punishment and deprivation continues...'* we tell ourselves. *'Screw you then,'* replies another part of ourselves, *'you can keep your stupid love if it's conditional. And I am having that cake as a love substitute...'*

Our resentment and sense of rejection hold the excess weight in place. So we do not nourish ourselves with wholefoods from Mother Earth, instead we cram our poor bodies with chemicals and junk in a bid to numb our painful feelings. The way out of this prison is to understand the difference between conditional love and unconditional Love; to reconnect with Spirit and with Mother Earth, and to feel worthy of receiving their unconditional Love.

It's about reconnecting with your own divinity and understanding at a cellular level that you were born magnificent and worthy with nothing to prove. Does a priceless diamond have to do anything to prove its 'diamondness'? No. It is a diamond pure and simple. It can be nothing other than a diamond. You could cover it in dirt to hide its brilliance but ultimately it remains a diamond underneath.

THE MANY FORMS OF LOVE

All the different ways people show positive emotion to us, are ultimately expressions of love. Affection is a form of love, as is help, compliments, gifts, attention, praise... if you have an issue with receiving any of these things then the thing you really can't fully receive is love.

I would extend this to also include nourishment and nurturing. To our subconscious mind, nurturing and nourishment is love. The first experience we had of being loved was bound up with being nurtured and nourished by our mothers and fathers.

All pleasures revolved around the mouth. Having something in our mouth, such as our mother's breast or a bottle teat, has us feeling loved and nourished. This is our first experience of nurturing. It's why we suck our thumbs as children.

If we experience a conflict or trauma at this early developmental stage, it can leave us with an oral fixation. Such a 'conflict' could be something as simple as being weaned from our mother's breast milk too early; having our hungry cries ignored, or just having our mum or our dad finish our feeding session too early, before we were satisfied.

People who did not, for whatever reason, experience being loved and nourished by their mothers and fathers as babies, may have issues with feeling worthy of love as adults. While at the same time they crave this loving connection and so offer themselves inadequate substitutes for love, such as food.

As we grow up, such an experience can manifest as an ongoing subconscious search for the oral stimulus and satisfaction that was denied us as babies. In other words, according to psychologists such as Dr Sigmund Freud, we have an oral fixation. From here we can manifest addictions from food to sex to shopping, and more.

BARRIERS TO RECEIVING LOVE

Perhaps we can't or won't receive love because, in our past, love was not given unconditionally by, say, our parents. Perhaps it was only fully offered to us on the condition we met certain expectations, or behaved in a certain way. Receiving love was conditional so now we refuse to accept love because either, we don't feel we've earned it, or because we fear it comes with obligations, ties, and conditions — such as having to behave in way we don't feel like behaving.

This is how our barriers to receiving love, even from ourselves, are built. The first foundation stone in our love barrier is distrust, explains Teal Swan in her video *How To Receive*[41].

"When we distrust someone's motive in offering love, we fear the consequences of letting our guard down so we cannot open up to receive anything from them. For many of us, the people who offered us love in our early life did not give this love freely or in a pure way. So now, when we are offered love, we feel panicked or obligated or unsafe," says Swan.

We believe, therefore, that we were flawed in order to justify the way we were treated as children. To let ourselves be loved and valued for who we really are means accepting that we were not loved like we deserved to be loved as children.

As children, we had to accept this flawed version of ourselves because we were so reliant on our parents for, literally, our survival. Also, we idolised our parents and so, if they treated us badly, we had to find a way to blame ourselves for it because it could not be our parents' fault. Our idols could not fall from their pedestals without our world crumbling with them. Blaming ourselves was the safer option. When children are abused by their parents, they do not stop loving their parents, they stop loving themselves.

So we install beliefs in our subconscious programming that then direct and shape our life and our experiences. Beliefs like, '*I am not enough*', '*I am invisible*', '*I am not worthy*', '*I am a disappointment*', '*I am a failure*' and so on. From here, we either decide that we do not deserve love, or we decide that we do not want love because it comes with painful consequences.

Both are intrinsically flawed because they do not allow for the reality that we ARE Love. Pure and unconditional Love. We are Love yet we have corrupted beliefs about love.

People who are unable to receive love also have a difficult time with receiving help. These people don't like to ask for help and so they don't get much help. Not because there is none available but they believe the world is against them and they must struggle uphill alone to get what they want. They don't even see help when it's offered. If they do see it, they don't trust it, thinking there's a dangerous ulterior motive.

---

[41] https://youtu.be/F6yiEuEYo3I

These people may feel unworthy of help (love), or they think that by accepting help they are showing they're incapable, or that by accepting help they are accepting the strings attached. So if someone offers them help, their first response is something like, 'oh no, I'm fine, honestly. Thanks anyway but I can manage. I wouldn't want to put you out...' etc. By responding in this way they also deny the person offering the help the chance to do something that makes them feel good about themself.

Love that is given to get something back is not love. It is an attempt to control, which is itself a symptom of fear. So fear is masked as love.

Beliefs that are barriers to love:

'Love makes me vulnerable and gives someone power over me'

This is true when the idea of love comes with leverage—guilt, duty, or debt. Strings attached, in other words. When someone gives you anything that comes with strings attached, it feels like entrapment. Love becomes a Trojan horse.

'I'm not worthy of love'

When we were treated in an unloving way by our parents, we decide something is wrong with us—there must be, we think, otherwise why would they treat us that way, we conclude. So we do not feel good enough for someone to love.

'I don't deserve the love I'm getting'

We believe we must earn or achieve something in order to be loved. If we don't, we are bad and will be punished by the Universe (God). So if we get love that we don't believe we deserve, we get panicked that punishment is soon to follow. This can be a reason for why people sabotage good relationships.

'I must reciprocate'

We believe love must be equal so we can't be guilted or entrapped. If someone gives us something, we think, 'oh no, what do I owe them in return?' We would prefer not to have love if there is a hefty or unpleasant price to pay for it.

'I always lose the people and things I love'

This is based on a previous experience where we lost love. One of the most painful experiences we can have is having love and then losing it. On a subconscious level, this creates a scar and a belief that it's better not to have love at all than to have it and lose it (death, divorce, disapproval, breakup). Or it's better and safer not to accept something that can be taken off us.

If you distrust love, do not expect yourself to trust love that is given to you. This can manifest in our physical lives as an ongoing commitment to dieting, which is, essentially, an ongoing commitment to rationing the supply of nourishment and love we offer to ourselves.

What do you do? First, you recognise all the ways you're turning away from love and support. In your Weight-Love Journal, write down this question:

'How do I turn away from receiving love and support?'

Then write down everything you can think of in answer to that question. Don't query what pops into your head, just write it all down, even if it's something *like 'I am a unicorn in a parallel dimension who farts love clouds to create the atmosphere'*. Who knows, maybe that's true... or maybe it's your ego throwing up screens to avoid you going deeper into your subconscious. In which case, you need to push through all those ego blocks to get to the layers beneath, so keep writing.

Maybe though, it's true in a metaphoric sense. Our subconscious, our Higher Selves, and Spirit often communicate with us in symbols, or images, or by sparking memories. Or perhaps Spirit is just trying to make you laugh, which will raise your vibration to allow deeper communication to follow. My point is, don't dismiss anything that pops into your head, it may be a piece of the jigsaw you're building, even if you don't understand it. To give you an example, here's what I wrote when I did this exercise:

Q. How do I turn away from receiving love and support?
A. I change the subject to deflect attention from myself. I'm uncomfortable about receiving compliments so usually dismiss the compliment in some way, like the other day when Haylie told me I looked good and in response I screwed up my face and replied, 'Hardly, I only changed my shirt...'
I steer clear of social media because I don't like the attention of Likes and comments. I don't bother with regular haircuts or buying myself

nice things, like pretty underwear because it seems like a waste of money.

I almost never ask for help and I'm uncomfortable with accepting help that is offered. I don't charge enough for my services and I never earned what I was worth when I worked for others, I was afraid to ask for more money for fear of losing my job. When I do work for someone, I over compensate. I do more than what is being paid for to exceed expectations.

When you start identifying and recognising some of the ways you're rejecting the various forms of love that are offered to you, the shift begins.

TAPPING SCRIPT: RECONNECTING TO MOTHER EARTH

TO TAP ON this issue, think about how disconnected you feel from your natural self, your body, and from Mother Earth. Then, choose a number from zero to 10 that matches this sense of disconnection, with 10 being the strongest.

Start tapping by saying the set-up statement three times on the karate chop point of either hand:

Even though I feel disconnected from my natural self, and my body, I relax and forgive myself.

Even though I feel disconnected from the Earth, I honour myself and my feelings.

Even though I feel disconnected from Love, I choose to love and accept myself completely.

Pause to take a breath and then continue tapping around the points on the face and torso:

EB: Somewhere down the track
SE: I disconnected from my natural self

UE: Sometime in my life
UN: I disconnected from Mother Earth
CH: I disconnected from my spiritual self
CB: I disconnected from Spirit
UA: I disconnected from Love
TH: I disconnected from who I really am

EB: I disconnected
SE: I feel separate
UE: I feel alone
UN: I feel isolated
CH: I feel judged
CB: I feel lacking
UA: I feel unworthy
TH: I feel disconnected

EB: I've forgotten who I really am
SE: Forgotten who I really am
UE: Forgotten who I really am
UN: Forgotten who I really am
CH: I've forgotten who I really am
CB: Forgotten
UA: Who I really am
TH: I've become disconnected from my natural self

EB: I've fed my body fake foods
SE: Artificial and synthetic foods
UE: Preservatives, pesticides, and chemicals
UN: Plastic-wrapped, food-like substances
CH: I forgot what a divine gift my body is
CB: But I'm starting to remember that now
UA: And I choose to reconnect
TH: To my natural self and the natural world

Pause to take several deep breaths before continuing tapping around the face and torso:

EB: What if
SE: ...the road back to reconnecting
UE: ...with who I really am
UN: Starts with reconnecting to the Earth

CH: *Remembering my connection to the planet*
CB: *Re-knowing my connection to the natural world*
UA: *What if my body is my reconnection point*
TH: *What if foods from Mother Earth*

EB: *Can awaken this connection*
SE: *Wholefoods made by Mother Earth*
UE: *Are Her gifts of Love*
UN: *To accept that nourishment*
CH: *Is to accept Love*
CB: *To be nourished*
UA: *Is to be loved*
TH: *By Mother Earth*

EB: *I choose to accept this love energy*
SE: *I choose to honour my body*
UE: *With foods from Mother Nature*
UN: *I choose to accept the energy of love*
CH: *From natural foods*
CB: *And I choose to*
UA: *Send this love back into the world*
TH: *Through my thoughts, words and actions*

EB: *I choose to appreciate*
SE: *The love I receive from the Earth*
UE: *I choose to be grateful*
UN: *For the nourishment offered to me*
CH: *By Mother Earth*
CB: *I am so grateful*
UA: *For Her abundance*
TH: *And the connection to my natural self*

EB: *I choose to honour the love*
SE: *I receive from Mother Earth*
UE: *By using the energy of that love*
UN: *To send more love out into the world*
CH: *I receive Her loving nourishment*
CB: *And I give love back*
UA: *Through my words and deeds*
TH: *I am part of this Divine flow*

Take a few deep breaths and check back in with your sense of disconnection. Look at your original number again, where is it now? Up, down or the same? If anything else came up for you while doing this script, tap on those new things, be they memories, emotions... keep tapping till you feel a shift.

When you're ending the session, close your eyes, cross your hands over your chest, take a breath and say 'transform'.

In your mind's eye, imagine this new knowledge of what it feels like and how to be connected to All That Is, pouring into every cell of your physical and energetic bodies until your whole being vibrates with this new frequency.

Take the time to visualise this happening. Watch as every cell of your body absorbs and reflects this new information. Watch your cells release the old patterns and witness the new choices being encoded into your DNA.

Slowly open your eyes onto a world in which you know what it feels like and how to be connected to who you really are.

EXERCISE: BLESS YOUR FOOD

IT WAS ONCE commonplace for people to sit together at meal times and, before eating, give thanks for the food they were about to receive.

As the popularity of organised religion has waned in mainstream culture, the practise of giving thanks and saying grace before eating has died away as well.

This is one of those 'throwing the baby out with the bath water' situations. I am not a big fan of organised religion. I believe the main religions of the world have managed to take something pure and beautiful and twist it into something oppressive, manipulative and controlling, at times downright hateful. They operate from a space of fear, offering us a false version of God that's essentially a Father Christmas figure for adults. *'He knows when you've been bad or good...'*

At the roots of all religion are the tenets of real spirituality, unconditional love, compassion, unity and inclusion. Unfortunately, we've lost sight of these values along the way and instead chosen to fixate on things like who, or how, other people choose to love. Rather than focus on our many similarities, we've chosen to focus on our minor differences. So I understand when people want to completely disassociate themselves from all the hypocrisy and trappings of organised religion. I understand, then, why prayer and the saying of grace, or giving thanks, before a meal has fallen out of favour.

However, we need to claim back the power of prayer. It has been usurped. The power of prayer does not belong to the organised religions that have so utterly corrupted the message of Creator / Divine Source / God / Goddess... the power of prayer belongs to every person on this planet. It is our divine birthright to communicate with the Divine and Compassionate Intelligent Energy that governs this universe. This Energy resides within every cell of our body. It is part of us. It is part of everything.

We are co-creators with this Energy and we are constantly channeling this Energy to create our lives. Food is connection to this Energy. Real food connects you to the planet, to Mother Earth, to the Divine Source that flows through these real foods.

Blessing your food is really important. By doing so you raise its vibration and show respect and gratitude to the Earth, the plants, the animals, the winds, waters, soils and sunlight that provided you with this nourishment. When we are thankful for our food abundance, we are spinning and weaving an experience of more appreciation and more abundance.

This is, again, part of the Law of Attraction and being in denial of its effects is as useful or effective as being in denial of gravity. Your exercise for this step, therefore, is to consciously bless and give thanks for everything you consume going forwards, from the water you drink to the food you eat.

The following is a prayer that can be used, adapted however you wish, to say before consuming anything. Don't just say grace before the healthy meals you eat though; give thanks for every food you choose to invite into your body. Yes, even if you're binge-eating a box of donuts, be thankful for their sweetness, for the pleasure of their smell and the hit of dopamine to your brain, be thankful for the abundance you enjoy that enabled you to buy them. Be mindful of each bite.

Dear Lord, Creator of All That Is, thank you for blessing this food I am about to eat.

Thank you for blessing all the people, plants, animals and insects whose efforts and sacrifice contributed to my receiving this nourishment. Thanks to the sun, the winds and the waters. Please help me use the energy of this sustenance to contribute to the world in a way that is worthy of these efforts and sacrifices.

Thank you for clearing, removing, the negative energies of people who have handled this food, as well as for clearing any negative energies within this food that have been transferred from any other living being.

Thank you for ensuring anything in this food that is detrimental to my health and wellbeing passes through my system harmlessly and is excreted.

Thank you for ensuring my body absorbs maximum nourishment and benefit from this food.

Thank you for energising this food with your unconditional Love and Light.

Amen

Now, with your eyes closed, visualise these things happening in your mind's eye. See the harmful energies from the food or water being cleansed, see the people and animals or plants involved in producing your food receiving unconditional love and light. This may include thousands of people - the farmers, the harvest labourers, the packers, the truck drivers, the shop staff who display it, the check-out staff who handle your money.

If you're drinking a cup of coffee, imagine the people who grew the plants, imagine the person picking the beans, imagine the beans being cleaned, roasted, ground, packaged, transported. Imagine the people who work in marketing and promotion of the final product. Imagine the drivers and pilots who haul the product between countries and cities. Imagine the people who stack it on the shop shelves.

Depending on what you're eating, you may see the bees and insects that helped pollinate the plants, you may see the rain that watered the soils, you may see the sunshine that nourished the plants—know too that you are consuming sunshine when you eat plants, and that the sun's rays contain information and healing properties of which our scientists, to date, remain completely clueless. This is why food grown under artificial lighting does not nourish us in the way that organic food grown in nature heals and nourishes us. Food isn't just about our physical bodies; food is spiritual energy that heals our spirits and souls. It rebalances our energy systems and reconnects us to All That Is.

Love yourself enough to nourish your divine body temple with the best foods you can find. When you do this you are, essentially, making an offering of love to God / Creator/ Spirit.

I would recommend doing the full prayer above whenever possible but at times when you need something quick and private, make an agreement with Creator / God / Allah / Divine Source / The Universe... that when you whisper, or think, or say, the first line, this is shorthand for the whole prayer.

If you eat something and forget to bless it first, no problem, just say *'Creator of All That Is, thank you for blessing the food I've just eaten...'* Make gratitude for your nourishment a habit.

ACTION AND AFFIRMATION

Action: Fruitful labours
Get a piece of fruit, something you can hold like a banana, apple, pear, strawberry, kiwifruit, etc. Close your eyes and hold it in your hands. Imagine that the cells of your body are communicating with the cells of the fruit. Imagine that the fruit is understanding what nutrition and healing you most need and is adjusting its cellular and energetic structure to be a better match to your needs on every level, emotionally, physically and spiritually. Deeply inhale the smell of this fruit. Send a prayer of thanks for this nourishment and slowly, mindfully, gratefully, eat the fruit. Imagine its energy merging with yours and raising your vibration.

Affirmation
Write the following affirmation on a postcard or post-it note and stick it where you'll see it at least once a day.

'I nourish my body and soul with the food and love provided by Mother Earth.'

STEP 16
RECONNECT WITH SPIRIT

"Why is there illness, why is there war? A malfunction in thinking. Humans do not think correctly, they think in opposition to themselves and therefore because God is within them, and God is a creator, God creates every thing they feel and think. When they realise that everything is being created because they want it to be created and when they take responsibility for that, they'll see the divinity in their creation and then their creation will move into divinity consciousness. God is everything. Everywhere around you, loving you unconditionally, always there." — Shamen Durek, spiritual guide and healer. @ShamenDurek

A message from the Spirit Collective: Reconnection
Dearest One
You are already always connected to God. You never stopped being connected to God.
You are like the drop of sea water that asks how it may reconnect with the ocean. It is already part of this awesome power. It has the full might of this awesome power at its disposal.
We suggest you ask a different question of yourself. Ask yourself, 'how am I choosing to disconnect from God?'
To feel your connection with All That Is, Divine Spirit, Source, we offer you these steps.
Sit quietly. Close your eyes.
Go within.
Ask that the energy of All That Is makes its presence felt in your body.

Ask this energy to fill you at a cellular level.
Notice the sensations.
Understand that this energy is always within you, whether or not you are aware of it.
This energy is part of you. Is you.
We love you.

AS I SAID towards the start of this book in chapter 10, 'Dieting, Domination and Disconnection', the obesity epidemic is a red herring. The real epidemic is disconnection, division, separation, isolation, despair, and loneliness through disconnection from our spiritual selves and from our natural selves. We believe ourselves to be separate from God and therefore we are in pain. Anything that is not true creates pain.

By putting all our focus on what goes in our mouths, we are looking in the wrong direction for the cure to our woes.

We have become disconnected from who we really are, which is divine sparks of God. We've forgotten that we are powerful co-creators who are in partnership with the intelligent consciousness of All That Is. That this intelligent consciousness flows through every cell of our body and is constantly creating our reality based on our vibration, our resonance.

Excess body fat is the physical manifestation of emotional and psychological baggage—both our individual separation from Spirit or Divine Source as well as our collective separation. When you lighten the load on your soul, this is reflected in your physical body.

When we lighten up emotionally, we lighten up physically. When we reconnect to Spirit, we enlighten. We let light in. We remove the blocks that are covering up our light. And our light is Divine Source.

Which is all well and good but how do you actually do that when you've got no idea how to start?

One way to start is by exploring and noticing all the ways you choose to disconnect from Divine Source, your natural self, the Earth, in every minute of every hour of every day.

Here are a few examples:

You disconnect when you abuse, criticise, or neglect to nourish, your body or yourself.

You disconnect when you collude in the harm done to Mother Earth.

You disconnect when you deny your divinity and magnificence.

You disconnect when you deny your spirituality.

You disconnect when you suppress your feelings.

You disconnect when you silence your voice.

You disconnect when you move away from what brings you joy.

You disconnect when you deny yourself pleasure.

You disconnect when you turn a blind eye to suffering.

You disconnect when you believe that you're powerless to alleviate suffering.

You disconnect when you blame God for your misfortune.

You disconnect when you place blame externally for your misfortune, be this your parents, the government, people on benefits, terrorists, gays, liberals, rednecks, gypsies, teenage mothers, etc.

You disconnect when you ignore the rhythms, cycles and seasons of Mother Nature.

You disconnect when you ignore your body's messages, for example, using stimulants to stay awake when your body wants to sleep, or forcing more food down when your stomach is full.

You disconnect when you become a slave to time, routine, or obligations.

You disconnect when you project hatred and judgment into the world in the form of thoughts, words or deeds. This includes everything from gossip and complaining, to physical violence.

You disconnect when you rebuff compliments.

You disconnect when you numb yourself with gambling, television, online gaming, food, drugs, stimulants, social media, shopping, etc.

You disconnect when you compare yourself with others, either favourably or unfavourably.

You disconnect when you make yourself and your needs a low priority.

You disconnect when you fill your life with clutter.

You disconnect when you cease to communicate with the people around you.

You disconnect when you rely on external sources for your information and opinions, your TV, social media, computer...

You disconnect when you consume hateful or fear-based media ('celebrities with cellulite'... for example)

You disconnect when you are a passive consumer instead of an active creator.

You disconnect when you deny another living creature's free will agency.

You disconnect when you deny another person's humanity.
You disconnect when you hold grudges and resentment.
You disconnect when you refuse to forgive. Especially yourself.

RECONNECT WITH THE NATURAL WORLD

Consciously connecting with Spirit (aka God, Great Mother, Allah, Creator, Divine Intelligence, Universe, All That Is...) is made out to be much more difficult than it needs to be.

The energy of All That Is flows through everything in the natural world so one of the most powerful ways to revive our connection to Spirit is through the power of nature.

Sadly, in our modern world of concrete skyscrapers we have forgotten just how potent, life-changing and healing it is to simply be in the natural world.

We are part of this universe and part of this planet. By just putting our bare feet on Mother Earth we 'plug in' to her energy. It rises up within us and rebalances our circadian rhythms, we are 'grounding' or 'earthing' when we do this.

Our bodies and our energy fields are part of the energy of the Earth. When we reconnect with this earth energy, our bodies and minds are reset and healed and we release any stored up negative energy—static electricity, if you will—back into the earth.

Mother Earth is endowed with electrons that we absorb through the soles of our feet. This is like taking antioxidants through your feet. It helps you sleep better and reduces the inflammation in the body that contributes to everything from arthritis to heart disease as well as excess weight. The arrival of the mass-produced rubber soled shoe in the 1960s, however, has meant that people are no longer grounding properly. Our shoes are literally preventing us from fully connecting to the Earth and this is negatively impacting our health and wellbeing. See the 'The Science of Grounding' documentary on YouTube.

So yes, if any alien species have been monitoring the development of the human race over the last few thousand years, they will probably be wondering why we're seemingly determined to pretend that we are not intrinsically connected to the planet we live on. They'll be scratching their huge green heads at why we're so set on proving that we are 'above' the patterns and rhythms of the natural world. It's like giraffes pretending they don't belong on the African savanna and have decided they're going to live in the ocean.

There's probably some board meeting of aliens going on in a conference room somewhere in the Pleides star system. One of the aliens will be presenting their findings on the earthling civilisation to the group with the help of an alien version of a PowerPoint presentation. This alien will be describing some of things earthlings get up to and the other aliens will be like, *'What!? Are you serious, Xodmogh? You're saying that those idiots actually poison the very soils and waters from which they eat and drink?'*

Xodmogh will sigh and say, *'I know, it's beyond belief. I think humans may be the dumbest species on this side of the universe. It's only those self-cannibalising Zothians that seem stupider. But if they can't stop eating themselves then the Zothians will have made themselves extinct by the end of this centrum. At which point, yes, earthlings will definitely be the dumbest species in this galaxy cluster, if not the whole universe.'*

ASK AND IT IS GIVEN

How to reconnect with Spirit? Ask to reconnect. Intend to reconnect.

Close your eyes and send up that request, 'Great Mother' or 'Creator' or 'Lord' or whatever name you choose to assign to the conscious intelligence that is the fabric of All That Is. Close your eyes and ask this intelligence to once again flow through your energetic bodies and to express itself in your life in the most beautiful and life-affirming ways.

Decide to be aware of the natural world. Open your eyes to the wonders of nature that are around you all the time. Observe. Notice.

In the next exercise, we're going to start noticing all the ways you are inadvertently disconnecting from your natural self, from the Earth and from Spirit.

EXERCISE: UNCOVER YOUR DISCONNECTION

AS PER THE suggestion from the Spirit Collective, this exercise is about bringing your awareness to all the ways you disconnect from your body, disconnect from your emotions and disconnect from God. At the most fundamental level, carrying excess weight on your body is ultimately the result of a disconnection from Divine Source.

Before we can turn that around and start reconnecting with Divine Source, we need to be aware of all the ways we are turning away. This exercise is about uncovering all the ways you're disconnecting from Source Consciousness and beginning the process of reconnecting.

Step 1: Exploring disconnection

In your Weight-Love journal, write a list of all the ways you perceive that you're disconnecting from life, Spirit, the planet, your natural self, God, etc.

For example, *'I disconnect when I join in on mean gossip about the new girl at work, I disconnect when I call myself stupid, I disconnect when I complain about other people, I disconnect when I blame others for my misfortune, I disconnect when I spend 10 hours sat at my desk in an office, I disconnect when I put artificial foods in my body, I disconnect when I complain about the weather, I disconnect when I choose plastic, I disconnect when I judge others...'*

Step 2: Exploring reconnection

In your Weight-Love journal, write a list of the times you connect with life, Spirit, the planet, your natural self, God, etc.

For example, *'I connect when I nourish my body with organic plant foods, I connect when I walk in bare feet on the sand or grass, I connect when I feel gratitude, I connect when I sing, I connect when I appreciate my family, I connect when I garden, I connect when I bake my special gingerbread cookies, I connect when I tell my parents I love them, I connect when I play with my cat, I connect when I pray or meditate...'*

Step 3: Choose reconnection

From now on, as you go about your day, notice when you're choosing disconnection or reconnection. Disconnection lowers your vibration while reconnection lifts your heart and feels beautiful. Consciously choose to add more reconnection into your daily life.

TAPPING SCRIPT: WEIGHT-LOSS BLUEPRINTS AND LIGHT CODES

THIS TAPPING SCRIPT is different to the usual format. It might seem odd but the idea is that this script works on an energetic level. You may love it, you may not, just give it a go. Start tapping on the meridian end point at the start of one or both eyebrows...

Even though, I'm not sure how to reclaim my body's most perfect blueprint, I love and accept myself anyway

Even though, I'm not sure how to reinstall my body's most ideal and original blueprint, I love and accept myself anyway

Even though, I'm not sure how to reconfigure my body's most perfect, original blueprint, I love and accept myself anyway

EB: I now command that...
SE: ... a weight-loss blueprint and new light codes
UE: ... are downloaded into my system now, through all my energy centres
UN: I now command that...
CH: ...neuro-circuitry for being my ideal natural weight
CB: ...is downloaded now into my system, and updated and renewed.
UA: I command that...
TH: ...old thought forms and ideas about my limitations

EB: ...are now pulled, cancelled and removed from my system
SE: ... and sent to the Light of Creator for transmutation.
UE: I now command that my energy channels...
UN: ...are cleared and enhanced
CH: ...so that my ideal weight is easily maintained.
CB: I command that all vows, oaths, obligations...
UA: ...agreements, contracts, and commitments I've ever made
TH: ...to hold onto excess weight be now pulled, resolved or completed

EB: ...on core, genetic, history and soul levels
SE: ...in all languages, lifetimes, dimensions and realities
UE: ...in whatever way is appropriate for my highest and best.
UN: I now command that all craving centres in my brain are balanced.
CH: I now command that...
CB: ...all my energy bodies receive blueprint updates or renewals
UA: ...for me to easily achieve my ideal body weight.
TH: I now command that...

EB: ...healthy digestion and flora light codes be
SE: ...brought into my digestive tract
UE: I command to know what it feels like and how to...
UN: ...easily reach and maintain my optimal body weight.

319

CH: I command to know what it feels like and how to be safe...
CB: ...at my optimal body weight.
UA: I command to know what it feels like to be safe...
TH: ...without needing excess body fat.

EB: I command to know what it feels like and how to...
SE: ...live my daily life without being in a battle with my weight.
UE: I command to know what it feels like and how to...
UN: ...find peace with my weight.
CH: I command to know what it feels like to know that...
CB: ...I am completely safe without excess body fat.
UA: I command that all these healings are integrated now in the highest and best way.
TH: Thank you. Thank you. Thank you. It is done.

Pause for a moment, close your eyes and take a long deep inhale then exhale through the mouth.

Imagine you can feel and imagine all these changes being made to your energetic and physical bodies. Take some time to let them take place. See them happening. Feel them happening.

Now, slowly open your eyes onto a whole new world of beauty, opportunity, happiness, and your own limitless potential.

ACTION AND AFFIRMATION

Action: Plant power

Go to your local garden centre and buy a plant and a pot. Go home and gently, lovingly, put the plant into its new pot, feeling the soil between your fingers. Show the plant around the house and ask where it would most like to be placed. Commit to talking to this new plant like a loved family member. Thank it regularly for the beauty it brings to your home and for cleansing the air you breathe.

Affirmation

Write the following affirmation on a postcard or post-it note and stick it where you'll see it at least once a day.

'Spirit and I are One. I am part of All That Is.'

THE WRAP UP

WELL DONE YOU absolute rock star! Give yourself a round of applause, you've made it to the end. You are awesome.

If you've made it this far, then you probably don't want to hear too much more from me so I'll keep this short. As a final note, just remember that you've begun a life-changing journey. A journey of liberation. This is not a 'lose 16 pounds in 16 weeks plan'. This is a long-term, seismic shift you're undertaking. There are no hacks. So, you may be working hard to rewire your brain, release limiting beliefs, and heal your gut, but the positive changes might not show on your bathroom scales for months. That's okay. I'm not bothered about what you weigh next week or next month. I'm bothered about you being healthier, happier and leaner in a year from now, in two years, five years, 10 years...

What I pray you're not doing in a year or two from now is still going round and round in dieting circles, losing a few pounds or kilograms, gaining them back a few months later, and still hating yourself.

However, although your body weight might take a while to reflect positive mental and emotional changes, I do hope that your happiness levels shift more quickly. While I'm not bothered about what you weigh next month, I am bothered about your happiness levels rising by next month.

Let me finish up by saying that I hope you're a little closer to dumping self-criticism forever and realising that you are more powerful and brilliant than you have ever imagined.

I hope you fall a little more in love with your incredible body every day and care for it with tenderness and respect. I hope you start to feel your angels and spirit friends around you (sorry, more hippie talk, can't help myself). I hope you open up your communication with your

Higher Power and allow this awesome and loving power into your heart and life.

If you want to keep in touch, head to my website at www.howtohealyourweight.com or www.tamarapitelen.com. I would love to hear from you.

If you liked this book, I would be monumentally grateful if you could give it a short review on Amazon.com, Amazon.co.uk, Amazon.ca, Amazon.com.au, Amazon.de... or whichever other version of Amazon is relevant to the country you live in.

Bless you, Tamara

P.S. Get yout FREE Weight-Love resources to help you on this journey. Go to www.howtohealyourweight.com/weightlove

HOW TO FAT TAP
The basics of EFT Tapping

EMOTIONAL FREEDOM TECHNIQUES (EFT), also known as tapping, is an energy psychology healing modality that combines aspects of traditional Chinese medicine with modern western psychology. It's also called meridian tapping therapy, emotional acupuncture, and acupressure psychology, amongst other things. To do it, we tap with our fingertips on the end points of the primary meridians, or energy channels, in our bodies. Tapping is a powerful tool for weight loss because the excess fat that we hold on our bodies is largely a result of the stress hormones keeping our bodies into fat storage mode.

In simple terms, tapping is like acupuncture without the needles and it can free you from persistent or inappropriate negative emotions. These thoughts and emotions become stuck or blocked nervous energy in one or more of your nerve channels, or meridians.

If you think of your energetic system as an energy motorway, then a past trauma is a little like a car crash, or traffic jam, on that motorway. Something is stopping the energy—or traffic–from flowing and this causes problems that can then manifest into physical issues.

WHERE IT ALL BEGAN

The process was originally conceived by clinical psychotherapist Roger Callahan in the 1980s. Basically, Callahan stumbled across the power of combining the energy meridian system and principles of acupuncture with psychology. He'd been working for more than two years with a client known as 'Mary' who had an overwhelming phobia of water. This fear of water was so intense that even having a bath could trigger an anxiety attack.

Callahan had tried all sorts of anxiety reduction techniques with her but nothing was shifting the phobia. Mary couldn't even walk near the swimming pool by his office without experiencing panic.

During one session, though, Mary mentioned that her fearful feeling was located in her stomach. Callahan had been studying kinesiology so he knew there was a meridian point located directly beneath the eye that, according to traditional acupuncture, is linked to the stomach.

As an experiment, Callahan asked Mary to tap on the end point of the meridian under her eye whilst talking about her fear and how it felt in her body. Mary experienced a dramatic shift. Her fear of water, she announced to Callahan, was simply gone and she ran to the swimming pool outside and splashed water on her face to prove it. Somehow, the process of tapping under her eyes while talking about her fear of water had permanently eliminated Mary's fear.

Callahan developed his new system, calling it Thought Field Therapy (TFT) but it was his student Gary Craig who created the system we now know as classical EFT or Emotional Freedom Techniques.

While Callahan's approach focused on using muscle testing to uncover which meridians were relevant to the issue presented by a client, Craig's approach was basically 'let's just tap on the end points of all the primary meridians and cover our bases'. It proved to be much quicker, easier, and very effective. Studies show that tapping significantly reduces levels of the stress hormone cortisol. This is the system that has spread all over the world thanks to its simplicity and its results.

TAPPING IN SUM

How does EFT Tapping work? Tapping is a pattern interrupt that shifts our thinking and the neural pathways in our brain so we cannot see a challenge or situation in the same way. It lowers the stress around a situation and then we think, *'why on earth was I so bothered by that?'*

This light tapping on the endpoints of the primary energy meridians in your body sends a calming signal to the amygdala – which is the brain's alarm bell and the trigger for the 'fight or flight' response. Whenever you're in a stressful situation, or you simply think of something that causes you stress, then your body responds to this thought by pumping out stress hormones like cortisol and adrenalin, by diverting resources to your extremities and away from your non-essential functions like digestion, by increasing your heart rate and breathing to pull in more oxygen so the muscles can fight or flee. This process also sees the more creative and lateral thinking parts of the brain shut down so you're operating from the primal lizard brain – in other words you actually become more stupid when you're in the stress response and are unable to think of solutions beyond 'run for your life!' or 'fight for your life!' Here is an outline of the steps to take in an EFT Tapping session:

1. Identify the issue

This could be any physical, emotional, mental or spiritual issue. For example, a sore shoulder, headache, fear of flying, anger over a childhood betrayal, or anxiety around losing a job. For people wanting to deal with weight, it could be *'I hate my fat belly'* or *'I'm terrified that I'll never find a soul mate until I lose this weight'*. Physically, it could be 'my back aches from all this excess weight'.

2. Rate the intensity of distress from 0-10

If it's physical pain, how sore is it on a scale from zero to 10? If it's an emotional challenge, how upset or distressed are you? If it's a belief how 'true' does it feel?

3. Set-up statement

While tapping with two or three fingers on the fleshy side of either hand, just below the little finger, also called the karate chop point, we just plainly state the issue. For example, *'I've got this chronic back ache'* or *'I'm really stressed about money'*. We say the set-up statement three times and there are two aims to achieve by doing this. First, you're acknowledging the problem or issue. You're shining the light on it and pulling it out from where it's been hiding in the dark. And, second, you're accepting and loving yourself in spite of it.

So a typical set-up statement would be: *'Even though I'm stressed to the max about all the debt I'm in and I can't see a way out of it, I accept that I feel this way and I completely love and forgive myself anyway.'* (Weight and abundance issues are often connected at a subconscious level. For example, if you feel like you never have enough money, you may be holding onto excess weight to ensure your survival through tough times, or to make you feel less like you have nothing. *'I may not have the money to pay rent this month but I've got this big belly!'*)

Another set-up statement could be: *'Even though I'm overweight and I hate having all this excess fat on my body, I accept that this is how I feel about it and I completely love and forgive myself anyway.'*

If you have a problem saying that you completely love and forgive yourself, then reframe it by saying something like, *'I choose to love and forgive myself'* or *'I am open to the possibility of loving and forgiving myself'*. Or simply, *'I'm okay.'*

4. The Sequence

This is the bit that stimulates and balances the body's energy pathways. We tap around the face and body, tapping with two, three or four fingers on the end points of the primary meridians While using our Reminder Phrase from the Set-up Statement and any other details that seem relevant – the more specific you can be, the more powerful the technique:

- Top of the Head (TH)
- Beginning of the Eyebrow (EB)
- Side of the Eye (SE)
- Under the Eye (UE)
- Under the Nose (UN)
- Chin Point (CH)
- Beginning of the Collarbone (CB)
- Under the Arm (UA)

The Reminder Phrase is simple as you need only identify the issue with some brief wording. Depending on your issue, you might say the following at each tapping point...

'This throbbing pain'
'My fat belly and huge thighs'
'Abandoned by my father'
'This stuttering in public'

There are two points to make here—it doesn't matter which hand you use to tap and it doesn't matter which side of your face and body you tap on. You can tap on either or both.

5. Re-assess the intensity

Finally, you establish an 'after' level of the issue's intensity by rating it on a scale from zero to 10. So, if your issue is a 2 it's not so strong but if it's a 9 or 10 it's as strong as it can be. Don't stress too much about this, just use your intuition and gut feeling, take the first number that pops into your head.

The reason for giving it a score or a number at the start is so that you have something to measure after a few rounds of tapping. You'll be able to see if your feelings get stronger or if they stay the same or lose their intensity. Ideally, the number will get to zero but you may find that it actually goes up initially as you focus on the feelings and thereby increase their intensity as you dive deeper into these emotions. That's all good! You've got to go into them in order to process and release them. Keep tapping until the number starts falling. Keep repeating the tapping process until you get to zero or you plateau at some level. When you get to a 2 or 3 on the zero to 10 scale, you can try bringing in positive statements, for example, staying with the theme of weight, you could say:

'I choose to love and appreciate my body for a change.'
'It's time to stop beating myself up about my weight and start recognising how incredible my body is.'
'I love and appreciate everything my brilliantly designed body does for me.'
'I am beautiful.'

What I like to do after each round of tapping is cross my hands over my heart, close my eyes and take a deep breath then say the word *'transform'*. Then, in my mind's eye, I imagine this new knowledge pouring into every cell of my body until my whole being vibrates at the frequency this new positive belief. I visualise this change happening. I visualise every cell of my body integrating this new positive belief system and vibrating at this new frequency. This part is really important. If you can 'see' this change taking place in your mind's eye, then your brain can 'see' it taking place and so it is done.

Another thing I like to do at the end of a session is, while tapping one by one on the right edge of the fingernails of my left hand, say:

Thumbnail: 'There's a Divine part of me...'
Index finger: 'That already knows how to honour, love, nourish and respect my body...'
Middle finger: 'That divine part of me is communicating this knowing to the rest of me now...'
Ring finger: 'This new knowing is uploaded into every cell of my mind and body now...'
Little finger: 'This process is now complete.'

Again, in your mind's eye, visualise this happening.

Just a small note on the fingernail tapping, some people prefer to skip the ring finger because that meridian is taken care of in the primary sequence, personally though, I like to do all five fingers. Make your tapping practise your own.

EXPLORE EFT TAPPING LAND

If you're new to the world of tapping, there are a myriad of excellent and free resources out there and I would encourage you to explore the wonderful work of the people who founded the method, in particular Gary Craig at www.emofree.com, the free resources and videos of Craig contain a priceless wealth of information.

As well take a look at the brilliant Dawson Church at www.eft-universe.com; Brad Yates at www.tapwithbrad.com; and Jessica and Nick Ortner at www.TheTappingSolution.com.

These are all excellent places for you to do further and more in-depth research.

Those are the basics in a nutshell. Head back to step one and let's get started...

ABOUT THE AUTHOR

With a media career spanning more than 20 years, Tamara Pitelen has written and edited for magazines, newspapers and online media in London, Sydney, Hong Kong, Dubai, New Zealand, and Bath.

While living in Dubai, she launched that region's first holistic health and wellness magazine, *Awakenings Middle East*, under her own publishing company.

Tamara is also a recovering dieter with decades of painful dieting self-abuse behind her.

On her long and winding personal journey out of the diet trap, she discovered the world of alternative healing and spirituality. As a result, Tamara is a certified practitioner of Theta Healing and EFT Tapping, as well as an RYT 500 yoga teacher, a medium-in-training, and general bleeding-heart hippie.

Previous books include *Spokes, Blokes and Blarney; Neanderthal Man Loves Tree Hugger; The Year I Went Pear-shaped,* and *Five Beliefs Keeping You Fat and How To Clear Them*. All available on Amazon.com.

Originally from Christchurch, New Zealand, Tamara now lives in Bath, England, with husband Adrian and cat Jake.

www.tamarapitelen.com

Acknowledgments

A shout out to the people who support me in every sense of the word. Here's to the lovelies who agreed to slog their way through early drafts to give me feedback, namely, Debbie Hucker, Su Saadeh, Raymond Ware, Verity Armstrong-Coop, and Adrian Maul. Thanks to the women who let me use them as guinea pigs on the first run through of the How To Heal Your Weight Support Circle and eight-week course – Lisa Pascoe, Kat Treagle, Ali Borgelin, Vicky Whipp, Khy Lovegood, Trish Fairbeard and Sarah Robinson. Thanks to my lovely Mum and Dad for once again putting up with me revealing family secrets and heartache to anyone who cares to read this. Thanks to Zoe Henderson and Vanya Silverten for the encouragement, inspiration and friendship. Thanks to my amazing husband Adrian Maul – for everything. Thanks and much love to all my friends and loved ones in Spirit for the encouraging messages and synchronicities.